Managing Information Technology in Turbulent Times

Managing Information Technology in Turbulent Times

Louis Fried

A Wiley–QED Publication

John Wiley & Sons, Inc.

New York • Chichester • Brisbane • Toronto • Singapore

Publisher: Katherine Schowalter
Editor: Theresa Hudson
Managing Editor: Mark Hayden
Composition: Publishers' Design and Production Services, Inc.

This text is printed on acid-free paper.

This publication is designed to provide accurate and authoritative information in regard to the subject matter covered. It is sold with the understanding that the publisher is not engaged in rendering legal, accounting, or other professional services. If legal advice or other expert assistance is required, the services of a competent professional person should be sought. FROM A DECLARATION OF PRINCIPLES JOINTLY ADOPTED BY A COMMITTEE OF THE AMERICAN BAR ASSOCIATION AND A COMMITTEE OF PUBLISHERS.

Library of Congress Cataloging-in-Publication Data:

Fried, Louis.
  Managing information technology in turbulent times / Louis Fried.
      p.   cm.
  Includes bibliographical references.
  ISBN 0-471-04742-2
  1. Management information systems.   I. Title.
T58.6.F75   1995
658.4'038—dc20   94-16470
                                                                                CIP

This book is dedicated to the memory of my mother,
Teriza Klein Fried
(1904–1993)

Contents

SECTION II

THE BUSINESS CONTEXT OF INFORMATION SYSTEMS   43

Chapter 2

The Business Climate at the Turn of the Century   45

Adapted from *Information Strategy: The Executive's Journal*
(New York: Auerbach Publications). © 1993 Warren Gorham Lamont.
Used with permission.

Chapter 3

Planning for Competitive Use of Information Technology   61

Adapted from *Information Systems Management*
(New York: Auerbach Publications), © 1991 Warren Gorham Lamont.
Used with permission.

SECTION III
MANAGING EMERGING TECHNOLOGIES   81

Chapter 4
Acquisition and Deployment of Information Technology   83

Chapter 5
Emerging Information Technologies' Impact on Business   99

Adapted from *Information Systems Management*
(New York: Auerbach Publications), © 1993 Warren Gorham Lamont.
Used with permission.

Acknowledgments

I wish to acknowledge the assistance of a number of parties who have made this book possible.

First, I wish to thank my wife for her patience during my years of long work hours and extensive global travel for consulting assignments. My career in information systems has been rewarding for me but stressful for her.

Next, I wish to acknowledge the enjoyable professional relationships that I have had with various editors who have published my articles and papers over the years. Especially outstanding are Karen Brogno of Auerbach Publishers, Joanne Kelleher and Lory Zottola Dix of *Computerworld* magazine, and Eilif Trondsen of SRI International's Business Intelligence Program. They have helped make my writing the pleasure for me that it is.

Some of the material used in this book has been drawn from various articles I have published. These articles are listed below:

- "Current IT Trends and Business Issues: An Executive Briefing." *Information Strategy: The Executive's Journal* (Spring 1993).
- "Gaining the Technology Advantage." *Information Systems Management* (Fall 1991).
- "Acquisition and Deployment of Advanced Information Technology." *Information Management* (Spring 1993).
- "From Here to 2000: IT's Impact on Business." *Information Strategy: The Executives' Journal* (Fall 1993).
- "The Rules of Project Management." *Information Systems Management* (Summer 1992).
- "When Bigger Is Not Better: Productivity and Team Size in Software Development." *Software Engineering* (May/June 1991).
- "Object Management and Security." *Data Base Management* (Spring 1993).

- "Planning for the Competitive Use of IT." *Productivity Improvement in IS* (December 1992), Auerbach Publishers.
- "Assigning Responsibility for Information Security in Distributed or Outsourced Environments." *Data Security Management* (March 1993).
- "The Flexible IS Organization." *Auerbach Information Management* (August 1992).
- "Logistical Positivism." *Information Week* (September 6, 1993).
- "Outsourcing Confessions." *Computerworld* (February 8, 1993).
- "A Blueprint for Change." *Computerworld*. (December 2, 1991).
- "Decision-Making Prowess." *Computerworld* (March 4, 1991).
- "Staying Ahead of the Pack: Managing Information Technology." *SRI International Datalog*, D93-1731 (April 1993).
- "Toward a Revolution in Information Systems Management." *SRI International Business Intelligence Program Report*, No. 825 (Fall 1993).
- "How to Succeed at MIS Outsourcing: Avoiding the Traps and Pitfalls." *SRI International Datalog*, D93-1721 (March 1993).
- "Business Process Redesign." *SRI International Datalog*, D91-1593 (December 1991).

Finally, I must thank all of my professional and business associates, especially those with whom I have worked at SRI International for over 18 years. The challenges they have posed, the solid advice they have provided, and the rewards of companionable professional relationships have made my life a continuous learning experience. That learning has resulted in this book.

Introduction

During the 1990s and the early twenty-first century, the management of information systems in enterprises will undergo a revolutionary change. Previous changes were evolutionary and largely driven by advances in technology—the introduction of operating systems in the 1960s, the introduction of minicomputers in the 1970s, and the introduction of personal computers in the 1980s. Now both technology and business directions are driving information systems management to a fundamentally new paradigm.

Information systems managers and those who aspire to such positions must prepare themselves for managing in an environment in which they may not directly control information resources—a corporate world in which the mystique of information technology is no longer the exclusive province of information systems specialists, line business managers increasingly take responsibility for information technology decisions, and computing and telecommunications are ubiquitous.

This book explores the new paradigm of information systems management from a management perspective and follows that with detailed approaches to solving a number of the major problems facing CIOs. Much of the material in this book is based on my observation of experiences and best practices among the largest 1,000 or so firms in the world that are SRI International's consulting clients, and for many of which I have conducted consulting assignments. As a result, the orientation of this book is toward managing information systems in larger, multidivisional, multinational companies. However, many of the management techniques described can be scaled down for use in smaller companies. The reader is expected to have a general knowledge of the terms used in information systems and an awareness of the technologies employed in such systems. However, no detailed technical knowledge is required. As a result, both those who make their careers in information systems and those who must use their services may find the book useful.

While this book is written for managers and those who aspire to be managers, it is also structured to be used as a textbook. Each chapter is followed by a short list of essay or discussion topics for use by a course instructor.

The terms *information technology* and *information systems* have become increasingly confused and are often used interchangeably. In this book, an attempt is made to preserve the distinction between the terms—*information technology* refers to matters concerning the technology itself or the general application of the technology; *information systems* refers to either an organization or to a specific application.

The thrust of this book is on *managing* information technology and information systems in a business environment during the 1990s and beyond.

A Revolution in Information Systems Management

This book is not intended to explore every aspect of information systems and technology management; nor does it treat every topic explored equally. Instead, it reflects my experience with those issues that have proven to be most troublesome to chief information officers and MIS managers.

In this vein, the first section is devoted to examining the future of the CIO in large corporations, illustrating the business and technological forces that are driving a dramatic change in the way information systems must be managed now and in the future. By setting forth both the driving forces and the best management methods for coping with them, it establishes the framework of which all the other sections of the book are components.

This section sets the stage for managing information technology in the turbulent times expected in the years before and after the turn of the century.

CHAPTER 1

A New Management Paradigm for Information Systems

THE DEMAND FOR CHANGE IN INFORMATION SYSTEMS MANAGEMENT

Internal Corporate Forces Acting on IS Management

Whether information systems (IS) managers like it or not, change is being thrust upon them by a combination of technological, business and social factors. Some evidence of this change may be noted from published surveys (see Table 1.1) that reveal the following:

- *People focus.* Concern is more frequently focused on people and business than on technology. Satisfying user needs continues to be a problem for corporate chief information officers (CIOs).
- *Cost effectiveness.* Companies continue to search for methods to prove information technology (IT) cost effectiveness and thus provide business credibility to the costs of the IS group. Alignment with corporate business strategy remains an elusive goal since such alignment can only be accomplished at the business unit or business process level, and IS policies have typically been developed at the corporate level.
- *Information dispersal.* Trends in technology acquisition are dominantly directed at the dispersal of information technology into the business units that use the information. CIOs who attempt to retain control are being forced to transfer IS functions to line managers (or being forced out of the company).
- *Business process redesign.* The demand for new, innovative applications continues and is being stimulated by business process redesign or

Table 1.1.   Selected IS Management Surveys and Studies: Findings and Implications

Survey/Study Findings	Implications
1991 Yankee Group survey of software development:[1]	

• CIOs feel they have least control over users and the development process.
• With 39% of software development justified by being critical to the core business, 27% for its bottom line impact, and 24% for gaining competitive advantage, CIOs' top problems in software development are viewed as
  • Management/people difficulties
  • Specification/design
  • Corporate intervention/instability
  • The software development process
  • The target audience.
	• Three of the five issues are nontechnical and relate to organization, staffing, user concerns, corporate directions, and politics.
	• Even the relatively technical concerns of specification/design and the software development process are dependent on close work with end users.
	• End users are rebelling against the "control" exercised by CIOs in the past.

1992 study by A. Yosri, New York University's Information Technologies Institute, of 31 firms with more than $500 million in annual sales:	
• 61% of CIOs used quantitative measures to evaluate information technology (IT) benefits, 55% said they were satisfied with the measurement methods they used. • 74% said they would use a new method if it were available.	• There is no good, reliable metric for proving the value of IT benefits, so the evaluation is subjective. • Subjective evaluation leads operating managers with bottom line responsibility to feel that they need to take control and use IT to meet the business needs they perceive.
1992 K. Redditt and T. Lodahl, Cognitech Services Corporation study of IT effectiveness:[2]	
• The key variables were organization alignment, IS and business cultures, and architecture alignment. • IS units judged to be highly effective mostly reported through the business unit organization rather than through an IS hierarchy. • Top performers dispersed client-sensitive functions close to the client and allowed the client day-to-day direction.	• Business unit managers are taking control of IT and making it work for them. • While the measures of "effectiveness" may be questioned, the perception of effectiveness has improved for those line managers who now have responsibility for their own information systems.

Table 1.1. *Continued*

Survey/Study Findings	Implications
***1992 Computerworld survey of 102 top IS executives:*[3]**	

• CIOs rate the following activities (in order) as most important to their company's business strategy: reengineering, total quality management, application downsizing, globalization, and decentralizing.
 • The most technological impact is expected from
   • High-speed networking
   • Client-server computing
   • Graphical user interfaces
   • Open systems
   • Portable computers
   • Image processing
   • Advanced desktop operating systems
   • Object-oriented programming.
	• CIOs of large corporations are increasingly recognizing the same key issues CEOs do.
	 • The thrust toward applications downsizing, globalization, and decentralization is a response to aligning IT organization and operations with corporate and business unit organization and operations.
	 • This recognition may be too late for some CIOs, as pointed out in the Computerworld/Andersen survey quoted below.

***1991 Information Week survey of Information Week 500 Awards finalists:*[4]**	
• 85% of the 116 top information management executives interviewed expect to invest in client-server computing in 1993.	• System architectures are following a path that is congruent with the shape of business units.
***1993 Computerworld survey of 120 major corporation CIOs:*[5]**	
• 82% plan to spend more money for local area networks and 66% expect to spend more on packaged software than they spent in 1992. • 42% plan to spend less on hardware, maintenance, and consultants. • IS budgets are generally flat, but when they do rise it is most frequently due to the demand for new applications, corporate growth, reengineering, and acquisition of new platforms.	• To reshape information systems organizations and improve responsiveness to users, corporations are investing in architectures and technology that will reduce long-term costs. • Centralized IS groups have had difficulty proving their cost-effectiveness and, as with other parts of companies, are under strong pressure to reduce costs. • IS groups that are part of business units tend to be perceived differently from centralized IS.

Table 1.1. Selected IS Management Surveys and Studies: Findings and Implications
Continued

Survey/Study Findings	Implications
1993 Computerworld/Andersen Consulting survey of 203 CEOs, COOs, and CFOs:[6]	
• U.S. businesses will spend over $200 billion on computers, telecommunications, and related services in 1993.	• As the pressures mount for IS to be more responsive to business unit needs CIOs who do not learn to relinquish "control" of IT are being replaced by those who do.
• Only about half of the companies feel they are getting their money's worth from IT investments.	
• In fact, according to a 1993 Deloitte & Touche study, CIO turnover in companies of over $5 billion in revenue hit 25% in 1992; one third replaced a predecessor who was fired.	

1. *Computerworld*, December 2, 1991.
2. *Information Week*, October 26, 1992.
3. *Computerworld*, October 19, 1992.
4. *Information Week*, December 7, 1992.
5. *Information Week*, February 22, 1993.
6. Computerworld, April 19, 1993

reengineering. Cost is not the only issue. When IS is a part of the business unit, alignment and effectiveness are easier to demonstrate.
• *Reporting relationships.* IS units are judged to be more effective if they report to the business units they serve rather than to a corporate IS chain of command.

The "glass house" mainframe computer center is not dead, nor is it dying; but it is becoming a smaller and smaller fraction of the focus of information systems management. In 1993, companies such as Associated Grocers, Inc., in Seattle decided to move all applications off mainframes within five years. Other companies expect that it will take longer to justify the move and that they may have mainframe applications running for 10 years or more.[1] Centralized information systems at a corporate level are rapidly becoming dinosaurs in many industries.

All this implies that a new paradigm is needed for IS management. But what will IS management look like in the future? I believe that previous changes were evolutionary, but the coming change is revolutionary, driven by a more computer-literate user community, new enabling technologies, and the movement toward leaner, meaner business organizations that are more competitive.

External Forces Acting on IS Management

One of the problems with most surveys is that they tend to reflect IS management looking at itself. In this, they are a mirror of what exists rather than a reflection of the external influences that will change both companies and IS management. Some of these external influences will have major impacts. (See Chapter 2.)

Corporate structures are changing as companies refocus on their core businesses. The 1970s and 1980s era of corporate adventurism has ended. Corporations that diversified in that 20-year period are, in the 1990s, divesting themselves of noncore business units. In fact, many corporations that vertically integrated their businesses in the past are now divesting themselves of parts of the value chain that do not contribute sufficient value and are purchasing product components instead. An article in *Fortune* magazine has named such companies "modular corporations," and described them as minimizing investment in plant and facilities by buying and assembling components so that they can focus their resources on product design, R&D, and marketing.[2] The article's examples include new companies that have been built on these principles as well as older companies that are redesigning themselves. Some of the new companies are Dell Computer, Nike, Exabyte, and Sun Microsystems. The older companies include Chrysler and Brooks Brothers. Even such venerable giants as IBM and General Motors are increasing their outsourcing of product components.

Another name for this business approach is the "virtual corporation." Malone and Davidow describe the virtual corporation as one that extends its influence upward through suppliers and downward through distribution channels to the end user or consumer. As customers and suppliers become greater participants in decision making for products and services, their personnel become integral to the functions of the company and make traditional organizations obsolete. Given a rapid pace of product and service evolution, even jobs often may become "virtual jobs," and corporations will need to plan continual employee training to fight skill obsolescence.[3]

Another advocate of the virtual corporation Byrne[4], has identified the attributes of such companies as

- A best-of-breed core competence and purchase of the rest
- Intensive electronic links with partners (suppliers, distribution channels, etc.)
- Opportunistic partnering, changing alliances
- Interdependence with allies and partners, requiring trusting relationships

- Cooperation across borders with suppliers, customers, and even competitors

These new approaches to designing the business architecture have led to a need for viewing the corporation and the business units as "extended enterprises;" that reach beyond company walls to include both suppliers and customers as a part of their business processes. For example, Ford Motor Company's design engineers team with suppliers at Ford sites to design specified parts of the products. GE Plastics' engineers and chemists team with customers to design new products for meeting the customers' end product needs. Just-in-time inventory management requires that suppliers have direct access to work-in-process inventory files to schedule parts deliveries. Suppliers to supermarkets and retail chains have direct access to inventory and sales records of their customers to better support the customers' sales requirements.

The extended enterprise is a reality in the early 1990s. We have entered an era of collaboration that is reflected in our business processes and the systems that support them. This collaboration must be reflected in the way IS is managed. (See Chapter 5.)

We are also facing a major shift in the way people work and live with computing and communications. Computing futurists have called this the era of ubiquitous computing. Ubiquitous computing means more than the expectation that computers will support every business function and more than the expectation that portable computing and communications will support business, social, and leisure applications. It means that an increasingly computer-literate society will expect computers to do what it wants, the way it wants it done. And it means that users will increasingly desire to create or tailor their own applications, often using objects created by computing professionals.

Ubiquitous computing implies that the "controls" over the use of computers by centralized IS management will erode to a few critical aspects. Amoco, headquartered in Chicago, has created relatively autonomous IS managers for each of its business units, and the corporate IS function now only sets standards for network connectivity. Perhaps the only corporate-wide IS controls left in some companies will be those that govern connectivity to networks, access to databases, and the use of objects. (*Objects* are discrete entities within computer systems that embody processes and data and that may be reused in a number of applications.)

REACTIONS TO FORCES SHAPING THE NEW PARADIGM

Reactions to the pressures just described have led to a new IS management paradigm with the following elements:

- *Changing application ownership.* Ownership of information resources by the business process managers rather than by a central IS department is a logical outcome of the ongoing dispersal of information systems resources to the business unit.
- *The emerging information utility.* Only resources or applications that transcend business units or business processes will reside with some corporate entity, which will provide services to dispersed users.
- *Growing IS outsourcing.* A variety of forces are supporting outsourcing and increased use of "shared services."
- A *new service culture.* Increased outsourcing and the implementation of the information utility concept, combined with the dispersal of responsibility and ownership of information resources, imply that corporate or business unit data centers will have to compete for business and will have to develop a new culture—a culture oriented to consumer service, competitive pricing, prompt and understandable service billing, and quick response to client requests. In other words, the data center will become just another vendor. (See Chapter 18.)
- *Changing responsibilities for IS planning and control.* Planning and control of information resources need to be in the hands of those directly responsible for the resources' profitable use. As ownership of IS changes hands, the functions traditionally performed will need to change to align with the management styles and needs of the new owners.

Application Ownership

In the past, when "integrated" applications were built to span the whole corporation with, for example, a single procurement system, ownership was diluted. Applications had so many owners (separate organizations within the corporation) that no single entity claimed clear title. As a result, ownership and its associated responsibility became so diffuse that the IS function, nominally the custodian of the application, was often viewed as the owner. The result was poor response to individual needs of users and a system design that was a suboptimization of the varied requirements of users from different business units.

We have learned from such techniques as *total quality management* and *information security management* that responsibility cannot be allocated without the authority that accompanies ownership. We have also learned, through the examples of *business process redesign*, that companies must abandon old hierarchical organization models and organize along lines that optimize business processes.[5] Command of a business process implies that the resources necessary to perform the process effectively are directed by the unified process-oriented organization.

The result of these lessons is a change in business organizations that must be paralleled by equivalent changes in IS organization to permit process managers to own all the resources that can reasonably be allocated to them. In many cases this will mean that economies of scale are no longer relevant incentives for centralization of resources. Instead, process effectiveness becomes the impetus for resource organization.

Much has been made of ensuring that IS strategy; matches the business strategy of the corporation. It is becoming clear, however, that to obtain true effectiveness, IS strategy must match the strategies of business units and the executives who have bottom-line responsibility for them. In fact, it is also becoming clear that simply "matching" the business unit strategy is not enough. IS executives must become an integral part of the unit's management team so that the competitive advantages of potential IT applications can influence the business unit strategy. (See Chapters 3 and 4.)

Dispersal of information systems resources to the business unit is only the first step. New technologies such as image processing with its accompanying workflow management systems, are inherently business process oriented. Collaborative processing, using workstations and local area networks, has the same orientation. As business units redesign their processes and change their organizations to support them, the ownership of information resources by the process managers is a logical outcome.

With technological capabilities moving hand in hand with business organization, and with the bottom-line pressure on business process managers, centralized IS management and operation is no longer consistent with the way the business operates. For example, when Xerox restructured its business into nine major business units in 1992, it moved responsibility for IS into each business unit, creating the position of divisional information officer (DIO). The DIOs report to business unit presidents with a dotted-line reporting relationship to the CIO. Examples of similar restructuring of IS are found throughout this chapter.

Application ownership, viewed as the ownership of all the resources required for IT support of the business process, will become the new driving force for IS management.

The Information Utility

Some resources or applications transcend business units or business processes. For some such applications—for example, the corporate consolidated general ledger—ownership is still clear. For others, such as electronic mail or bulletin boards, access to network gateways, wide area network management, and other facilities that may be classified as "utilities" in the same sense as a telephone is a utility, ownership must reside with some corporate entity. That entity may be "corporate information systems" or "corporate telecommunications."

Several companies, including Shell Oil of Houston, Texas, have adopted the concept of the "computing utility," in which a centralized computing facility serves the diverse needs for computing power of the company's divisions in addition to the corporate types of applications described above. The divisions use the computing utility to run applications for which they have insufficient local capacity.

Outsourcing

Outsourcing—defined as including consulting, applications development, applications maintenance and enhancement, computer operations, data communications network operations, and voice communications network management—is here to stay.[6] In most European countries, the relative difficulty of reducing staff (because of employment laws) when needs diminish has encouraged the substantial use of consultants and systems developers/integrators on contract. In many other countries, severe shortages of highly skilled professionals, combined with the peaks and valleys in business systems development requirements, have also stimulated the use of contractors. Furthermore, assumed economies of outsourcing computer operations and telecommunications management have stimulated interest in outsourcing these functions. (See Chapter 9.)

A growing trend related to outsourcing is the use of "shared services." Outstanding examples of such an approach are the consortia-operated airline reservation systems GALILEO and AMADEUS in Europe. Other examples abound, such as shared services for bank accounting, automated teller machine systems and check clearinghouses. In addition to shared services are specialized services provided by vendors for specific applications such as payroll operations, truck routing and scheduling, electronic data interchange (EDI) services, and a host of value-added network services. Shared services and the use of specialized services are attractive because

- Such arrangements usually provide the ability to deliver application services at costs substantially below in-house efforts.
- Either the services are in noncompetitive areas or the cost savings outweigh the competitive advantages of in-house operation.
- The cost of independent development of the capability is prohibitive for a single company (or a single company may not have the technical expertise and depth to develop the capability).
- Extensive distribution of access to the information is necessary to the success of the participant's business and difficult or impossible to attain alone.

The result of the trend toward shared services is that corporations or business units will tend to operate with smaller permanent staffs of systems developers and often may not have mainframes or computer operations of their own. Those corporations that continue to operate their own data centers may tend to view the mainframes as large servers, another part of the information utility.

Planning and Control

CIOs of major corporations have been accustomed to managing the tactical and strategic planning of IS; budgeting capital and expenses; and controlling the technology used, the development of applications, and the levels of resources made available to users. With decentralization to the business unit, this same management pattern has frequently been adopted at the next lower level of the corporation—the strategic business unit. However, the pattern reflects either a "mainframe" mentality or the tendency of IS to follow the organization patterns of the company it serves. As these organization patterns change for the business, IS must follow.

Where IS has been viewed by top management as a barely controllable cost of doing business, there has a been a tendency to develop an IS bureaucracy that is focused on detailed planning and budgeting, recovery of costs from users, and detailed justifications of new or modified applications. Such control has added little to the value of information systems, and the justifications for additional systems are rarely realized. Paul Strassmann, *The Business Value of Computers*[7] has done a superb job of debunking the myth that computer applications and the growth in the use of information technology are related to profitability.

A substantial part of the failure of systems to pay off must be attributed to the analytic methods of the past, in which applications were designed to automate the business processes as they existed rather than to redesign the business processes first. Application users felt that systems analysts did not really understand their business needs, while systems analysts felt that users did not understand their methods or the technologies involved. This analytic approach was partly a product of the relative intellectual isolation of the central IS function.

Overall cost control of information systems remains a concern, but when one cannot correlate IS costs with profitability, simply controlling costs per se is not meaningful. In fact, a primary emphasis on cost control may be detrimental to the success of the business. When IS costs become a directly controllable part of the bottom line calculation for each strategic business unit, they will vary in proportion to income as the business unit's strategic deployment of information systems varies to meet its needs. For example, there is no inherent reason that a business unit operating in a lower-wage area of the country should pay the high wages of systems development personnel from a corporate headquarters located in a major metropolitan area. Similarly, if a business unit can operate successfully with low-cost client-server-based systems, there is no reason that they should pay the higher cost of mainframe-based operations.

Planning and control of information resources need to be in the hands of those directly responsible for their profitable use. As ownership of IS changes hands, the functions IS has traditionally performed will need to change to align with the management styles and needs of the new owners. How these functions change is the topic of the next section.

IS ORGANIZATION IN THE FUTURE

In 1991 SRI International conducted an in-depth survey of 16 major multinational corporations.[8] Among the findings was that 12 of the 16 companies had decentralized their information resources to the strategic business unit level *or below*. With increasing frequency, perceptive CIOs like Jim Newman of Precision Castparts Corporation of Portland, Oregon, are leading the way to dispersal of their centralized IS organizations to the command of line managers in business units.

The implications of this trend, and of the other observations cited previously, are that IS organization and management must change. Whereas alignment of IS with corporate strategy was a major problem of the 1970s and 1980s because of the diversity of communities that corporate IS was attempting to serve, such alignment with business strategy is natural at the business unit or business process level. As this alignment takes place, it will force rethinking of such functions as systems development, computer operations, user support, technical support, communications, information security, standards, and strategic planning. Furthermore, IS management will recognize needs that have been too long ignored or that are created by implementation of the new IS management paradigm. These new or dramatically changed functions include technology management, information management, quality management, and software logistics management.

Systems Development

> *Systems development will be decentralized, reporting to business units, but inherent disadvantages will have to be overcome.*

Almost every organizational option has been tried by one company or another at some time—centralized analysis and programming, decentralized analysis and centralized programming, decentralized analysis and programming, distributed analysis and programming reporting to a centralized IS organization, and so forth. Each option has advantages and disadvantages that have been explored in the literature.

The primary advantage of decentralized systems development is unquestionably the responsiveness of such IS units to their host organization. Analysts and programmers become intimately familiar with their users' personnel, problems, and business requirements. The primary disadvantages are in introducing new technology and methods (such as business process redesign), maintaining specialized skills, ensuring conformity to corporate standards, and providing a long-term career path for professionals. (See Table 1.2.) Each of these disadvantages can be overcome by intelligent corporate planning, coordination, and technical support. For example, to ensure long-term career paths, one corporation requires that IS job openings be posted company-wide before outside recruiting is done. Given equal qualifications, current employees receive preference for jobs regardless of their location.

Computer Operations

> *Computer operations will combine both decentralized and centralized approaches, based on the nature of applications.*

Reduced cost of random access storage (reducing the need for tape mounting) and the gradual improvement in operatorless computer operations imply future reductions in the size of operations staffs. This, combined with the lack of operator requirements for workstations and local area networks, indicates that "computer operations" is becoming an obsolete concept except in mainframe-based systems. Even in mainframe-based systems, "lights-out" operations are becoming more feasible as online applications convert mainframes to large "servers." As a concept and as a management function, computer operations is shrinking in importance. In fact, as previously described, computer operations will increasingly fall into the category of outsourced services.

Ernest M. von Simson, in his *Harvard Business Review* article "The Centrally Decentralized 'IS Organization',"[9] indicated that the "pendulum" is swinging back from decentralization to centralization of IS. He found that 16 of 17 companies surveyed that had recently reorganized IS had moved toward centralization. One of the principal reasons for this move, he found, was the substantial savings in site license costs resulting from the elimination of multiple computer center sites. He further pointed out that lower-cost telecommunications also exerted a strong influence on data center consolidation, making it possible for a single, centralized site to economically serve widespread users.

Table 1.2.   Remedying the Disadvantages of Decentralized Systems Development

Disadvantages	Remedies
• Difficulty in introducing new methods and/or technology	• Retain centralized technology planning. • Provide education and technology training to distributed systems development (SD) groups and users. • Provide technical advice to SD groups. • Conduct periodic seminars for SD groups and users.
• Difficulty in maintaining specialized skills due to lack of use or inadequate staff depth	• Provide specialized skills from a central IS organization on a "contract" basis. • Conduct periodic refresher courses or seminars. • Establish electronic bulletin boards for staff with special interests to share experiences.
• Inability to ensure conformity to corporate standards	• Reduce corporate IT standards to the minimum necessary to enable communications connectivity.
• Difficulty in providing long-term career paths for personnel in small SD groups	• Inform all SD employees of position openings anywhere in the company. • Assuming equivalent qualifications, give preference to current employees for new openings. • Publicize employee career policies. • Provide a dual career ladder (both professional and management). • Support specialized training for qualified employees.

The von Simson findings contrast sharply with the previously mentioned SRI International survey, and evidence for moves to client-server technology in decentralized form appears in almost every issue of IS trade publications. For example, the Turner Corporation, one of the largest non-residential construction companies in the United States, headquartered in New York City, claimed in 1993 to have cut its IS budget nearly in half (by $2.5 million per year) by downsizing to a client-server environment.

These two apparently contradictory trends—toward distributed client-server systems and toward corporate consolidation of data centers—are really a part of the same phenomenon of downsizing. The rationale for consolidation of large mainframe-based data centers is based on cost reduction and efficiencies of scale. In reality, many opportunities for data center consolidation exist because new applications, redevelopment of current applications, and software development activities are moving to client-server environments, reducing the need for the excess capacity represented by multiple large-scale data centers. In addition, the human interfaces to the old "legacy" applications are being moved to more friendly personal computers, further reducing the processing cycles needed on the mainframes, even though the basic legacy application survives until it is economically and/or technically feasible to convert it.

Incidentally, although von Simson points to the reduced costs of telecommunications as aiding centralization, in reality this cost reduction helps both strategies. Distributed, low-cost client-server systems, using distributed database management systems software, can support the coordination of databases across wide area networks while avoiding the communication expense for transactions that are completely local. From the data center consolidation perspective, one must recognize that good managers of distributed data centers have long maintained some level of overcapacity to allow for recovery in the event of failure, for meeting unanticipated peak loads, and for potential new applications. This mainframe overcapacity may range from 20 percent to 40 percent for each data center. As new applications are directed to client-server systems, some of the overcapacity becomes unnecessary. Since it is also unlikely that data centers serving different business units will simultaneously experience peak loads or the need for failure recovery, a major part of this overcapacity may be eliminated by consolidation, which will result in substantial savings.

Considering the trend toward an information systems architecture that views the mainframe as a large server, recentralization of mainframe power leads to the future creation of the information utility or computing utility previously described (although this concept may also be implemented with distributed large data centers). The information utility concept is completely consistent with the new IS management paradigm.

In a number of instances, the centralization of data centers has been concurrent with, or a precursor to, outsourcing of the centralized data center operation or of major applications.

User Support

> *Personal computer users' demands for support will require innovative approaches reaching all parts of the organization.*

In an era of spreadsheets, natural language queries, automated screen design tools, prototyping methods, fourth-generation languages, and object-oriented programming, users are increasingly able to help themselves. In fact, it is almost impossible to discourage or prevent user self-support.

For example, in 1993 Owens-Corning Fiberglas, replaced more than 370 disparate databases that had evolved over time with one integrated client-server system. End users are now managing and modifying their own applications using this database, without the intervention of IS programmers.

Many centralized IS organizations have already realized the futility of opposing the trend toward user self-support and now try to assist their users by providing consulting teams and hotlines to help users become more self-sufficient. Although current experience shows that development backlogs for major systems applications have not been reduced by increased user self-support, there have been two major benefits to the IS professional organization:

- User satisfaction increases as the IS organization becomes more helpful.
- Users are becoming better able to define system needs as they learn more about the potentials and constraints of information systems. In effect, they become more knowledgeable buyers of IS services.

User support takes several forms: personal hands-on attention requiring the local presence of the support team; training requiring occasional local presence; and hotline services (either by telephone or electronic mail). Because local presence is required "as-needed," economy often dictates that the same support function handle the hotline services as well.

User support contains a new element in which users contribute to their own support. Every office or plant seems to have its share of employees who have become fascinated with their personal computers or workstations, and smart managers are taking advantage of this situation. Rather than complain that the employee is spending too much time on the technology and not enough on his or her assigned task, these companies are surveying the skills of the "experts" and appointing them as "gurus" to provide technical support to other users in their department or division.

Satisfying users with the levels of support they think they require is no easy task. John P. Halloran and Brian S. Pappas, writing in *CIO*,[10] recommend establishing clear-cut, formally defined services and service agreements to prevent user support services from degrading into a "reactive free-for-all." Such agreements should set forth a definition of the services, the business-related goals of the services, and the measures by which satisfactory performance will be judged. (See Chapter 18.)

Information Management

> *Users' needs to access information will create new functions and introduce new specialists to support information-intensive processes in the company.*

A new concept and a position are growing out of the need for corporations to share critical information among appropriate managers and professionals. A few research-oriented organizations (such as pharmaceutical companies) have recognized this need and created the position of director of information management (IM). One such company has over 100 employees in the IM department serving its R&D organization. Several concerns drive the need for this position and the department that supports it:

- For technology-based companies, the growing flood of internal and external information is too much for individual users to digest and determine its relevance to their work.
- In many instances, technology workers have difficulty in accessing information, do not understand how to phrase queries for the various access methods, or do not know all the possible sources for pertinent information.
- A "due-diligence" search of records is needed to protect potential patents or proprietary developments of the company.
- Indexing stored information to enable appropriate retrieval requires standards that are difficult to control if left to researchers, engineers, and others who may be information providers.
- In the litigious society of the United States, the availability of information often mandates its use. For example, a doctor who prescribes a medication is expected to know the potential reactions to the medication as described in the *Physician's Desk Reference*. Prescribing the wrong medication for the circumstances can lead to a suit based on the concept that the physician possessed the information and did not use it. Similarly, class action suits over defective products have been based on the defendant's possession of information that related to the defects. Corporate officers are liable even if they were not aware of the availability of the information. The corporation may need a means to

ensure that critical information is brought to the attention of those who need to know.

To answer these concerns, the IM function needs to be established in functional groups or processes that require information storage and access. Such organizations may be R&D groups, patent attorneys' offices, legal departments, marketing departments, and other information-intensive operations. IM groups should be organizationally (and often physically) close to the organizations they support. Their functions include

- Defining the information storage and retrieval requirements of their "clients" to information systems providers
- Identifying internal and external sources of information and making appropriate arrangements for access to the information
- Establishing standards and procedures for the classification, indexing, and storage of information
- Classifying, indexing, and storing information
- Assisting in formulating queries for information
- Retrieving and disseminating requested information
- Establishing an "alert service" for clients to identify, retrieve, and disseminate information critical to their needs when it first appears
- Maintaining a close liaison with IS, external information sources, and users to anticipate needs and resolve problems

Technical Support

Specialized technical support will need to combine both centralized and decentralized approaches to provide needed service effectively.

Technical support (a function often referred to as "systems programming" in mainframe language) used to be charged with the tasks of installing and maintaining operating systems or other systems software; solving problems created by systems software failures; training and advising applications developers; developing standards; installing new equipment and reconfiguring equipment; evaluating new technology or products; and providing technical advise to IS, systems development, and operations management. Technical support also frequently acted as an interpreter between the vendors of equipment and/or software and the IS organization.

In the new paradigm, the role of technical support is changing dramatically because of new responsibilities, the need for distribution of some activities, and economies of centralization for others. New responsibilities may include managing the distribution of personal computer-based software over the corporation's network to ensure that consistent versions are used throughout the company. Technical support may also take on the duties of user support and of training departmental user support personnel.

Technical support duties in the future (currently, with some firms) in a large, complex, heterogeneous environment may be organized and located at different places, as follows:

Business unit, division, or plant:
- Providing technical support beyond the skills of user specialists
- Installing or reconfiguring of hardware and local area networks or gateways
- Solving problems created by systems software failures
- Training departmental support personnel
- Installing and maintaining operating systems or other systems software
- Training and advising applications developers
- Providing technical advice to IS, systems development, and operations management
- Managing IT standards for the business unit
- Managing the distribution of personal-computer-based software (business unit applications)

Corporate:
- Managing the distribution of personal-computer-based software (corporate-wide)
- Developing corporate information systems standards
- Evaluating new technology or products (See Chapter 4.)
- Providing the activities listed above but to the corporate group and corporate data center

Communications

> *Centralized communications management will remain the most cost-effective approach.*

Communications technology and the communications carriers, pushed by the increasing demands of users, are responding with a range of competitively priced offerings to permit their customers better global connectivity. The demand for additional communications capacity is created by several trends and expectations, including

- Increased volumes of information exchanged
- Greater use of electronic data interchange (EDI)
- Transmission of graphic materials

- Increasing use of videoconferencing
- Anticipation of multimedia systems
- Trends toward groupware
- Telecommuting for workers
- Implementation of the "extended enterprise" concept

In these applications, efficiency and lower cost are often gained through use of the same networks for combinations of voice and data transmission. In fact, this combined capability is critical for future adoption of multimedia technology and tools.

Because data and voice communications are truly a utility for all users, it makes eminent sense to centralize these functions. Skilled telecommunications planners, network designers, and network managers are scarce, and centralization requires fewer such specialists. The very nature of networks allows these specialists to be located at almost any facility of the company. Furthermore, centralized management of communications permits better deals to be made with carriers. Some companies have found that once they have centralized their communications network management and really understand the scope and usage of the network, they are in a better position to outsource network management and operations, saving even more money.

When operations such as telecommunications management are outsourced, the management functions and the work performed by employees change. No longer do managers direct large numbers of employees, plan their activities, evaluate and select equipment and tools, and so forth. No longer do employees directly plan and manage the facilities and routes, implement network facilities, and assist in network recovery. With outsourcing, managers evaluate contractors, arrange contracts, plan for future demand, establish performance measurement criteria and agreements, and monitor the performance of the contractors. The few technical employees remaining assist the manager with contract management functions. These new duties require new skills and may mean the retraining or replacement of personnel.

Information Security

> *Both users and IS professionals will be required to assume responsibility for ensuring information security.*

Maintaining the availability of information and information processing resources; ensuring the integrity of information during processing, storage and transmission; and ensuring the confidentiality of information throughout the company have long been the domain of the information security organization within IS. With the increasing distribution of information processing resources, there is a growing need to classify the functions that should be centralized, those that should be dispersed, and those that should not be a part of information security. The basic principle of such reorganization is ownership of information systems and data.

Figure 1.1 illustrates the manner in which large multidivision companies are beginning to allocate the responsibility for the services required to preserve information security.[11] In many instances, an organization that bears a specific responsibility, such as an application owner, does not have all the resources or skills necessary to carry out its responsibilities. In such cases, the organization bearing primary responsibility is designated by a "P" in the appropriate matrix cell. Organizations that support the primary responsibilities are designated by an "S" in the matrix. Several activities require coordination among various groups. As such coordination must be designated by policies and procedures that need to be developed by each company, the coordination activity is not shown in the matrix.

In this matrix, the only organizations that typically reside at the corporate level are the network provider, internal audit, and the corporate information security function. All others either reside at business units or serve the corporate-level functions of the company. There are many variations in reporting relationships for the corporate information security (CIS) function, including being a part of the overall security function or reporting to the CIO. CIS has responsibility for coordinating a company-wide information security program; this unit's manager should be responsible for program coordination. The CIS unit should do the following:

- Ensure that information security policy, procedures, and standards are complete and correct.
- Facilitate identifying information asset ownership and sensitivity classifications of applications or information by owners.
- Advise senior management of information security issues affecting the corporation.
- Establish and coordinate the information security standards-setting process by creating a corporate information security standards document. This document should define program elements, responsibilities, and high-level control requirements, with appropriate references to the information systems standards document and a section that identifies specific technical and procedural controls for information security in various types of information systems environments.
- Provide information security training and support to the group coordinators.
- Establish and sustain a corporate-wide information security awareness program.

Organizations Responsible

Services Required	Network Provider	Application Owner	Application Developer	System Operator	Corporate Information Security	Security Coordinator	Internal Audit
Policy and procedure development	S			S	P	S	S
Employee security training and awareness					P	S	
Establishment of security facilities	P	S				S	
Security development for applications		P	S	S	S		
Ongoing operational administration and control:							
Network availability	P			S		S	
Information confidentiality and integrity		P	S	S		S	
Resource availability			S	P			
Procedural advisory services					P	S	
Technical advisory services	P						
Emergency response support	P			S			
Compliance monitoring	S		S		S		P

P–primary responsibility; S–support responsibility.

Figure 1.1. Security Responsibility Matrix

23

See Section 5 for a more extensive discussion of information security functions and methods.

Standards

> In many organizations, the only corporate IT standards that remain may be those that ensure connectivity among users and systems.

Standards for hardware, software, and development methods have long been a concern of IS heads. The rationale for standards is clear: They tend to lessen the variability of results. In doing this, good standards reduce complexity, make maintenance easier, reduce the numbers of technical support specialists required, and save costs. Poor standards, on the other hand, may paralyze an organization with paperwork and procedures or lead to ingrained thinking and methods that prevent or slow the adoption of new techniques and technology.

At their worst, standards are an excuse for not thinking and for "playing it safe." The old argument of the managers who elected to create "true blue" shops that only bought from IBM was based on this type of "standard": "If you buy from IBM, no one can fault you if something goes wrong."

However, as users become increasingly aggressive in choosing their information systems solutions, and as application packages become an increasingly viable solution to specialized user needs, the selection of a package may drive the selection of the hardware and systems software that supports the package. Furthermore, as prices for desktop and portable computers drop into the range of purchasing approval by lower-level managers, these managers become quite willing to select equipment and solutions that provide the most for their money, regardless of so-called corporate standards.

New applications using advanced technology such as artificial intelligence, image processing, and groupware have forced both users and IS groups to seek alternatives among potential suppliers and to create or adopt new methods for application development.

Considering all these impacts in combination with the decentralization of information systems resources, it is not surprising that standards have become a major point of contention in many corporations. In diversified corporations, many business units feel that corporate standards inhibit their ability to respond to competitive needs and changing markets. One basic management principle must be observed in regard to standards—don't make rules if you can not enforce them.

In a new information systems management paradigm, responsibility for the development, promulgation, and enforcement of standards will need to be changed radically. This change will require a fundamentally new philosophy for IT standards in a corporation, a philosophy that might be termed "standards by exception" and "self-enforcing standards."

Rethinking standards requires that we reestablish the premises on which they are based. Standards are useful for

- Ensuring the ability to exchange and distribute information among members of a group who have common requirements to access the information
- Minimizing the need for scarce or expensive skills required to maintain the operating capability of information processing resources
- Reducing the complexity (and therefore the cost) of providing interconnectivity for a community of users (or devices) who must communicate with each other
- Minimizing the ongoing cost of maintaining and enhancing applications
- Ensuring timely responsiveness to business needs
- Ensuring the pertinence, accuracy, and quality (and therefore the long-term costs) of new applications developed or acquired by the company

If this view of basic premises is adopted, the first consideration in establishing standards becomes the identification of the communities of users; the second becomes the maximization of the business unit's ability to respond to changing business needs; and the third becomes the minimization of long-term costs. These considerations, or imperatives, mean that different standards may be required for different business units, processes, or functions within a corporation. A corollary imperative is that corporate standards be limited to those necessary to ensure the objectives of *corporate* functions.

By this logic we can see that corporate standards should apply to those functions, applications, or resources that are either supported for the entire company as a "community" or required for the operation of the corporation as a coherent entity. As a result, it becomes apparent that interfacing equipment, systems software, or applications to a corporate wide area network that all business units share will require that connectivity standards be developed and promulgated from a corporate level. For example, the corporate IS group of RAND Corporation, a research and development company based in Santa Monica, California, allows its distributed users to buy any of the widely available desktop computers as long as the machines' communications capabilities are compatible with corporate network standards. This type of standard is self-enforcing, since nonstandard connectivity is not supported and nonstandard devices cannot use the network.

Some large corporations face a struggle with the standardization of electronic mail and electronic data interchange (EDI) after permitting random adoption and growth of different systems by the business units. The problem exists because of a lack of foresight and a failure to recognize appropriate corporate standards compared to business unit standards. Identifying the community of users when the adoption of this application began would have led to the development of corporate standards. On the other hand, identifying the community of users for image processing systems that will have application only within a business unit leads to development of standards within the business unit, since the requirements for such systems in other business units may be different.

Standards for application development may present a different kind of problem. Obviously, it is in the interest of the corporation to obtain all the advantages of standards globally. However, unless these standards can be enforced, they are worthless. Clearly, interfaces to corporate applications such as general ledger accounting can be self-enforced—if the format is not correct, the transaction will be rejected. But other issues are more troublesome.

Just as users have become aware of the advantages of packaged software use, companies are realizing the advantages of reusing proven software. Many companies make a serious effort to transfer applications from the business unit responsible for original development to other business units that will find the application suitable. Such transferability requires that the application be developed according to an implicit "commercial" standard so that subsequent users can support future enhancement as their needs diverge. Failure to meet this commercial standard reduces opportunities for transferability. Although the cost savings to the corporation alone may not impose an overriding need for standards, self-enforcement may come from the developers' desire to share the cost of development by "reselling" the application.

Packages are becoming both larger and smaller. Total applications have become more ambitious in scope, producing larger packages of code and documentation. Conversely, the growing use of object-oriented design and object-oriented programming (OOP), and the resulting objects, provide smaller packages of proven code that may be reused effectively to reduce development costs.[12]

As the use of "object technology" gradually grows, we can expect attempts to expand this use from single applications to broad application suites and from sharing of objects among a limited group of application developers to use by application developers (and users) throughout the company. In order to accomplish this expansion of use, companies will need to use OOP within a development framework that is composed of CASE tools implemented in a distributed, cooperative processing environment. Effective use of OOP will require that two major concerns be addressed: management of the object inventory and preservation of information security in an object-oriented development environment. This implies that standards for the development and management of objects will need to be created for the community of potential users of the objects. (See Chapter 8.)

In sum, both standards and standards management will need to be rethought and redesigned by almost all computer-using companies.

Quality Management

> The new CIO will need to lead the drive to quality management in information systems.

Quality management is closely associated with both standards and the functions of information security; however, it deserves to be addressed separately because too little attention has been given to the issues of quality per se in the past.

Quality management techniques (often under the title of total quality management, or TQM) have been successfully employed throughout many company operations not only to improve the quality of products and process results but to improve the spirit in which these are delivered to both internal and external customers. IS needs to adopt these techniques, in both service and product aspects, for computer and communications operations and for applications development, maintenance, and enhancement.

Implementation and management of quality management techniques will require development of procedures, training, and monitoring of results. They will require that service providers and recipients work together to clearly delineate their respective roles and responsibilities and to set up means to ensure that objectives are consistently met.

Quality management must address relevance, timeliness, accuracy, cost, and user satisfaction with the IS services. From an operations perspective, this means that criteria for measurement of services and procedures to report results and deal with discrepancies will need to be established. From a systems development perspective, it additionally requires that users be prepared to take a major role in IS strategic planning, defining application requirements, redesigning business processes, monitoring project progress, and conducting acceptance testing.

Quality management techniques go beyond simple evaluation of performance measures. (See Chapter 18.) With a goal of "customer satisfaction," IS management is finding it necessary to view its functions as "processes" in the same way that other corporate functions have done. Ernst & Young[13] have divided the IS function into seven key processes that it feels create business value, provide ongoing business support, or do both. Each process may include subprocesses, but each defines specific customers and products. These processes are

- IT-enabled business opportunity identification
- IT infrastructure stewardship
- IT component delivery and evolution
- IS operations
- IS customer support
- IS strategy development
- IS management

In 1993 the Society for Information Management, with a membership of over 2,700 IS managers, launched several quality-related studies, including one to identify IS processes, one to create a matrix evaluation tool for rating levels of quality, and one to examine business process redesign methods and identify prominent practitioners.

Quality management will need to start at the top of the organization through leadership and example, but it will need to be implemented at the level where the work is performed (including the same vision of the extended enterprise as that adopted by the rest of the company).

Software Logistics Management

> *The complexity of software management and the benefits available from reuse of proven software will force IS managers to control software inventories in a new way.*

Another function closely allied to standards is software logistics management (SLM), which consists of three elements:

- Enabling application software developed by one owner to be used by another owner. For example, a materials inventory control system developed by one business unit may be suitable, with little or no modification, to the needs of another business unit. Coordination through an SLM function is necessary if the availability of the application is to be made known and the potential for reuse (and the consequent savings to the company) realized.
- Ensuring version control of popular software packages. In many companies, the use of text editing or spreadsheet software, for example, has proliferated throughout the personal computer user community. The SLM function can coordinate purchases of commonly used soft-

ware packages to obtain better prices. In addition, over telecommunications facilities, SLM can distribute new releases of the software to ensure that users maintain compatibility and are using the latest approved version.

- As the use of object-oriented programming increases, anticipating that end users as well as analysts and programmers will reuse objects to reduce the time and cost necessary to develop applications. Objects that are required to be standard across the corporation will need to be managed and controlled at the corporate level. The SLM function will need to manage object libraries, ensure the integrity of the objects, facilitate access to objects by authorized users, and provide support for modification and reuse of objects.

SLM functions may be established at both a corporate level and a business unit level depending on the size of the business units and their needs. (See Chapter 8.)

Technology Management

Technology management will need to leverage the talents of a few skilled planners, but find ways to involve users more than in the past.

Competitive pressures have awakened executives to the knowledge that technology management is as important for their information systems as it is for their manufacturing facilities and products. As a result, IS executives are under increasing pressure to meet the same goals of efficiency, cost reduction, and responsiveness other organizations within their companies must meet.

Many companies, having dedicated years to the development and implementation of mainframe-oriented business systems, have hundreds of millions of dollars invested in hardware and huge application software libraries. Mainframe-based systems will be with us for many years to come; however, newer technologies are very attractive to hard-pressed IS directors because of better price/performance ratios, faster software development paradigms, specialized application capabilities, smaller increments of capacity increases, and improved architectural flexibility. In addition, the efforts of many companies to redesign their business processes have resulted in a surge of interest in new information technologies.

Business needs have spurred the adoption of new information technology, but in many cases, IS departments are poorly equipped to deal with the entire scope of managing the introduction of new technology to the firm. IS executives must learn how to successfully introduce new information technologies to the firm, how to unify IS and information systems users into a cooperative technology planning team, and how to take advantage of the new disciplines of business process redesign by using the enabling power of advanced information technology.[14]

Users who are taking charge of their information processing, combined with the view of information technology as an enabling capability for business process redesign, have changed the approach to technology management from one in which IS "introduced" new technology to the company to one in which the users set the requirements for new technology—that is, from technology *push* to demand *pull*. In this new environment, the functions and roles associated with technology planning must be closer to the user than ever. But this is not to say that the CIO does not have a role.

IS needs to perform certain functions to ensure that the technology knowledge and skills are in place when they are called for by users. Issues that will have to be faced and the methods by which they may be addressed are described extensively in Chapter 4.

As a part of overall strategic planning and assisting business units with strategic IT planning, the CIO must maintain a realistic awareness of the company's position in the use of IT. Increasingly, CIOs are turning to consultants to perform benchmarks in which the company's performance is compared to that of competitors. Such benchmarks not only are concerned with technology adoption, but also may provide insight into the company's relative position in software development methods, project management, quality management, and user satisfaction. In addition, in the search for new ideas, some CIOs have asked that benchmarks go beyond the usual comparison to competitors and include firms from other industries from which the company can adapt payoff ideas.

Strategic Planning

> *Strategic IT planning will be performed primarily at the business unit level.*

It is apparent from the preceding discussion that strategic planning for information systems in large corporations must take place at two coordinated levels. The bulk of strategic planning must take place at the business unit level. At this level it is most closely related to the demand rising from the processes of the business that IS serves. At the corporate level, strategic planning must take a new form. If corporate functions such as accounting, finance, treasury, and legal, are considered to be another type of business unit, the CIO may be responsible for strategic planning of IS for these—just as the CIO may carry out all the other functions of IS management for the corporate-level operations. However, in the context of supporting IS planning for strategic business units, and for the corporation as a whole, the CIO must operate in a different mode.

In the new paradigm, the CIO's duties focus on policy and strategy concerns rather than on operational concerns. This means that the strategic planning activities of the CIO will be related to

- Planning for support of centralized IS functions
- Planning overall IT policy for the corporation
- Advising business units on their strategic IS plans
- Influencing the corporate strategy to take advantage of IT to maintain the company's competitive advantage

Of these duties, the latter two may be the most critical. That is because strategic business plans developed without regard to the competitive threats and opportunities supported by technology advances can be blindsided by more aggressive users of technology.

HOW INFORMATION SYSTEMS MANAGEMENT IS CHANGING

The Stages of IS Management

When told by an advisor that his proposed actions would alienate the Pope, Joseph Stalin is supposed to have asked, "How many divisions has the Pope?" Stalin's thinking assumed that power is the product of the numbers of people reporting to an individual. The Pope, on the other hand, is powerful because of the numbers of people he *influences*.

Future CIOs, and current CIOs who intend to survive the paradigm shift, must divest themselves of the misconception that power comes from direct command of resources. The power of the new CIO will come from knowledge of the technology, knowledge of the business, and the skill to combine the two and influence the strategic directions of the company and its business units.

Companies that currently face the issue of centralization versus decentralization must realize that the onslaught of technology and the consequent empowerment of end users is more powerful than any desire for IS management control. Managers must be cognizant of the reality of decentralized processing—it has invaded all organizations. However, it is not technology alone that is driving the IS organization toward decentralization; it is the customers of the IS function who are trying to find ways to better satisfy their business needs for information and business process support.

Since the 1950s, IS management has evolved as the technology has enabled changes. The five stages through which IS management has moved tend to overlap, as early adopters of technology move more quickly than technology followers. These stages are described in Figure 1.2, which illus-

	Stage 1 1950–1970	Stage 2 1965–1975	Stage 3 1975–1985	Stage 4 1980–1995	Stage 5 1990–Future
Technology	Mainframe batch operations	Mainframe with connected terminals, batch, and online operations	Mainframe, PCs, telecommunications, minicomputers, primarily online operations	Mainframe, PCs, workstations, wide area networks, local area networks, online operations	Client-server workstations/PCs, wide area and local area networks, cooperative processing, wireless portable computing, online operations, lights-out data centers
Organization	Centralized two-level structure	Centralized two-level structure	Centralized control with distributed operations, two- to three-level structure	Centralized control, distributed computing, some distributed system development, two- to three-level structure	Limited centralized control, business unit ownership of IS; dispersed, heterogeneous interconnected systems; dispersed systems development; four-level structure
CIO's role	EDP manager, hands-on management and supervision	MIS director, IS management	Director or vice president of MIS, management and control of all IS resources	Vice president of MIS or CIO, management of centralized resources, some control of distributed resources	CIO, limited management of resources, leadership role in technology strategy and management, power through influence

EDP—electronic data processing; MIS—management information systems; PC—personal computer;
CIO—chief information officer

Figure 1.2.   The Stages of Information Systems Management

trates the technology enablers, the changes in organization, and the changes in the CIO's role during each stage.

The future shape of IS management involves not one level of IS organization or even two (as in the earlier versions of distributed computing), but three or four. These levels depend on the scope and size of the business units they serve. A brief description of each of these levels provides an idea of how the new paradigm may be implemented.

Level One: The End User

Driven by trends toward client-server architectures, groupware, cooperative processing, and specialized systems such as image processing or CAD, the "MIPS (millions of instructions per second) on desktops" promise to outweigh the "MIPS in the glass house." With the raw power now in the hands of the users, the responsibility for creation and enhancement of applications will soon follow. This combination of trends will be fostered through a flood of new tools that allow users to design and enhance their own applications. New applications built out of spreadsheets, personal computer database management systems, or text editors are appearing with increasing frequency as this book is written. Since most of these applications support business activities within a limited work function or business process, any standards applied or any sharing of applications will need to be managed within the process level or the business unit level.

Level Two: The Business Process

Business processes may be somewhat arbitrarily defined by business units, although the need for a continuous flow of work or information often creates a "natural" boundary. Processes may be as small as a business unit's human resources function or as large as a procurement and inventory control function that includes material requirements generation, procurement, receiving and inspection, accounts payable, and inventory control. As companies abandon the inefficiencies and turf battles connected with the classical hierarchical and function-oriented organization, and reorganize along business process lines, the management of these processes will demand control of the information resources necessary for their operation. At this level, the architectures will contain specialized systems, mini- or mid-range computers, and client-server systems. The issues will be to manage internal resources and outsourcing, develop standards and manage conformity to standards, continue to be responsive to business needs, control costs, plan future use of IT, ensure information security, provide technical support to users, and operate computers (servers) that are commonly used by all participants of the process.

Level Three: The Business Unit

A small business unit may have all the responsibilities delineated for the process level. In larger business units, where responsibility for process information systems is taken by process managers, the head of IS for the unit may act as the unit's CIO. At this level the responsibilities may include wide area communications management and unit-wide standards and policies. In order to minimize redundant staffing and cope with the shortage of highly trained technicians, technical support, technical and end user training, information systems R&D, and highly specialized information technology expertise will be relatively centralized at the strategic business unit level, if the unit is large enough and autonomous enough. If the business unit is too small to effectively support these functions, they will reside at the corporate level. This level may also include responsibility for specialized technical support, strategic planning, coordination with the corporate CIO, and other duties typical of a CIO.

Note that in very large business units, the responsibilities and functions normally conducted at a business unit level may be allotted to plants or divisions.

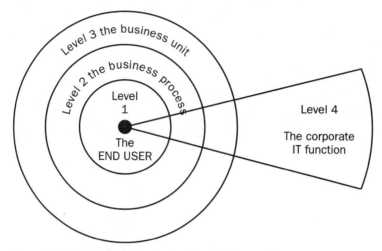

Figure 1.3.   Relationships in the New IS Management Structure

Level Four: The Corporation

Aside from being responsible for IS support for corporate functions (which may be delegated to a corporate IS manager), the corporate CIO of the future will directly manage few functions. Instead, he or she should expect to be an advisor, a strategist, a business executive, a salesperson, and a missionary. These new roles lead naturally into a discussion of the functions for which the CIO of the future may expect to be responsible.

The relative relationships and the leadership influence of the corporate level is illustrated in Figure 3. Each of the concentric circles, represent levels within the business unit, exert management control or ownership of resources from level 3 down to level 1. The level-4 corporate IS function (or the CIO) exerts a leadership influence that permeates the organization (in addition to direct management of the functions retained for corporate information systems).

THE FUNCTIONS OF THE FUTURE CIO

The CIO of the future should expect to focus attention on four key objectives of IS that

- Influence the ability of the corporation to gain competitive advantage from IT
- Maximize the effective utilization of scarce resources

- Ensure the ability of the business to avoid or recover from business interruption
- Ensure the ability of the corporation to effectively communicate information

The functions and responsibilities of the CIO in regard to meeting these objectives should include the following:

- *Participating in development of corporate strategy.* A key function of the CIO is to establish the corporate strategic technology position (adopter, adapter, or inventor, as described in Chapter 8) for IT use. Since this may vary by business unit, it will require that the CIO be familiar with the business needs of the units and be prepared to advise them on technology positioning and strategic planning for their IS functions. In addition to this function, the CIO of the future must be a direct participant in corporate strategy development, advising the CEO and COO on potential threats or opportunities arising from the introduction of new technology to the market or from competitors' use of information technology.

- *Leading IS quality management.* While much of the implementation for IS will be at a business unit level, the corporate level must set the pace by defining objectives, creating standards and methods, conducting training, implementing reward and penalty incentives, establishing quality councils, and recommending appropriate process redesign.

- *Managing the development and promulgation of corporate IT standards.* Corporate standards will still be required in a decentralized world. They must start with development and maintenance of corporate IS policies, then address standard practices and procedures (such as capital expense control), and finally deal with technical standards. Individual business units may have differing business needs; may be positioned differently in regard to competition; may apply different levels of sophistication to systems development; or may differ in their use of outsourcing. For this reason, corporate policies, procedures, and standards must be restricted to those absolutely necessary to ensure communication through interconnectivity and to ensure effective business practices. In some corporations, standards may be used to ensure the effective transferability of applications from the developer to other potential users. Strategic business unit executives who are responsible for their unit's bottom line must be granted maximum control over their resources.

- *Ensuring career development paths for IS personnel.* A significant challenge to the success of IS decentralization is that career paths may be limited by the scope and resources of business units. As a result, the corporation may lose valuable talent. The CIO must establish policies that give preference to qualified current employees for openings anywhere in the corporation. Furthermore, the CIO should establish training programs and facilities and promote their active use by IS professionals in the corporation. Such efforts and expense are more than offset by the preservation of the professional capital of the corporation.

• *Establishing and directing corporate IT research and development.* This function also will require that the CIO establish and conduct meetings for a corporate IT R&D council composed of business unit IS directors and COOs. The R&D Council will set the directions of R&D to conform with corporate strategy and business unit needs. The IT R&D function in many companies may provide a resource for the development of applications using new or advanced technology for which the business units do not yet have the skills. Examples include applications of artificial intelligence, modeling, and statistical analysis techniques.

• *Supporting information technology management and transfer.* Closely allied to the IT R&D function is the technology management function. The scarcity of talented IT planners means that corporate support will be necessary to the business units. A corporate information technology management group can aid in ensuring that IS functions in business units remain current with technology trends and with new practices in business process redesign or systems development.

• *Directing the management of the corporate wide area telecommunications network.* The network, as previously noted, is a utility that provides connectivity throughout the corporation. Whether operated by internal resources or outsourced, it will require management.

• *Directing corporate information security.* The corporate information security function is responsible for development and promulgation of information security policy, and it may take other roles when economy or scarcity of resources dictate. Supporting information security requirements may also require the creation of a computer emergency response team. Such teams, composed of a few highly trained individuals, have become increasingly popular in combating the affects of computer virus infection or assisting in the recovery from disasters.

• *Directing the corporate information processing utility.* Although directing the management of the corporate IS function may be included in the list of CIO functions, actual management is usually delegated to a corporate IS director. As a result, that function has been excluded from this list in favor of the CIO's role in directing the management of a corporate IS utility that acts an an outsourcing contractor to provide processing capacity to business units. The corporate information processing utility offers value in providing regular operational capacity beyond that owned by some business units, capacity for unusual or sporadic workloads, a backup or warm-site facility for disaster recovery, or technical support to meet occasional business unit needs.

• *Aiding in minimizing business and technical risk.* The CIO, as the most senior IS executive, will be a member of any IS steering committees in the company's business units. In this capacity, the CIO will provide strategic guidance and the benefit of experience to the committee's deliberations and decisions.

• *Coordinating purchase agreements to obtain the best prices.* Rather than setting detailed standards, the CIO is in a position to use the large purchasing power of the corporation to obtain the best prices by coordinating purchase agreements. The prices that business units can obtain for isolated and small-volume purchases of equipment, compared to the prices of consolidated purchases of popular equipment, is greater incentive than standards for conformity.

• *Directing software logistics management.* This function will be required at a corporate level and may be required by business units as well.

The functions described above generally meet more than one of the key objectives of the CIO. This relationship between functions and objectives may best be illustrated by the matrix shown in Figure 1.4.

Democratization or Balkanization?

Depending on perspective, the future path of IS management may appear to be either democratization or Balkanization. In either case, the populist movement is coming to IS rapidly. In a 1993 survey by *CIO* magazine of 110 IS executives in companies with over $500 million in annual revenues,[15] 46 percent of those who had distributed their computing said that the general managers of business units were the driving force behind the change. This was more than twice the number of any other groups cited as the prime movers.

The challenge for CIOs is to manage the transition in a fashion that leads to user control and responsibility for information and information resources, without the internecine warfare and chaos implied by Balkanization. Thomas Kiely has described the IS management structures of PepsiCo, Inc. of Purchase, New York, Marion Merrell Dow Inc. of Kansas City, Missouri, and Rockwell International of Seal Beach, California.[16] Each of these companies found a slightly different path to an IS organizational infrastructure that closely approximates the new paradigm described here. The route taken by each mirrors the organization and business strategies of the corporation. For example, PepsiCo's IS manage-

Objectives

Functions	Help to Gain Competitive Advantage	Maximize Use of Scarce Resources	Avoid/Recover from Business Interruption	Ensure Effective Communication
Participating in development of corporate strategy	•	•	•	•
Leading IS quality management	•			
Managing the development and promulgation of corporate IT standards		•	•	•
Ensuring career development paths for IS personnel		•		
Establishing and directing corporate IT research and development	•	•		•
Supporting information technology management and transfer	•	•		
Directing the management of the corporate wide area telecommunications network		•	•	•
Directing corporate information security		•	•	
Directing the corporate information processing utility		•	•	
Aiding in minimizing business and technical risk	•	•	•	
Coordinating purchase agreements to obtain the best prices		•		•
Directing software logistics management	•			•

Figure 1.4. Matrix of CIO Objectives and Functions

Table 1.3. Comparative IS Management Approaches

Functional Approach	PepsiCo	Marion Merrell Dow	Rockwell
Business unit controls IS resources:			
Computers	Yes	Partial	Yes
Software development	Yes	Partial	Yes
CIO manages corporate IS	Yes	Yes	Yes
CIO's leadership role is facilitation, not control	Yes	—	—
CIO's leadership role is coordination and control	—	Yes	Partial
CIO sets standards	No	No	Yes
CIO coordinates procurement	Yes	Yes	Yes
CIO is responsible for technology management	Yes	No	Yes
CIO manages telecommunications	No	Yes	Yes
CIO provides common core applications	No	Yes	Partial

ment reflects the fact that several of its business units compete with each other. Table 1.3 indicates how these corporations differ in their implementations of new IS management approaches.

In general, the new paradigm contains four roles that are played by the different levels:

- *Primary responsibility*—the ownership and direct management of information resources
- *Alternate or similar responsibility*—in which ownership and management are delegated or restricted to a given level
- *Leadership*—in which leadership and influence replace direct ownership and management
- *Support*—in which organizations may have limited resources (e.g., at the desktop) and must support the levels with broader responsibility

Table 1.4 illustrates this new alignment of IS management responsibility under the overall ownership of the responsible user management at the corporate, business unit, business process or end user level.

Transition to this new role will require that CIOs display true leader-

Table 1.4.   New Roles for the Four Levels of IS Management

Function Performed	IS Level			
	1	2	3	4
Information utility operation			A	P
Information security management	S	S	S	L
Standards development		A	P	L
Quality management	S	S	A	L
Technology management		S	A	L
Strategic IS planning		A	P	L
Strategic business planning		S	P	L
Software logistics management		A	A	P
Procurement management			P	L
Employee career maintenance	S	S	P	L
Communications operation/management			A	P
Computer operations		A	P	A
Systems development	S	A	P	A
Technical support	S	A	P	L
User support	A	A	P	A
Information management		A	P	

P—primary responsibility; A—alternate or similar responsibility limited to designated level; L—leadership role; S—support role.

ship for the benefit of their company and for their own survival. Leadership, rather than rear-guard actions to preserve territory, will be the key to success.

DISCUSSION TOPICS

- How does the IS management paradigm described in this chapter compare to IS organizations with which you are familiar?
- Are the functions described in this chapter carried out in organizations that you have observed?
- To what organization or management structure do these functions report?
- Do you feel that any of the functions described are unnecessary? Why?
- What are the forces that are driving IS organizations?
- What is the future for the "information management" concept?

REFERENCES:

1. "Study Sees Long Life for Mainframe Apps." *Computerworld*, April 12, 1993.
2. Tully, S. "The Modular Corporation." *Fortune*, February 8, 1993.
3. Malone, M., and Davidow, W. "Virtual Corporation." *Forbes ASAP*, February 1993.
4. Byrne, J. "The Virtual Corporation." *Business Week*, February 8, 1993.
5. Fried, L. "A Blueprint for Change. "*Computerworld*, December 2, 1991, 91–95.
6. Fried, L. "Outsourcing Confessions." *Computerworld*, February 8, 1993 and Fried, L. *How to Succeed at MIS Outsourcing*. Menlo Park, CA: SRI International Business Intelligence Program, March 1993.
7. Strassmann, P. *The Business Value of Computers*. New Canaan, CT: The Information Economics Press, 1990.
8. Fried, L. *Information Technology Adoption: A Survey of Advanced Information Technology Use in Multinational Corporations*. Menlo Park, CA: SRI International Business Intelligence Program, June 1992, and Fried, L. "Advanced Information Technology Use." *Information Systems Management*, Spring 1993.
9. von Simson, E.M. "The 'Centrally Decentralized' IS Organization." *Harvard Business Review*, July-August 1990.
10. Halloran, J.P., and Pappas, B.S. "Micro Management." *CIO*, April 15,1993.
11. For further information on the Security Matrix, see Fried, L. "Assigning the Responsibility for Security in Distributed or Outsourced Environments." *Data Security Management*, March 1993, or Fried, L. "Responsibility for Security in Distributed or Outsourced Environments." *Datalog*, Menlo Park, CA: December, 1992.
12. Fried, L. "Management and Security Issues in Object-Oriented Programming." *Software Engineering Strategies*, March/April 1993.
13. Ernst & Young. "IS Quality." *CIO*, April 15, 1993.
14. Fried, L. "Staying Ahead of the Pack: Managing Information Technology." *Datalog*, April 1993.
15. "The Democratic Process." *CIO*, May 1991.
16. Kiely, T. "The Best of Both Worlds." *CIO*, February 1993.

The Business Context of Information Systems

Information technology supports the operations and activities of the enterprise that is the host for information systems. Professionals and information systems (IS) managers who fail to understand the goals of the enterprise and orient their efforts to reaching those goals do so at peril to their jobs.

This section establishes the context in which businesses will operate in the decade beginning in the mid-1990s. Economic forces of the early 1990s have driven companies to massive "downsizing" of their workforces, reorientation of their businesses through acquisition and diversification, and globalization to secure markets. The section addresses two major issues with which CIOs are faced as a result of such changes:

- What will be the business climate that the IS organization must support, and how will it affect the companies that supply information technology products?
- How can a CIO help the company stay competitive by using information technology?

By addressing these issues, this section addresses a broader issue touched on throughout this book—how to align IS strategy with business strategy.

CHAPTER 2

The Business Climate at the Turn of the Century

To make the right strategic choices in vendor selection and in the selection of information systems application development priorities, managers need to understand not only their own company's needs, but the major issues facing their industries and their information technology suppliers.

THE SCOPE OF INFORMATION TECHNOLOGY ISSUES

In the rest of the 1990s and beyond, information technology will present perhaps more management challenges than ever to business. In order to build a logical view of information technology issues, it is necessary to divide the broad scope of this problem into two principal segments. First is the *suppliers* of information technology products and services; second is the *users* of those products and services. Suppliers include computer manufacturers, manufacturers of computer-related products, systems integrators, software package vendors, telecommunications carriers, value-added network suppliers, and many others. Users include manufacturers, financial services companies, government agencies, travel companies, and almost every other business imaginable. A large market segment has grown since the early 1980s among private individuals using personal computers and networks. While this market clearly is influencing both supplier and user organizations, this chapter does not attempt to address the private user segment.

The issues addressed here are segregated into those of primary interest in the short term (until 1999) and those that will become challenges in the early years of the twenty-first century. Corporate managers are responsible for making decisions about how they will invest in information technology for their business. Clearly, they must make such investments within the context of their company's needs, but those needs are conditioned by general industry trends as well as the unique characteristics of their company. The sometimes huge investments in information technology must also be made with a view toward the life cycle of the investment—that is, not only the payback for the investment but the profit derived from the continued viability of the system. For this reason, the selection of suppliers may be critical to obtaining the maximum benefit from an IT investment. It is thus almost equally important to understand the issues facing suppliers and to evaluate suppliers according to their demonstrated ability to respond to the challenges raised by these issues.

THE ISSUES FOR SUPPLIERS OF IT PRODUCTS AND SERVICES

The critical issues for most suppliers are strategic business issues rather than technical issues. They center on the supplier's ability to advance its competitive position in a highly innovative field.

Short-Term (before 1999)

1.   Consolidation of the industry through mergers, acquisitions, and failures, combined with expansion of the industry through new start-up businesses.

Although the number of companies in the IT field has continued to expand in the 1980s and early 1990s and promises further expansion, this growth is mostly due to start-ups. Start-ups enter the field primarily in two venture areas: new technology-based products for either hardware or software and new service companies, primarily in software development or system integration. These areas have the common characteristic of not being burdened with a prior customer base of products that must continue to be maintained or for which compatibility must be ensured. In addition, software and service companies often have the advantage of low start-up investment. For the buyer of their products and services, the start-ups may provide advanced technology or innovative applications that can improve the buyer's competitive position. On the other hand, start-ups carry the risk that they may not survive to support their products over the useful life of the application. Nevertheless, the competitive advantages to be gained are often worth that risk.

At the other end of the industry are larger firms that are heavily involved in mergers, acquisitions, alliances, divestitures, and investments. During the 1980s, IBM poured billions of dollars into investments in software firms that market application packages or utility software. While other manufacturers have not been able to invest on the same scale or breadth, they are hard at work forming alliances with systems integrators and software developers. Now, a troubled IBM has started to question its array of investments and withdraw support from some. In the software area, Computer Associates has grown to a billion-dollar business by buying up their financially weaker competitors. In both the hardware and software areas, financially weak firms are tempting takeover targets, especially as product markets reach a plateau in sales and expansion is needed. In fact, as the AT&T acquisition of NCR shows, a takeover target need not be financially weak, it only has to be desired by a stronger company. Mergers and acquisitions often increase the financial strength of the supplier, but the buyer must be aware that specific products may be discontinued or lose support as a result.

2.   Globalization of competition as suppliers strive to keep pace with their customers' businesses.

Clients and customers are globalizing, and it is clearly necessary for their suppliers to globalize as well if they expect to retain their preferred positions. This represents a major problem for companies that are primarily local or regional such as Seimens/Nixdorf, Bull, NEC, Toshiba, and NTT. In order to enter new markets, these companies often resort to acquisition, but many times this strategy is dangerous. A company that does well before acquisition may be a disaster after acquisition and the attempt to integrate it into the acquiring company. One example of such an acquisition gone awry is the acquisition of Rolm by IBM. Zenith Data Systems' acquisition by Bull is another example.

The major concern of companies that intend to deploy a new technology globally is the ability of the vendor to ensure continuing support for purchased products wherever they may be installed.

3.   Vertical consolidation as suppliers try to more comprehensively meet the needs of customers for overall solutions to problems. Examples are EDS buying a major interest in National Data Systems, IBM buying minority shares in many software houses, and Unisys's move into the systems integration business.

Every hardware manufacturer has recognized that software and services will provide more revenues than will hardware in the future. Furthermore, as the increasing influence of open systems is felt in the market, hardware becomes more of a commodity, with attendant lower profit margins. From the supplier side, vertical expansion is seen as needed to maintain profit margins; however, vendors also seem to believe that there is a market "pull" for them to enter the services business. Continued strong competition from existing service companies, despite the favorable marketing position of the manufacturers, seems to bring market pull into question. The buyer can benefit from this situation in two ways. First, a long-range strategy of moving to open systems away from proprietary systems can lead to dramatic reductions in hardware costs and software development and maintenance costs. Second, the buyer may take advantage of "one-stop shopping" and obtain the application development, system integration, and hardware from a single source. On the other hand, the experience of computer manufacturers in supplying the application needs of users has not been an unqualified success. Application implementation is a different business from computer manufacturing; one with which many manufacturers are not familiar.

4.   Sustaining the pace of product innovation.

As previously indicated, new product entries into the field from new vendors do not have to be concerned about maintaining "backward compatibility" to old products. On the other hand, established vendors must ensure that new products do not destroy their customer base by making old products obsolete before their useful life is finished. A prime example is IBM's introduction of OS/2 for its line of PCs. The DOS market had become so large that IBM, in the short term, was unable to drag its old customers away from it. As a result, the clone makers that continue to produce DOS systems have profited at the expense of IBM, and Microsoft, the vendor of DOS, has become a multibillion dollar company.

All established hardware and software manufacturers face the problem of maintaining the pace of innovation (to attract new customers and maintain their image in the market) while not damaging their customer base. This situation has often led to substantial delay in new product introduction.

Another factor is financial strength, which primarily affects packaged software vendors. Many software packages, especially in the mainframe market, become technologically obsolete because of the inability of the seller to reinvest the sums necessary to rewrite the package.

New suppliers of new products face the problems of educating potential customers, sustaining revenues during their early years, and avoiding premature market entry. Most of their problems focus on cash flow. Existing strong suppliers can sustain a long market entry period when they introduce products with new capabilities that do not affect their products already in the hands of customers.

5.   Understanding customer needs.

One of the weakest areas for hardware manufacturers has traditionally been understanding customer needs. All suppliers have access to reports from IDC and other survey firms that describe markets and attempt to forecast trends. Still, they repeatedly encounter surprises because of the inherent limitations of trend-based forecasting. It is necessary to examine customer needs in depth and to understand how industries apply technology. Many firms attempt to remedy the shortcomings of trend-based forecasting by using input from their own sales force. Unfortunately, internal sources are biased for several reasons. Sales personnel often respond in terms of the deficiency that caused them to lose the last major sale. Frequently, they are "brainwashed" into believing the excellence of their own company's products and services. Finally, in many supplier organizations, sales personnel are subject to considerable turnover and rarely get to know a single customer's industry in depth.

Even in instances where suppliers' marketing groups have performed in-depth analyses of customers' industries and needs, the product planning results are often heavily biased toward existing products, services, and internal organization and methods. It is hard for these groups to adopt new thinking without outside help, massive management change, or dramatic market pressures.

In acquiring new products, especially applications, the buyer is well advised to make sure that the vendor's staff supporting the product has a good understanding of the buyer's industry and business needs. Most successful procurements are based on buyers protecting themselves through a careful specification of requirements, evaluation of alternatives, and evaluation of the vendor's ability to provide long-term support for the product.

6. A slower market, especially in mainframe computers, compounded by the need to invest in R&D for new products.

Technological advances during the late 1980s and early 1990s in computers and telecommunications dramatically affected the mainframe market and had similar impact on the minicomputer market as applications and the resultant equipment purchases moved toward greater distribution to desktop systems, workstations, and client-server systems. In the late 1980s, the plateau in mainframe sales had already become a reality. In the rest of the 1990s, a similar plateau is very likely for minicomputers. At the same time, the sales of personal computers, workstations, local area networks (LANs), and server devices are increasing. These trends are causing computer vendors to reexamine their product lines and place greater R&D emphasis on the "low end" of the hardware spectrum.

Similarly, software vendors are finding that the greatest increase in sales is for applications and utilities that reside on low-end equipment. Mainframe application sales are reaching a plateau (and it is logical to expect minicomputer-based applications to do the same). Another problem faces the established vendors of application packages. Many of these applications were developed during the heyday of mainframes, in the 1970s and early 1980s, and they are therefore architecturally obsolete. The cost of redesigning and rebuilding major applications to take advantage of up-to-date hardware and software technology is prohibitive. In fact, many such firms cannot afford the investment.

It is important for the buyer to examine the architectural basis for products (both hardware and software) to ensure that it is not investing in a technologically obsolescent product that may lose its competitive benefits in a short time.

7. Erosion of the proprietary operating system marketplace and the need to develop open systems offerings.

The financially weaker computer manufacturers, most start-up manufacturers, and even some larger vendors such as Hewlett-Packard and NCR (now AT & T Global Systems) have moved to UNIX as a "standard" operating system. Furthermore, vendors are trying to position themselves for the next generation of "open" operating systems through such efforts as the joint IBM, Apple, and Hewlett-Packard operating system development through Taligent, and other efforts by Sun Microsystems and Next, Inc., or Microsoft. This move is taking place for several reasons:

- The cost of developing and supporting a proprietary operating system has become prohibitive and, for start-ups, out of reach.
- There is an increasing market demand for heterogeneous "open" systems that permit portability of applications among a variety of computers and that support easy connectivity.
- Customers are seeking solutions that require both hardware and application software. Most third-party software package vendors need to find the largest potential market base for their products. As a result, they have built applications primarily for such major vendors as IBM or DEC. One of the few ways that a hardware vendor can entice software vendors to build applications, or take advantage of existing applications, is to provide an application environment that has a less restricted potential market than that of the hardware vendors' proprietary operating system.

As the demand for open systems increases, even the biggest computer vendors have had to respond. This creates two dilemmas for these manufacturers: first, how to migrate to open systems without making their existing customer base vulnerable to intrusion by other vendors offering similar products; second, how to prevent the erosion of profit margins as hardware becomes more of a commodity. As previously mentioned, these dilemmas are forcing computer vendors into greater horizontal integration of their businesses by moving into software and service sales.

From a buyer perspective, the question appears to be how to take advantage of this trend toward open systems without unnecessarily discarding existing systems. A well-planned migration strategy is needed.

8.   Managing a large, vertically integrated business over diverse geographic regions.

As an outgrowth of the trends of horizontal integration, globalization, acquisition, and investment during the early 1990s, one may expect the larger surviving IT suppliers to encounter the same problem that many of their customers encountered in the 1980s—how to manage and control a diversified group of businesses spread around the world? One may expect to see repeated organization change as these companies try to meet this challenge and as the situation is further compounded by the demands and regulations imposed by the governments of the countries or regions in which the companies operate.

Evidence of the need to abandon outdated hierarchical management structures has been developed by the Stanford University Graduate School of Business under a grant from the Alfred P. Sloan Foundation. The article "Researchers gather data to profile computer firms" (*Stanford Business School Magazine*, December 1993)[1] describes how computer and electronics firms changed their organizations between 1988 and 1994. Over this period, the firms studied showed a shift away from business units organized by function (the traditional system) to units organized around product or customer segments, as shown in Table 2.1.

Long-Term (after 1999)

1.   Maintaining the customer base through a transition from proprietary operating systems, which locked the customer in, to open operating systems; which permit customers to integrate hardware from any supplier or move applications among hardware sets.

Continuing the trends started in the late 1980s, it is expected that this transition will have its greatest impact on suppliers in the late 1990s. As computer manufacturers begin a major shift away from proprietary systems, there will be an even greater impact on packaged software suppliers. Ap-

Table 2.1.   Business Unit Organization, 1988–1994

Organization by	Year Surveyed		
	1988	1991	1994
Function	92%	74%	57%
Product	7%	23%	28%
Customer segment	1%	3%	14%
Geographic Region	—	—	1%

plications designed for proprietary operating systems will need to be entirely reconstructed to take advantage of new technology as well as to operate in an open systems environment. The scale of investment required will create turmoil in the software industry and a new wave of failures, consolidations, mergers, and acquisitions.

2.   Introducing new technology for new applications or enhancements of old applications while preserving the customer's investments in existing applications.

An abrupt change from proprietary operating systems would create havoc among users who have huge sunk costs in application software. Therefore, one can expect transition strategies that permit continued operation of existing applications while new applications are constructed in open systems environments. One may also expect new paradigms in software development to appear in time to meet the conversion needs of users. However, there will also be a demand for the introduction of new technology into business use. Further distribution of applications, organizational restructuring to take advantage of "groupware," use of imaging technology, extended use of artificial intelligence, integration of varied systems, and rapid adoption of hand-held computer devices will all serve to pull vendors into new product and service areas as they strive to retain their customer base.

3.   Transforming the skills of marketing and technical support staffs from selling and supporting hardware to selling and supporting integrated systems solutions (mostly software).

Obviously, as vendors look to horizontal integration of software and service sales to maintain their margins, they will need to modify the skills of their sales and marketing forces. Such previously ignored areas as in-depth knowledge of customer industries and project management for large implementation projects will become critical to expansion (or even survival). Suppliers may recruiting professional personnel from their customers or developing in-house training programs to meet these needs. They may also find themselves more frequently forming alliances with consulting firms that already have those skills.

4.   Expansion into new business areas to address added markets (e.g., consulting services, systems integration, facilities management, value-added networks, public databases, entertainment).

Again, expansion represents continuation of a trend beginning in 1989–90. Horizontal integration will take computer and telecommunications vendors into such areas as supplying information and entertainment to their customers as well as providing hardware, software, systems integration, and facilities management. Buyers of such services need to remain alert to changes in the services offered by their current suppliers and potential new suppliers.

THE ISSUES FOR USERS OF IT PRODUCTS AND SERVICES

Users of information technology in business and industry must contend with many of the same broad issues that confront suppliers of IT products and services. However, within those broad issues lie a range of challenges that affect the manner in which IT is applied to enhancing the firms' competitive posture. The 1990s are the decade in which it has become impossible for a business or a government agency of any size to exist without being dependent upon information systems for its operation and management.

The issues described here are necessarily generalized. They have been identified though numerous consulting assignments with large, often global corporations and through published surveys of the IS concerns of top executives.

Short-Term (before 1999)

1.   Controlling IS costs while reshaping business processes through the use of information technology.

The 1990s vogue is "restructuring," "reengineering," or "operations redesign" of the corporation through information technology. This is not new; the capabilities have existed (and have been applied since the early 1960s) for information technology to reshape the corporation. One has only to realize that today's large financial institutions and airlines could not operate on their present scale without the intensive use of information systems. The combination of communications and computers that exists today has created new opportunities in corporate organization. For example, in the past, large, global corporations had to balance their organizational form against their need to respond quickly to market conditions throughout the world. With today's technology, the corporation is free to choose among centralized or decentralized forms for any function to suit any management style. Rather than be constrained by traditional organizational forms, through information technology corporations can address real issues such as time to market, customer relationships, cost tradeoffs, or competitive positioning, to name a few.

Within this context of restructuring the organization and its functions, business conditions make it imperative that the costs of information technology be controlled to maintain the profitability of the firm. Executives responsible for information systems in most companies have always had difficulty justifying the apparently high costs of information technology as compared to the costs of other functions in the firm. On the other hand, investments in computer integrated manufacturing (CIM) or process control, for example, have been viewed as a capital investment in production capability. To relieve this cost-control pressure, many IS executives have implemented cost charge-back procedures in which the user is budgeted and charged for the development and use of information systems. Theoretically, this should work; however, when the total IS budget is presented each year for approval, the number still appears larger than top management wishes. It is time for IS management to adopt the accounting conventions that drive much of the rest of the firm. Not only should IS costs be charged back to the users (application owners), but IS budgets should be related to business costs on the basis of direct cost, indirect cost, and general and administrative overhead. In this manner, it becomes clearer to management how IS costs relate to the production and delivery functions of the company.

Whatever conventions are adopted, there will always be countervailing pressures in the firm when it comes to allocation of investment and operating funds. The job of management is to make the investment decisions that will be of most benefit to the firm. Considering the size of IT investments and their usual life span, it is often necessary for management to take the long-range view of benefit to the firm rather than the unfortunately short-range view of responding to quarterly or annual profit performance needs. European and Japanese firms show a greater propensity to take that long-range view than American firms do.

2.   Meeting the need of executives for "real-time" management information from both internal and external sources.

Size and global span have changed the firm from one in which the president could "walk the floor" of the company to take its "temperature" to one in which the executive staff is separated by many layers and miles from their operations and field conditions. Nevertheless, the ability of top management to respond quickly to tactical needs and to develop the understanding to conduct strategic planning is vital to their success. IT now provides a range of tools for improving the information flow to top management. These include executive information systems (EIS), database access, videoconferencing, and others based on related technologies. In addition to internal information, it is now more necessary for the executive to have access to external information such as stock market reports, competitive information, and news. Managing the corporation in "real time" requires a blend of internal and external information. To continue managing the widespread business interests of the firm by reading monthly or quarterly reports is like trying to drive a car by looking in the rearview mirror.

Unfortunately, more than ever the executive is open to "information overload" from these various sources. Current technology requires substantial intervention by staff personnel or the careful design of management information systems to screen and reduce the information finally presented to top executives. Such intervention in the information flow creates a risk that vital decision-making information may not reach the correct level in the organization. By the late 1990s, artificial intelligence tools will likely improve the ability of executives to establish their own information screening criteria (through so-called software agents) and to view only that information they consider important.

Management must establish mechanisms to ensure that appropriate technology is introduced into the firm on a timely basis and in an effective manner.

3.   Creating information systems that provide the corporation with a strategic advantage.

A constant complaint by line executives is that information systems analysts do not understand the business, thus making it difficult to create systems that bring strategic advantage to the firm. This complaint is coupled with a similar complaint from systems analysts that executives do not understand IT or have the patience and commitment to adequately define their requirements. In Japan, many corporations rotate personnel on the "management track" through successive promotions and tours of duty with the different functional areas of the company (a "spiral" of training and promotion). One of those tours of duty is usually in the information systems organization. Over the long run, this rotation (from an IS viewpoint) helps managers become knowledgeable users, but it has the offsetting disadvantage that very few persons in the management track achieve any substantive level of technical proficiency. In the West, the pervasive distribution of personal computers to middle management, combined with their need to work with information systems, is gradually breeding a corps of management with a deeper understanding of the uses of IT.

In spite of this progress, it remains true that the language of a business is the language of specialized industry terms and conditions, which many information technologists do not understand. User management has become increasingly favorable to bringing in external consultants to help bridge the gap between IT knowledge and business knowledge. This use of consultants has in part accounted for the phenomenal growth of the consulting industry.

4.   Aligning IT strategy with corporate goals.

Alignment of IT strategy with corporate goals and strategic objectives faces still another problem. In many cases, the goals and objectives of corporations are not clearly set forth and documented, rather, they are "understood" (or misunderstood) by management. It is often necessary to first obtain a clear statement of goals and objectives before any reliable planning can be accomplished for the use of IT. More important, as discussed in later chapters, chief information officers (CIOs) and other IS managers have attempted to align IT strategy with the overall corporate strategy. However, since few corporations are monolithic and involved in only one business, this rarely works. Alignment is only possible with one business. As a result, alignment of IT strategy with business strategy is best accomplished for single strategic business units.

5.   Rationalizing information systems as a result of mergers, acquisitions, or divestitures, and instituting cross-functional systems in the corporation.

As competition increases, some firms divest themselves of holdings or divisions and return to their concentration on a core business. Other firms find it necessary to capture broader markets through vertical or horizontal integration. Still others acquire companies with some major focus on their core business and spin off or sell those divisions or product lines in which they have no interest.

During the 1980s, MIS organizations made significant efforts to minimize cost and improve effectiveness through development of integrated information systems or the use of common systems for serving common functions throughout the company. However, when presented with the need to isolate a segment of their systems to accommodate a divestiture, or to incorporate the systems of an acquisition into existing systems, their response was tragically slow. Most applications had not been designed to take such potential conditions into account. This situation has added further complexity to the already complex processes of acquisition or divestiture.

Cross-functional systems may exacerbate the problem, but if properly designed, they provide significant advantages. For example, over many years the computer-integrated manufacturing (CIM) and process control systems of companies have been developed and managed separately from the management information systems. It has become increasingly clear to management that these formerly disparate developments have neglected to satisfy the needs of management for real-time operating information. There is a demonstrable need for integration of manufacturing information with management information. In banking, there is a pressing need to integrate marketing and sales information systems with operational systems such as demand-deposit accounting. In fact, cross-functional systems design presents the potential for aiding the restructuring of the firm. Modern data-flow analysis techniques can be applied to the design of cross-functional systems.

Managers in companies that are strategically inclined to modify their "portfolios" of strategic business units must be especially wary when "integrated corporate-wide systems" are proposed. A key to their success will be the ability to easily divest the company of business units that no longer meet portfolio needs and to sell them as "intact businesses," not as divisions that have little or no independent information systems to support them. Similarly, an integrated systems solution must not be so "closed" that it presents major problems in smoothly embedding a new acquisition in the company.

6. **Improving the effectiveness of systems development activities.**

The 1980s witnessed the introduction and gradual acceptance of computer-aided software engineering (CASE) tools intended to improve the effectiveness of application development. These tools have proven to be most effective in the initial stages of application development—that is, in requirements definition and application specification as contrasted to coding and testing. Many adopters of these new tools have been disappointed in their implementation, since the tools do not generally address the maintenance of old applications well and seem to add to the cost of development of new applications. While the first of these objections is generally valid, the second is deceptive. The true cost of application development must include maintenance and enhancement of the application over its lifetime. In fact, history has shown that maintenance and enhancement activities represent over 70 percent of the lifetime cost of an application. CASE tools that combine with appropriate methodology to provide more precise definition of the application from inception may dramatically reduce the lifetime cost of the application.

Other advances in query languages and fourth-generation languages (4GLs) have made it easier for MIS to respond quickly to user requests for new functionality and, many times, for entire applications. However, in spite of these advances in tools, system developers are often perceived as being unresponsive in terms of quality, timeliness, and meeting business requirements. Tools and methodology are of some help, but the basic problems are frequently found in organization, management, and resource availability.

For the foreseeable future, even with the promise of object-oriented methods to increase the reusability of code, a shortage of capable software application developers will continue. Management will increasingly be forced to turn to "packaged" application solutions or to external systems development resources to meet their needs.

7. **Maintaining the security and integrity of corporate information.**

In the United States, as court decisions have increasingly made corporate board members responsible for the prudent management of their company's assets, the issue of protecting the company's information assets and its capability to do business has become critically important. Significant losses of information or information processing capabilities can irreparably damage the competitive position of a firm or its financial condition. Guidelines for protecting these assets have been developed, audit procedures have become more important, and security functions have been established in many organizations to ensure the security and integrity of information. Despite these moves, many companies remain deficient in their protection of these critical assets.

To ensure against loss, managers must see that their internal audit and information security capabilities are sufficient to evaluate and maintain the security of the company's information assets, information processing, and information transmission. If this capability is deemed insufficient, management should rely on external consulting support to establish appropriate safeguards.

Long-Term (after 1999)

1. Creating "transparent" communications and information processing "utilities" for end users.

The increasing capability of users to develop their own applications, the increasing cooperative use of computing among users with common projects, the expanding use of telecommuting (through electronic mail, video-conferencing, and other means), and the need to link heterogeneous equipment into commonly accessed media and information will force IS functions in companies to take another look at how they provide services to users. Users will demand that their applications operate responsively without regard to the physical platform on which those applications reside or to the location(s) of those devices. Corporate information resources will sometimes become "utilities" in the same way that we view telephone service. These utilities will be expected to work reliably, respond immediately, provide sufficient capacity, and protect the information of the user.

Again, users of information technology should establish regular programs to monitor technology and to introduce appropriate technology to the firm. Such programs are also useful to support the requirements of meeting competitive threats as well. Top management must reexamine the relationships between the IS organization and its "customers" to prepare for the changes that are coming.

2. Creating applications that will enhance the competitive stance of corporations.

Business and industry will grow more dependent on information technology to deliver goods and services to their customers. Trends indicate that customers are demanding not only more responsiveness and quality but increasingly customized and personalized goods and services. Information technology will be critical in meeting these demands and in maintaining the competitive position of the business. Customers will also be expecting greater ease of use and flexibility in products, so one may expect to see explosive growth in the use of small computers embedded in products and hand-held devices.

3. Creating information bases and integrating tools that permit end users to meet their own needs for information access and manipulation.

In conjunction with trends toward transparent information utilities, client-server architectures introduced in the early 1990s will come into widespread use. The client-server architecture assumes that a repository (the server) exists for large volumes of data and can provide extra processing capacity if required. Concurrently, smaller amounts of data and significant processing capacity exist on the client machine on the desktop of the end user. Clients and servers are linked by local area networks, which are in turn linked to similar client-server groups, to large computers as required, and to external data services. In fact, in many instances the mainframe computer acts as a server to provide a computing utility.

Management must be alert to opportunities for using information technology to improve the performance of cooperative work groups by making them independent of the separations created by time and distance.

4. Introducing tools that enhance international communication and reduce the need to travel (for example, video-conferencing, multimedia workstations, and automated voice language translation.)

Again, following trends initiated in the early 1990s, it is anticipated that telecommunication will become less costly and more effective than the heavy travel schedules previously imposed on executives and professionals in many industries. In addition, as fiber optic channels and satellite links proliferate, it is expected that the cost of telecommunication will continue to drop. Low-cost information superhighways like Internet lead in this direction.

5. Obtaining skilled software application developers and system integrators.

The shortage of application developers will persist for the foreseeable future, forcing users to continue to turn to outside resources to supplement their major application development and implementation efforts. Planning and design for overall system architectures, long-range application planning, judicious introduction of new technology, and prioritization of application development and enhancement activities will become critically important to the firm.

6.   Managing contractors that supply software and systems integration services.

As a corollary to the shortage of application developers, the use of external resources requires a different form of management than that required by internal application development. Greater stress will be placed on contract management and on the specification of work to be performed in order to successfully purchase services and control the results.

CONCLUSION

Each year various computer industry publications and consulting organizations conduct surveys about the issues and concerns of the industry and of IS executives in user organizations. The rankings of these issues in terms of importance vary each year, but the issues identified in our short-term view seem to have remained within the top ten for several years. The long-term issues are, of course, harder to predict. They may be affected by world economic conditions, major changes in technology, and a host of other factors. Such issues must be addressed on the basis of assumptions about trends and technological advances.

There are clearly a number of intelligent steps that may be taken by top management to minimize the risks associated with their investments and continuing operational costs for information technology. Some of these have been set forth above.

From any perspective, 1995 to 2005 promises to be a decade of accelerating change and challenge for both suppliers and users of information technology.

DISCUSSION TOPICS:

- This book is written in 1994. Have business issues changed?
- How have the predictions made in this chapter held up over time?
- Has the availability of new technology modified any of the issues identified in the chapter?
- Have developments in economic conditions, trade agreements, or other national or international areas changed or added to the issues described?
- How do the issues for suppliers and users differ?

REFERENCE

1. "Researchers Gather Data to Profile Computer Firms." *Stanford Business School Magazine* (December 1993).

CHAPTER 3

Planning for Competitive Use of Information Technology

In the current economic climate, most businesses must struggle to maintain or enhance their competitive position. Information technology, which has become an integral part of the corporate infrastructure, is increasingly recognized as a competitive weapon in this struggle. The pace of technological change demands a major commitment of company funds to planning and the acquisition of up-to-date equipment and expertise. Without this commitment, corporations lose the competitive advantage that superior technology confers.

This chapter discusses approaches a corporation can take to ensure that its information technology will be adequate to maintain or improve its competitive business position. Companies should rank themselves and their competitors according to their current use of information technology to achieve corporate objectives. An "assessment cycle" and a "planning/development/implementation cycle" should be adopted as bases for effective information technology acquisition and use that increase the competitive edge.

STRATEGIC USE OF INFORMATION TECHNOLOGY

Information technology (IT) is a common denominator in the growth and competitive stance of all types of businesses, from retailers to manufacturers and large service industry organizations. Many firms have made massive investments in and have become dependent on information technology. In most cases, such investments result in information systems that last for years. For example, the major airline reservation systems operating today have a core of program code that was developed in the mid-1960s.

On the other hand, in many cases the competitive advantage provided by an IT investment can be short-lived. This is especially true for information-technology-based products. Computer games, for example, often have only a three-to-six-month opportunity window before their capabilities are matched by competitors.

Still, the potential competitive advantage could make a crucial difference in the marketplace, even though the investment may be large.

Information technology affects both internal operations and products or services. The internal operations can include traditional data processing and communications functions, optimized over a global market, as well as enhancements of manufacturing and marketing. Products and services can range from embedded information technologies for manufactured equipment to software-based services. Effective technology investment strategy pursues development options in all dimensions relevant to corporate competitiveness.

For years, top executives thought of information technology as an accounting tool or a data source for decision making. Today the emphasis has moved to "operational systems" that actively transact business rather than passively observe and record its results. In a 1992 survey of business managers, use of information technologies for competitive advantage was ranked first (up from fourth place in 1987) and alignment of information systems with corporate goals was ranked second. Operational systems have become weapons in the corporate arsenal.

A second, growing emphasis is on embedded systems, in which computers become a part of traditional products. Automobile ignition systems, for example, are now controlled by microcomputers, and computer-driven displays and alarms are featured in many cars.

Some businesses are totally dependent on information systems. Airlines rely on advanced information technology for reservations, frequent-flyer promotions, route scheduling and optimization, billing, training by flight simulator, parts logistics, payroll, and air traffic control—not to mention the myriad of systems embedded in the aircraft themselves. Banks, too, have long been users of information technology. In the early 1950s, the magnetic ink character recognition (MICR) printing method for checks was a precursor of electronic information technology functions that now include online automated tellers, electronic funds transfer, extensive credit card operations, foreign exchange trading, and demand-deposit accounting systems.

Interest in strategic planning for the use of information technology continues to grow as new products and new business situations create new opportunities. Trend-setting organizations like American Express,

General Motors, and Chemical Bank, as well as their competitors throughout the world, have been stimulated to formulate strategies for information technology development, not only by the realization of their dependence on IT, but also by their recognition of the competitive threats and opportunities IT affords. (See box, "Examples of Strategic Application of Information Technology.")

Examples of Strategic Application of Information Technology

The new uses of information technology can give a corporation a several-year lead over its competitors. Some cogent examples follow.

- In 1977 SRI International and Merrill Lynch jointly developed the concept of the Cash Management Account (CMA), which used computer and communications technology to provide new levels of customer service to investors (and incidentally captured most of the investment business of their clients). It took five to seven years for Merrill Lynch's competitors to catch up and offer the same services—long enough for Merrill Lynch to become dominant in the market.
- Just-in-time (JIT), the computer-coordinated delivery of parts to manufacturing companies, has become well known through its widespread use in Japan. The IT concept of electronic data interchange (EDI) significantly improves the efficiency of the JIT approach; in fact, by linking suppliers, manufacturers, distributors, and retailers, EDI revolutionizes the process of delivering goods to consumers. For example, by 1992 Toyota was reputedly able to deliver an automobile with colors and accessories to customer specifications within five days of when the order was placed. General Motors has created a pan-European EDI system to link its suppliers, factories, and distributors in a manner similar to that of its U.S.-based system.
- Clothing manufacturers are turning to computer-aided design (CAD) to improve the speed with which they modify products to conform to style changes or retailers' specific orders; furthermore, they rely on computer-aided control of laser pattern cutters. The most competitive companies use on large computer- and communication-based product distribution systems to optimally speed time-sensitive merchandise to retail outlets.

- Some scientific companies now rely on computers rather than laboratory experiments for research. Chemical and pharmaceutical manufacturers use computer modeling techniques to design new chemicals and drugs and to predict their effects or likely interactions.
- Graphics-based models for laminar flow and turbulent flow allow designers of airplanes, automobiles, and ships to develop new configurations on the computer and to "test" their operating characteristics in days rather than the months or years it took with physical models.
- A major U.S. fast-food chain was among the first to install a company-wide broadband communications system to enhance its ability to control its widespread operations. The same company was among the first to make use of a PC-based expert system to schedule part-time employees so as to insure coverage on all shifts.
- The Campbell Soup Company, which is heavily engaged in marketing, has used the sophistication and power of information systems to refine its marketing analysis. Instead of treating sales as a nationwide phenomenon, Campbell has collected effective sales data for each product in each neighborhood market. Thus, it is able to build accurate models of market dynamics at very intimate levels of customer interaction for both its own and competitors' products, and to correlate them with the corresponding promotional actions occurring in specific local environments. This systems yields detailed and timely information about which products and which actions contribute most to profits.
- In 1983, faced with a combination of economic problems and aging systems designed for high-volume production, Jaguar P.L.C. made a strategic decision to invest in a new computer-integrated manufacturing system (CIM) to support low-volume production of luxury cars. The system included just-in-time delivery of parts from suppliers and a closed-loop manufacturing system that enabled all its operations to feed information back into the process. Jaguar credits this system with aiding its competitive posture and financial success and with improving product quality.
- Other examples of innovative retailing of goods and services are increasing. As two-income families now dominate the consumer market in some countries, shopping habits have changed and consumers are more demanding. These trends have given rise to schemes for measuring consumer prefer-

ences and catering to the needs of families with no time to waste. Electronic shopping, whose use by affluent consumers is growing, is a full-spectrum technological means of presenting data and goods to customers, recording their preferences, and delivering data to suppliers. At the same time it directs physical delivery of goods to the electronic participant-consumers and simultaneously records detailed marketing information in large databases. Time-based competition is becoming the wave of the future.

CLASSIFICATION OF INFORMATION TECHNOLOGY STATUS

Experience with many large multinational enterprises indicates that in terms of the competitive use of information technology, corporations usually take one of three fundamental positions: adopter, adapter, or inventor.

- *Adopters* make poor use of information technology, usually just adopting off-the-shelf products. Adopters are simply buyers, and they do not undertake more than routine application of their purchased systems. Their goal usually is short-term survival or simply catching up with competitors. At this level, virtually any company can increase its business advantage by proper application of IT products, but most adopters must build (or rebuild) a basic technological foundation.

Adopters may be found in stagnant industries, in areas of depressed economy, or in companies with insufficient capital resources. However, an organization can find itself in this position simply through the failure of management to recognize the competitive value of information technology. In such cases, the solution may be heightened management awareness of the competitive changes that can be wrought by obtaining the technology advantage, plus the vision to enter the technological arena with vigor and commitment.

To obtain IT resources at minimal cost, a company can purchase application software packages, use a service bureau, contract for resources, or employ temporary professional staff. Full-scale business alternatives might include merger with a competitor, sale of the company to a more technologically advanced firm or one with greater financial resources, or acquisition of a smaller but more technologically advanced company.

- *Adapters* are developers and users that have already made information technology an essential element of their value-based planning. They have the awareness, capability, and funds to undertake internal development. Adapters cultivate close working relationships with suppliers that allow them to take advantage of developments in which timing is critical.

Adaptive companies generally use information technology at a level close to that of their competitors. Although they invest significantly in maintenance and enhancement of existing applications, they also focus on adapting emerging technology through expansion and innovation. Frequently they invest in applied research for product or process innovation.

Adapters are found in expanding markets that are often global in business scope. They face strong competition from companies with dynamically changing products and services. Generally profitable, with the financial strength to compete in their chosen sector, they frequently seek acquisitions that will bring them new markets. Formally and informally, these companies make use of the latest technology, often retaining external consultants to ensure an objective view of their status or to introduce new concepts.

Top management in adaptive enterprises recognizes the competitive value of information technology and increasingly involves itself in the planning process. Adaptive companies maintain an up-to-date awareness of their competitors' technological development. Their principal strategy is to remain at the forefront of the state of the practice vis-à-vis their competitors, and to make every possible use of existing and emerging information technology to obtain competitive advantage.

- *Inventors* are technology creators. Such companies seek unique opportunities that depend on significant departures from current practice, scientific breakthroughs, or very innovative use of state-of-the-art information technology. Their successes come from their ability to leapfrog the competition and gain significant advantage or to create new markets.

Inventive companies maintain their advantage through research and development—by participating in the discovery and earliest use of advanced information technology tools, techniques, and products. They are not afraid to deviate from current practice or to pursue a fundamental transformation of products and processes. Such companies are aggressive leaders in dynamic industries that are experiencing volatile product and service changes. In addition to research spending, their strategies include encouraging management to use the latest technology, creating spin-off companies in new product or service areas, and participating with technology leaders in joint ventures for new product development.

Inventors can be found in various areas of the information technology industry (computer manufacturers, software suppliers, etc.). However, being inventive and innovative is not enough. Inventors must have the ability to interpret market needs and to bring their products or services to the market in time and at a competitive cost.

An individual company may find that it fits all three of the above categories—adoptive, adaptive, and inventive—according to product lines or lines of business and the corresponding IT applications in those areas. The objective is to tailor the application to the company's needs in a given area or strategic business unit—seeking to develop the resources for competitive technological advantage as appropriate to the enterprise.

THE INFORMATION TECHNOLOGY DEVELOPMENT CYCLES

Companies can maximize the benefits of information technology by applying two technology development cycles, as follows:

The Assessment Cycle

- Evaluate the position and approach used by competitors.
- Evaluate the company's current IT status.
- Develop an understanding of ways in which information technology can be applied to achieve or enhance corporate business strategy.
- Assess environmental factors that reflect changes in industry structure, customer preference, technology development and usage, and global economic conditions.

The Planning/Development/Implementation Cycle

- Identify major threats and opportunities.
- Develop an IT strategy for competitive advantage.
- Develop an implementation infrastructure.
- Elaborate the details of planning and implementation.
- Install the strategic applications or bring the product to the market.
- Evaluate the realized returns on investment.

To use information technology successfully for competitive advantage, the company must iterate these two cycles of activity continuously. Most companies undertake one or more of the above steps, but they vary considerably in follow-through. Objective evaluation of the company's status vis-à-vis the competition, and of the company's ability to use information technology, is the key to meeting competitive threats.

Each of the steps in the IT development cycles provides some of the vital intelligence needed for management decision making and improved use of technology. A successful technology strategy is linked to the company's overall business strategy. Astute investment of corporate resources is re-

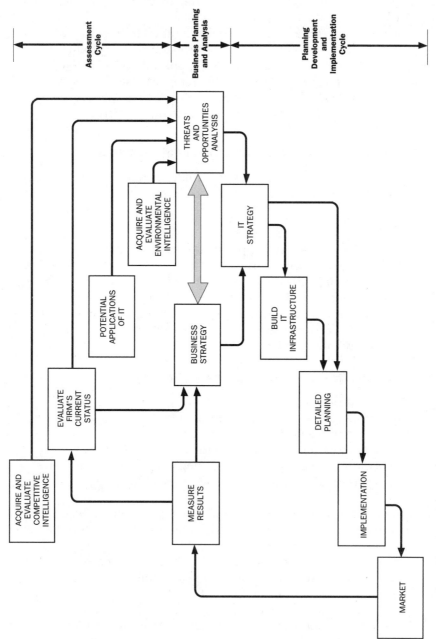

Figure 3.1. Planning and Implementing Information Technology

quired to obtain an enhanced technological position. As indicated in following sections, investors must also be prepared to define their expectations of return on investment and to ensure that the return is obtained.

The schematic outline of this two-cycle approach is shown in Figure 3.1.

USING THE CYCLES TO ACHIEVE MARKET ADVANTAGE

The Steps in the Assessment Cycle

The first technology development cycle involves assessment of the company's situation, with respect to internal and external environments. The cycle is a series of events that drive development and implementation of the technology strategy. Whether or not senior managers understand information technology, they can generally be counted on to understand the economics of their industry and potential competitive threats. For this reason, an analysis of threats from the competition is a good way to gain senior management's attention to issues and needs.

Evaluate the position and approach used by competitors. Competitive threats to the firm's products and services, as related to information technology, may be derived from several primary and secondary sources. First, it is necessary to understand the specific industry the firm is in and the competitive environment of the industry, as follows:

- Identify and describe key competitors' strong and weak points as to products or services.
- Identify and characterize key competitors' major applications of information technology.
- Identify key competitors' technical and financial strength and their ability to invest in information technology.

This intelligence should be updated at least annually and provided to senior managers at briefings to maintain the "technology watch" needed for the decision-making process.

It is possible to learn about competitors' use of information technology through external observation. Sufficient public data about competitive status can be gathered, so there is no need to engage in industrial espionage. Articles in trade magazines describe the innovative use of information technology by certain companies. Customers, suppliers, and distributors rapidly become aware of new applications, and surveys of such sources can reveal how the new technology is being used. New products or services can be analyzed to identify the introduction of new technology or the innovative use of existing technology. New employees can be debriefed on entry into the company. In short, intelligence analysis can provide a reliable understanding of the ways in which the competition uses information technology. (See box, "Corporate Competitive Intelligence Programs.")

Evaluate the company's current IT status. Evaluation of IT status requires an objective view of the company's use of information technology and of its capacity to advance beyond the competition in the use of technology. The appraisal must overcome the potentially defensive (and frequently typical) postures of the organizations within the company that are responsible for the development of IT applications. For this reason, this step should be the responsibility either of an independent group within the company or of a consulting organization with a good knowledge of the industry.

Corporate Competitive Intelligence Programs

In a 1988 study, The Conference Board, a New York-based business research organization, surveyed 308 companies about their activities in competitive intelligence programs. Of those surveyed, two-thirds indicated that they were planning to increase their monitoring efforts during the next few years. The Conference Board identified the following characteristics of most competitive intelligence programs:

- The objectives of the programs were to identify threats and opportunities, improve planning, and avoid management surprises.
- Intelligence efforts focused on gathering information about competitors' sales, pricing, and corporate strategy.
- The intelligence groups published regular reports and ad hoc papers. A few companies provided user access to online databases.
- The intelligence groups gathered data through interviews with their own sales force and with customers and competitors, and through press releases, annual reports, the trade press, newspaper clipping services, and other sources.

News reports indicate that intelligence groups often report to the corporate marketing or strategic planning department. Many and diverse companies—for example, Adolph Coors, Upjohn, AT&T, and Honeywell—have competitive intelligence units. Some consulting firms specialize in competitive intelligence, and there is even a Society of Competitor Intelligence Professionals (SCIP).

First, the evaluators should construct an "application status statement" describing the application of information technology to critical operations or products and the gaps that exist in the application's ability to meet its objectives. The statement should include the function of the application, the performance of the application relative to expressed or potential needs; the level of the technology (off-the-shelf, state-of-the-practice, state-of-the-art, or advanced innovative concepts); the age of the application software and its maintainability and flexibility; and the computer hardware, telecommunications, staff, and other resources used in the application.

Next, the evaluators should appraise the skills and experience of the application developers and the methods and tools used for application design and development. Embedded in this appraisal should be an evaluation of the staff's knowledge of the end functions for which applications are intended and of information technology tools. The evaluators should review recent development projects to determine the project management skills of the developers and their ability to interface with users and understand user requirements.

The evaluators should review the work mix of the development organizations. The percentage of MIS resources dedicated to the maintenance of information systems is growing steadily, and it is estimated that a full 70 to 80 percent of MIS efforts are devoted to applications enhancement, maintenance, and migration, while only 20 to 30 percent are dedicated to the development of new applications.

Finally, the evaluators should draw a composite picture for management of the company's IT status and make a rough comparison of this status to that of major competitors.

Understand how information technology could be applied. This step demands knowledge of the potential application of the technology to the company's business processes, products, services, and industry. Equally important is a clear perspective of the company's products or services and the major trends in the market. The major tasks are to

- Appraise the available information technology that could be used for competitive advantage now.
- Appraise anticipated changes or new developments that could be used for competitive advantage over the next three to five years.
- Identify potential applications of current and future technology and how such applications might affect the competition.
- Identify potential changes in current applications driven by market demands or technology development.

For companies not in the computer or telecommunications business, these tasks require the assistance of professional information systems analysts and engineers who are capable of conceiving innovative uses for information technology. Companies that are in the information technology business will need the services of research scientists and marketing professionals.

Assess environmental factors. The operating environment represents a wide range of threats and opportunities. The main elements to be scrutinized are

- Technology
- Industry structure
- External economic and political forces

To assess technological changes requires long- and short-term insight into the state of the art. Management needs this intelligence in order to evaluate investment alternatives, so scheduled management briefings should be held at least twice a year to keep decision makers apprised of new options. Possible uses of information technology should be forecast for three to five years, which period approximates a reasonable length of time for application development. Computer and telecommunications vendors may need to look at a five- to eight-year forecast as well, since these time intervals are more representative of the product engineering cycle.

Changes in the industry structure can be analyzed in terms of Michael E. Porter's popular 1985 model, which examines changes in buyers, suppliers, substitutes, and new entrants for their potential impact on the value chain and on the characteristics of products and services. Although the discussion here gives special consideration to competitor analysis and customer focus, is important also to keep the big picture of the industry in view and to have a perspective on the pattern of shifts under way from all elements, as depicted in Porter's approach. Numerous other approaches to competitive advantage have been suggested, see, for example, Shill, 1986, and Bakopoulos and Treacy, 1985, in the selected readings at the end of the chapter.

Other important elements to watch in the external environment are the legislative and political climates and the effects of global economic pressures such as trade imbalance, investment, and the pricing of fundamental commodities (e.g., oil stocks). Such external factors may influence the organization's ability to carry out investment plans to a successful conclusion, or they may influence the need for the investment in a changed competitive environment.

Steps in the Planning/Development/Implementation Cycle

Identify major threats and opportunities. This step consists of summarizing the results of the assessment cycle. Using these results, the company should identify the areas in which improved use of information technology would be of greatest value. This investigation must be directly related to business objectives, and if the company has more than one line of business, information must be segregated accordingly and an analysis performed for each principal area of application.

Develop an IT strategy. The knowledge of threats and opportunities should be used first to identify those areas that deserve high-priority attention. The ways in which competitors maximize their use of information technology in these areas should be described, and the company's ability to respond to the competition should be detailed. Important threats from other sources should be treated in a similar fashion. Next, new uses of more advanced information technology for products and services should be identified and analyzed. Each type of corporation or product line—adapter, adopter, inventor—demands a different level of analysis. Finally, new opportunities and potential diversification pathways should be identified. These options should be evaluated in light of the overall corporate business strategy with respect to potential return and enhancement of competitive position. Scenario preparation and value chain analysis are useful techniques for the evaluation.

To the extent possible, threats should be assessed in terms of probability of occurrence and potential financial or market position impact. The probable costs and benefits of responding to each threat should be estimated and compared. Opportunities should be assessed in terms of competitive benefit, development risk, risk of impact on existing product lines, and implementation investment. (See box, "Linking Technology to Corporate Strategy.")

Finally, the infrastructural improvements necessary to respond to threats or to take advantage of opportunities must be identified.

Company management should review the findings of this investigation, set priorities, and allocate funds for more advanced information technology and development of applications within a framework of economic constraints and expectations. On the basis of the priorities and the level of funding initially established, a plan should be created to upgrade the information technology infrastructure or to develop specific technology-intensive products or services. This upgrading or new development can be done through acquisition of the appropriate hardware and tools or through internal development.

The candidate list of IT development items should be narrowed to a final slate for development and implementation. Some items may require research, initial development, or further study before final implementation can be approved; others may move directly to implementation.

As a final step in this process, the criteria for measuring success should be specified. Examples of such criteria are specific quantitative or qualitative measures relating to savings, profits, cash flow, revenue improvement, share of market, market entry, and defense against competitive threat.

Develop the infrastructure to implement the plans. A general implementation plan should be drawn up to achieve the company's information technology objectives. The goals, strategy, approach, expected results, critical milestones, and requisite resources must be specified. In some cases, it may be necessary to change the company's information systems development infrastructure to accommodate the new technology and achieve the desired results.

The decision to implement plans that will move the company or segments of the company to higher technological levels must address

- Personnel resources and skill levels
- Available software for application support
- Computer and telecommunications requirements
- Application development methods and tools
- Project planning control methods and tools
- Project management resources and skills
- Organization to support improvements
- Management oversight and progress reporting
- Involvement of nontechnical resources

Linking Technology to Corporate Strategy

While many companies go through the fundamentals of planning outlined in the text, few attempt to make the connection to strategy or to correlate technology investment with return. However, some major companies are applying the concepts discussed here.

In a 1988 *Information Week* article, Pillsbury's vice president of information management described Pillsbury's corporate information planning approach, which is analogous to the process recommended in this chapter. Information technology investments are divided into foundation, tactical, and strategic categories. Pillsbury looks to its multiyear strategic programs for the major payoff from IT investment. By increasing its ability to use the technology, Pillsbury covers an ever-wider and varying range of targets.

Chrysler's IT strategy is to employ a focused "rifle" (as opposed to "shotgun") approach, coupled with company-wide commonality and integration of systems. The latter is illustrated by Chrysler's approach to computer-integrated manufacturing (CIM), which is applied across the board for the most fundamental parts of its operations. Rather than applying CIM to its operations only in a theoretical sense, Chrysler has succeeded in linking the consumer, manufacturing, and supplier sectors. Buyers' orders activate planning at the factories, which in turn stimulates a JIT system linking 1,200 suppliers. Each car in the manufacturing line is tracked with respect to progress and problems that would result in defects or schedule delays. Chrysler is linking electronic funds transfer into this overall process.

In the late 1980s, American Express used a small corporate core group in technology strategy to follow IT activities at subordinate companies. This group attempts to achieve synergies and economies of scale while allowing subordinates to remain decentralized. Advanced competitive developments include use of image processing and voice systems for the company's travel business, laser printing and consolidated statements for financial services subsidiaries, and expert systems for credit and charge authorization.

Perform detailed planning and implementation. Once management has allocated funding, improvements to the IT infrastructure can proceed; detailed planning for application must take place in parallel. This extensive process needs to reach beyond application of the technology to the installation of new applications in the firm or the introduction of new or enhanced products to the market. It may require many years of effort to bring such plans to fruition. (Detailed planning and implementation, as well as installation and market introduction, are not trivial exercises; they are beyond the scope of this book.)

Often, the organizations within a company have different interests and functions in the implementation process. For example, an MIS group may be charged with implementation of a project sponsored by a customer division that will use or market the resulting product. Large corporate development efforts may be shared by several internal "customer" bases, each with different missions and objectives, and the total effort may have inherent weaknesses from several points of view. The MIS group may advocate technology that is beyond what is needed or, conversely, the customer groups may be too shortsighted and advocate solutions that lack the appropriate technological underpinnings. It often falls upon someone such as the corporate technology officer, or perhaps the corporate planning division, to see that a steering group representing all interests is established to oversee development planning.

When the development process is completed, the processes for introduction may diverge. For product development, the company may choose various approaches to test-marketing or initial, limited release to "friendly" customers before final release. If the application is internal, a pilot operation is often used to determine whether or not the application satisfactorily meets user needs before company-wide implementation is permitted.

Evaluate the realized returns on the investment. If the development has resulted in an improved internal application of information systems, migration to the new application may take several months. Problems not identified and corrected in the testing process will arise during this time. Evaluation of the success of the application may not be possible until after it has been operating satisfactorily for three to six months. An even longer period may be required if business processes have been substantially redesigned.

If the development has resulted in a new or enhanced service or product, test-marketing may precede market release. An early assessment of probable success or failure may result in product or service changes or cancellation. A final evaluation may not be possible until several months after market release.

Companies must maintain updated estimates of return on technology investments, so that the data can be used to prioritize implementation and to improve the planning methodology.

"Success criteria" should be identified at the time the project is approved and should be applied by means of one of the numerous current methodologies for measurement of return on technology.

Reiterate these cycles to maintain the competitive position. The result of the investigative and planning phases just described is a strategic plan for competitive use of information technology at a specific point in time. In order to be effective, the development cycle must be continued and updated at least annually, providing both knowledge for management investment decisions and critical input to the annual budget and to tactical planning for application development.

The strategic plan should be viewed as a method for increasing the responsiveness of the IS organization to the company's competitive needs. It must be reviewed and updated annually and modified if events occur that seriously affect the ability of the information systems developers to meet the plan's objectives. The learning process and the skills gained during the development of the first strategic plan should reduce the effort necessary to prepare or alter subsequent plans.

It is equally important that the competitive assessment cycle be continually maintained and updated. External events may well require changes in tactics or in products that will be overlooked if the company relaxes its monitoring of the competition.

SUMMARY

During the next decade, corporations will need every competitive weapon at their command to achieve their strategic goals. Information technology is one of the most powerful weapons available. Strategic goals can range from survival to a leapfrogging of the competition, but it is important that the goals be within reach given the resources the company can devote to attaining them. Companies must seek an expert and impartial evaluation of their technological position vis-à-vis that of their competitors. Using the classifications of *adopters, adaptors,* and *inventors,* companies can gauge their technological styles and those of the competition and strategically plan how to improve their competitive edge.

Adopters often lack the technological infrastructure to appropriately adapt current technology. Because they are often substantially behind the competition, they are unable to retain the skilled professional employees needed to upgrade their status. Without quick action, such companies may continue to see their business stagnate or be overwhelmed by more aware and aggressive competitors.

Adapters, on the other hand, usually have a well-developed infrastructure that keeps abreast of competitive development and actively seeks new technology for application to operations, products, or services. Adapters are generally able to retain good-quality professional IT employees through adequate compensation and sufficient technical challenge. Nevertheless, in order to retain their competitive position, adapters need to activate the technology development cycle. They must be alert to unexpected competitive threats both from the inventors in their industry and from substitutions based on different technologies.

Inventors generally are leaders in their industry and are committed to maintaining their leadership through investment in technology. Primary threats to inventors are complacency, the "not-invented-here" syndrome, and a lack of objectivity in evaluating their status. Scientific breakthroughs rarely pose a threat to inventors, because the time lag from breakthrough to market application may be as long as ten years. On the other hand, the innovation cycle is much shorter and the competition can occasionally surprise even the most dedicated inventor. Inventors must carefully balance research investments against securing potential patent positions, the cost of development and manufacture against market acceptance, and the cost of development and implementation against the competitive advantage to be gained.

The cycles of assessment and planning/development/implementation should be applied to achieve the maximum advantage. The model provided here can serve as a basis for information gathering in the service of competitive strategy. Clearly, the task of corporate management does not end with goal setting. Development and implementation, planning, infrastructure improvement, and applications can present a monumental challenge.

DISCUSSION TOPICS

- Is your company an adopter, an adapter, or an inventor?
- Should your company be changing its technology strategy?
- How can senior management be convinced to make a technology strategy shift?
- What competitive threats from the use of information technology does your company face?
- How do you currently gain information about competitive use of information technology?
- How should the assessment, analysis, and implementation cycles described in this chapter be adapted for your company's culture?
- Would you use the same team for the assessment cycle as for the planning/development/implementation cycle?
- How should these teams be staffed? (What skills, what organizations, etc?)

SELECTED READING

Bakopoulos, J.A.Y., and Treacy, M.E. "Information Technology and Corporate Strategy: A Research Perspective," Sloan Working Paper No. 1639–85, Cambridge, Mass: Sloan School of Management, Massachusetts Institute of Technology (1985).

Bard, J.F. "An Interactive Approach to R&D Project Selection and Termination." *IEEE Transactions on Engineering Management* 35 (August 1988).

Betts, M. "Snoopers See MIS As Dr. No." *Computerworld* 23 (December 1988): 1.

"Campbell's Marketing Bites into MIS." *Information Week* (June 20, 1988): 28–32.

Connolly, J. "Study: Spending Up; Stress on Strategy." *Computerworld* 22 (November, 1988): 8.

Connolly, J., and Horwitt, E. "American Express Sets Own Limits." *Computerworld* 22 (December, 1988).

Foster, R.N. *et al.* "Improving the Return on R&D—I." *Research Management* (January-February 1985): 12–17.

———. "Improving the Return on R&D—II." *Research Management* (January-February 1985): 13–22.

Mitchell, G.R., and Hamilton, W.F. "Managing R&D As A Strategic Option." *Research Management* (May-June 1988).

"Nick Simonds Driving Chrysler's MIS." *Information Week* (February 29, 1988): 24-29.

Patterson, W.C. "Evaluating R&D Performance at Alcoa Laboratories." *Research Management* (March-April, 1983).

"Pillsbury's Talent Recipe." *Information Week* (March 28, 1988): 24–28.

Porter, J.G., Jr. "Post Audits—An Aid to Research Planning." *Research Management* (January 1978): 28–30.

Porter, M.E. *Competitive Advantage.* New York: The Free Press, 1985.

Shill, R.L. "Managing Technology for Competitive Advantage in Interindustry Markets." *R&D Management* 16 no. 2 (1986) 103–116.

Managing Emerging Technologies

With the background of the previous section, it is now appropriate to go into further detail about the process of aligning information technology with business strategy.

This section describes how to identify and track the information technologies that will be most useful to the enterprise. It then describes the paths to successful deployment of new information technology.

This procedural detail leaves out one aspect: What will those technologies be and how will they impact the business? Chapter 5 takes a "futurist's" view of information technologies emerging in 1994 and shows how they may affect the business, the society in which the business exists, employees' work habits, and the bottom line.

CHAPTER 4

Acquisition and Deployment of Information Technology

Chapter 3 dealt with determining what competitive threats exist and how to plan countermeasures. This chapter explores in more detail the aspects of introducing new technology to the firm.

THE BUSINESS PROBLEM

As previously stated, the global business environment is becoming more competitive than ever, forcing companies to seek ways to improve efficiency, lower operating costs, be more responsive to customers, and bring new products to market faster. This drive to improve has resulted in a burgeoning interest in technology management, ranging from acquisition through exploitation of new technologies. While many technologies are of primary interest to one or two industries, all industries have a interest in information technology.

It is generally accepted that most major corporations would not be able to operate their businesses without computer systems. Top executives are also becoming increasingly aware that their competitive advantage may depend on the ability of their computer and communications systems to respond quickly to changing business needs. This means that companies must keep abreast of competitive moves in the use of computers and, in many cases, be prepared to stay ahead of their competitors.

These pressures have awakened executives to the knowledge that technology management is as important for their information systems as it is for their manufacturing facilities and products.

Two major issues, inexorably linked together, trouble management information systems (MIS) directors of major corporations throughout the world. These issues are (1) supporting the redesign of company business processes, and (2) replacing "legacy" systems that are impeding the MIS function's ability to respond flexibly to business needs. What links these two issues is the ability of the MIS function to plan for, acquire, and deploy new information technology for the development and operation of new applications.

Having dedicated years to the implementation of mainframe-oriented business systems, many companies have hundreds of millions of dollars invested in hardware and huge applications software libraries. Mainframe-based systems will be with us for many years to come. However, better price/performance ratios, faster software development paradigms, specialized application capabilities, smaller increments of capacity increase, and improved architectural flexibility promised by newer technologies are very attractive to hard-pressed MIS directors. These "internal" infrastructure improvements of MIS generally require a substantial short-term increase in costs before the long-term benefits can be realized.

Unfortunately, unless the company's CEO is oriented to the strategic use of information technology, or the MIS head is a great salesperson, meeting the internal needs of MIS for new and advanced technology is hard to justify. However, there are signs that this situation is changing. For example, an *Information Week* survey (December 7, 1992)[1] indicates that 85 percent of the 116 top information management executives interviewed expect to invest in client-server computing in 1993. Nevertheless, the justification for these and other investments in advanced information technology must be related to business needs.

The efforts of many companies to redesign their business processes; have resulted in a surge of interest in new information technologies. First USA Bank in Wilmington, Deleware, has implemented a neural-network-based system for fraud detection in patterns of credit card use. USAA, a San Antonio, Texas, insurer, has started a full-service banking operation based entirely on automated teller machines (ATMs) and telephones, with no branch offices. Several major banks have converted their loan application processing to image-processing systems with workflow management software. Portable and hand-held computers are popping up in applications throughout the country, and most pharmaceutical companies' sales representatives are equipped with notebook computers. The Chicago Board of Trade and the Chicago Merchantile Exchange have a system that allows floor traders to register transactions through hand-held wireless computers.

Business needs have spurred the adoption of new information technology, but in many cases MIS departments are poorly equipped to deal with the entire scope of managing the introduction of new technology to the firm. Technology management is not only a problem for information systems. Fast-paced industries such as biotechnology and electronics, have dealt with the issue almost from their inception. Now, with the pressures of global competition, old-line manufacturing companies in such industries as automobile, glass, and many others have been learning that technology management is critical to their continued survival. These companies have discovered that the scope of technology management includes a broad range of activities, such as

- Strategic technology positioning
- Tracking technology trends
- Aligning technology needs with business needs
- Identifying appropriate new technology
- Identifying the "technology rendezvous"
- Justifying technology acquisition
- Acquiring new technology
- Introducing new technology
- Adapting technology to business needs
- Deploying new technology

STRATEGIC TECHNOLOGY POSITIONING

While many aspects of technology management could be subsumed under positioning, here we have taken a narrower view: Strategic technology positioning consists of adopting policies and procedures that set forth the management position regarding technology. A firm may determine that its competitive position is best served by being an adopter, an adapter, or an inventor of technology. (See Chapter 3.) Adopters tend to use off-the-shelf products and thus trail others in technology acquisition; adapters tend to make technology an essential element of their value-based planning and use new technology in innovative ways; and inventors tend to seek opportunities by creating new or innovative technology to stay far ahead of competition.

Furthermore, procedures must accommodate the feedback of technology opportunities to the business plans. Strategic business plans developed without regard to the competitive threats and opportunities supported by technology advances can be blindsided by more aggressive users of technology. The clearly stated positions embodied in policies and procedures reinforce a strategic approach to technology planning and acquisition. They also ensure that valuable employee time is spent in accord with corporate policy.

TRACKING TECHNOLOGY TRENDS

Large MIS groups frequently have specific positions created to track technology. The MIS group in several major petrochemical companies have such positions; in addition, the exploration and production groups of these companies usually have a similar function embedded in their R&D divisions, which are heavy users of advanced information technology for systems such as seismic analysis and well-head logging analysis.

Technology tracking activities are often part of a "technology planning" or "systems architecture" group within the MIS division. Although some managers feel that technology tracking is a part of every systems analyst's job, more successful results are obtained when the effort is not so diffused. Diffusion of this task so that it is "everyone's responsibility" often results in it being "no one's responsibility." Since successful technology planning must be continuous, specific assignment of responsibility is necessary. In smaller companies that cannot dedicate full-time personnel to tracking, the responsibility should be made explicit for one or two individuals as a part-time function, with defined results expected.

Tracking may be done a number of ways. The information technology (IT) field is rife with industry publications, many of them free, that provide insight into commercially available products and their applications. and specialized publications present research results that allow prediction of the availability of technology. Conferences and membership in professional associations also provide access to technology trend information. Occasional use of external consultants may supplement the insight into technology trends and provide innovative ideas for using emerging technologies.

Technology tracking can only work properly in the framework of strategic technology positioning. It is futile to track emerging technologies if the company's position is that of adopter; however, for adapters and inventors, a vision and understanding of the future and of technology life cycles is imperative.

This understanding serves as a means to determine areas in which skills need to be developed, to identify new projects for clients, to improve productivity and quality, to and anticipate potential competitive advantages and disadvantages.

The technological life cycle may be described as consisting of six stages, as follows:

1. *Breakthrough and basic research,* in which the technology is invented and advanced to a stage at which product development is feasible.
2. *Research and development,* in which initial products are developed.
3. *Emergence,* in which products are introduced and the market is educated to accept them.
4. *Growth,* in which the market advances most rapidly and new products using the technology continue to be offered at a rapid pace.
5. *Maturity,* in which the market for the technology stabilizes and products become commonly applied.
6. *Decline,* in which the technology is being superseded by newer technologies that have functional, cost, or performance advantages.

For most businesses that use information technology, stages 2 through 6 are of particular interest. Technologies that fall into these stages tend to overlap them, however. For example, while multimedia can still be viewed as a major research topic (stage 2), initial products have been introduced to the market and are gaining acceptance by early adopters (stage 3). On the other hand, even though new wide area network (WAN) products are continually being introduced, users have clearly adopted WANs; thus, the technology can be viewed as moving from the growth stage (4) to the maturity stage (5).

In some instances we must consider technology applications rather than simply technologies. Technology applications are generally constructed when individual technologies are blended. The 1980s witnessed the "PC revolution," which was actually a composite of technology trends involving miniaturization of components, local area networking, graphical user interfaces, and so on. In the 1990s, we can expect several other "revolutions":

- *Multimedia* involve the blending of images, graphics, sound, voice, video, text, and tabular information within a human interface that uses these capabilities to access and present information. This revolution will achieve its major market impact by the late 1990s and will have a substantial effect on the online information and CD-ROM information industries.
- *Workgroup applications,* based on local area network (LAN) and client-server technologies, remove the constraints of time and distance and allow ad hoc or permanent workgroups to focus concurrently on particular tasks. Because this application requires the sharing of information among group members, we can expect that some of the information shared will come from external resources such as online database services. These applications are beginning today and will become widespread by the late 1990s.
- *Portable computing,* involving miniaturization of computers and storage media combined with wireless communications, will lead to the ubiquitous presence of computers as personal aids by the end of the 1990s.

As examples, listed here are 28 information technologies that will have an impact on many large multinational businesses during the 1990s:

- Automated multimedia indexing
- Automated text indexing
- CASE tools
- Client-server systems
- Compression technologies

- Cooperative workgroup systems (groupware)
- Distributed processing
- Expert systems
- Graphical user interfaces (GUI)
- High-speed wide area networks (WANs)
- Image systems
- Information security
- Intelligent agents
- Intelligent user interfaces
- Knowledge understanding
- LAN and inter-LAN networks
- Multimedia systems
- Natural language understanding
- Object-oriented programming
- Parallel computing systems
- Personal digital assistants (PDA), or hand-held PCs
- Portable computers
- Rapid prototyping
- Relational database management systems (RDBMS)
- Search engines and indexing
- Speech generation
- Speech recognition
- Text storage and retrieval systems

Figure 4.1 shows the relative maturity of the 28 technologies at this time. Technology trackers need to monitor information technologies continually because they tend to develop at different speeds. For example, imaging systems reached the market in 1989 and are already moving into the growth stage. In contrast, expert systems reached the market in the early 1980s, but are in approximately the same stage imaging systems in 1994.

Monitoring the stages of information technologies provides yet another advantage. By observing the applications to which technologies are applied (as described in trade journals), ideas can be found that will be useful to a company and its clients.

ALIGNING TECHNOLOGY STRATEGY WITH BUSINESS NEEDS

Tracking technology without regard to the needs of the business can waste much time and money. It is absolutely critical that those tracking the technology be aware of the potential uses of technology in the processes and products or services of the company or the strategic business unit. Basi-

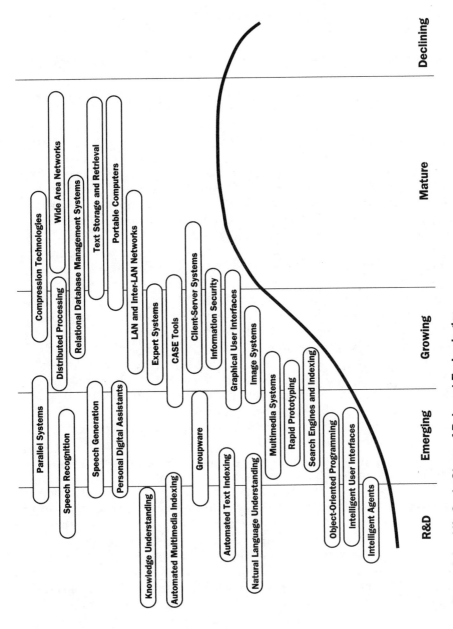

Figure 4.1. Life-Cycle Stage of Relevant Technologies

cally, this means that technologists cannot be *only* technologists; rather, they must understand the business they are charged with supporting.

This understanding enables technology planners to

- Appraise technologies that may be used immediately for competitive advantage
- Appraise changes or new developments that may be used for competitive advantage over the next three to five years
- Identify potential applications of current and future technology and how such applications may affect the competition
- Identify potential changes in current applications driven by market demands or technology developments

Aligning technology strategy with business needs rates as one of the most frequently identified problems confronting corporate MIS heads. This alignment requires knowledge of the business operations of each strategic business unit in the corporation and their competitive business strategies, and the best available knowledge of the technology and business strategies of competitors. In addition, it requires the active participation of both information technologists and users to develop an understanding of the potential of information technology use and a consistent vision of the future.

It is important to recognize that we are in an era of "demand pull" rather than "technology push." Research in technology management and product development has shown the success of *triad management*. Triad management techniques create teams of marketing representatives, technology suppliers (such as engineering or R&D), and manufacturing representatives to rapidly introduce new technologies or bring new products to market. Similarly, MIS experience has shown that the most successful implementations are those that are wanted by and driven by users. Alignment requires that MIS form alliances and occasional task forces or teams with user organizations. Technology planning is no exception if the alignment of technology and business strategy is the goal.

Actually, alignment of technology strategy with business strategy requires two modes of operation: (1) the technology strategy must be able to respond quickly to changing business needs, and (2) the technology potential and vision must be able to influence the development of business strategy. Such alignment does not come easily, and a number of tactics must be used concurrently to address the problem.

The MIS function must take an active role in educating management about the potentials for information technology. Since corporate managers have little time or patience for formal education, informal means generally work best. One company's MIS executive makes a point of meeting with other top managers for lunch in the executive dining room to informally discuss what competitors or other firms are doing with information technology. Another director of MIS uses a combination of a periodic newsletter about intriguing uses of information technology and a monthly meeting with user executives. This meeting is ostensibly to discuss project progress or service satisfaction, but the director also uses the opportunity to convey technology application ideas of interest and to discover unmet needs.

On a more formal basis, the chief information officer (CIO) or head of MIS should be (and more frequently is) a member of the corporate strategic planning committee and has the opportunity to directly influence the resulting business strategies. Also on a more formal basis, many MIS executives have found that publishing a brief annual executive summary of MIS activities and plans and/or conducting a semi-annual or annual management briefing provides education opportunities.

Even though schools and colleges are increasing their computer training courses, and the profusion of personal computers has forced employees and managers to become more computer literate, most noncomputing professionals are not aware of the full potential of computing and communications technology. College courses grow out of date and fade from memory. The use of personal computers rarely provides managers or professionals with insight into the potentials of such technologies as knowledge-based systems, imaging technology, or many other emerging or current technologies that could be used to advantage.

Technology planning must continue to be the responsibility of technology planners, but the planners need to become more than technologists. Technology planners should make a point of meeting with user managers, not only to educate them informally but to learn about their business operations and needs. It is almost always flattering to be asked about one's job. Most line managers will spend their time and the time of their employees to respond to requests from MIS personnel to learn more about business operations. In fact, they may find it a refreshing change.

Technology planners also need to discover how competing companies are using information technology. This does not imply industrial espionage, but simply tracking articles in the trade press, attending industry or information technology conferences, talking with prospective vendors and suppliers, and so forth, as described in Chapter 3. Innovative applications can arise outside the company's industry and be applicable to company needs, so this "intelligence" effort should not be confined to the company's industry.

In today's global markets, very few firms are self-sufficient. Many

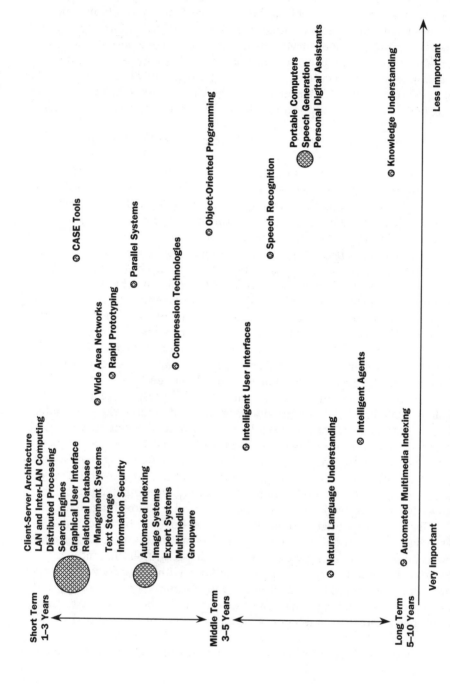

Figure 4.2. Relative Importance of Technologies (Technology Rendezvous)

never were. Increasingly close cooperation with both suppliers and customers is needed to be competitive and to respond to market conditions in a timely manner. As a result, it is now necessary to view the firm and its business processes as part of an "extended enterprise," composed of the firm, its allies, to suppliers, and its major customers. Technology planners must create relationships within the firm that will provide the perspective of the extended enterprise, or they must initiate relationships with key suppliers and customers to understand how they use information technology and how the company's processes will need with interface to those of its "business partners."

As technology planners acquire a knowledge of the industry and the business, they will need to document this knowledge in notes that may be used for building a business case for new applications. They will also need to find a way to translate the needs of strategic business units into a projection of when and how new or emerging technologies will influence the company's industry.

First, with a knowledge of the industry's business processes, technology planners can construct a value chain. In a manufacturing company, for example, the value chain may contain the major elements of R&D, engineering, logistics, operations and manufacturing, marketing, distribution, sales, and service. New technology can affect any aspect of this chain through product design tools, materials or components procurement, inventory management, manufacturing methods and controls, maintenance of plant and equipment, packaging processes, sales and service tracking, and so forth. The potential applications that can provide leverage and maximize the contribution from technology investment can be recognized, and the technologies supporting those applications can be identified.

Working with user managers, technology planners can gain an understanding of both the leverage points and the managers' perceived priorities. These factors drive the identification of the relative importance of various technologies to the firm. This "technology rendezvous" illustrates the relative importance of technologies to the business compared to the time at which the technology should be adopted by the company.

Figure 4.2 illustrates how the technology rendezvous may be shown to management in an imaginary multinational company. From that example, it is possible to identify "clusters" of technology that must be introduced over time to keep the company competitive. The cluster of technologies in the upper left corner of Figure 4.2 indicates those technologies that will be most important in the shortest period of time. The immediate and short-term very important technologies must be considered in the early stages of implementing a technology plan.

The plan must consider other technologies in an evolutionary fashion, as follows:

Immediate/great importance:

Client-server systems

Local area networks and inter-LAN networks

Distributed processing

Search engines

Graphical user interfaces

Relational database management systems

Text storage and retrieval

Information security

Short-term/great importance:

Automated text indexing

Image systems

Expert systems

Multimedia systems

Groupware

Short-term/medium importance:

High-speed wide area networks

Rapid prototyping

CASE tools

Compression technologies

Massively parallel systems

Medium-term/medium importance:

Intelligent user interfaces

Object-oriented development

Speech recognition

Intelligent agents

Language translation

Long-term/great importance:

Natural language understanding

Automated multimedia indexing

Long-term/less importance:

Speech generation

Personal digital assistants

Portable and hand-held computers

Knowledge understanding

The technology rendezvous is important for meeting both modes of strategic planning discussed above: IT strategy for rapid response to business needs and a way to influence the strategy of the business. When constructed on the basis of knowledge of the industry and competition, it provides a top executive view of the need for introducing new technology or for extending the use of currently available technology to remain competitive. Thus, it influences corporate business strategy. Simultaneously, it provides MIS with a view of when and how it should anticipate training, experimentation, and application development using these technologies. This knowledge directly influences long-range application planning, MIS budgeting, and hardware and software selection. Note that both the technologies being tracked (Figure 4.1) and the technology rendezvous (Figure 4.2) will be different for each industry and, to some extent, for each company or strategic business unit on the basis of the technology position maintained and the relative level of technology already in place.

INFORMATION TECHNOLOGY DEPLOYMENT

Professionals involved in technology management have discovered that technology *per se* is rarely deployable; instead, it is deployed through application. A new technology for the manufacture of integrated circuits, for example, is deployed through the change of processes and equipment on the production line; a new materials technology for the manufacture of automobile fenders is deployed through changes in the molding equipment and the manufacturing and assembly processes. Similarly, new information technology is deployed through its application for the benefit of the company and the user.

Information technology deployment through applications means changes and requisite training for the application designers and developers as well as for the users. The processes that will change may include requirements definition, system design specification, programming, user documentation development, application testing, system installation, system support, and end user business processes.

Such changes may result in organizational change in the systems development and maintenance function to permit more rapid application development and better field support of users. Substantive changes that allow companies to take full advantage of enabling IS technology will almost invariably require changes in business processes and in the organizations that perform these processes. For example, one major bank adopted an image-processing-based application for loan application review and approval. Prior to installation of the new system, loans had been approved by a sequential process in which different specialist groups handled different aspects of the loan application. After installation of the system, a "case" method was introduced in which loan officers were assigned specific loan applications to handle from start to finish. The specialist groups were disbanded and the entire loan processing function reorganized.

INTRODUCING NEW INFORMATION TECHNOLOGY

To this point, this chapter has dealt primarily with technology planning, including identification of business needs and identification of appropriate new technologies to support these needs. Next, it is necessary to deal with the actual introduction of IT to the business.

The acquisition and introduction of new technology requires justification in terms that will meet the approval of senior management. Even if the planning has been carried out with appropriate involvement and approval by top management, the introduction of specific elements of the plan will require detailed justification based on their benefits to the business.

Two types of technology introduction predominate those that do not have an impact that is visible to users and those that do. In the first type, for example, an MIS department may introduce a subsystem for massively parallel processing that adds capacity to process additional transactions of the same nature, and in the same apparent manner, as current transactions. Such a technology introduction may be invisible to the end users of the systems (other than the impact from system testing prior to implementation), but it will be highly visible to the MIS department as new design and programming techniques are introduced.

However, many introductions of new technology will change the way employees perform their tasks. Corporations and whole industries throughout the world are restructuring and downsizing to improve their efficiency and competitiveness. In many instances, they are finding that they must adopt new information technology to carry out their goals.

Replacing legacy systems has therefore become a critical concern to many companies. With perhaps tens of millions of dollars invested in mainframe-based systems, MIS chiefs in many companies are finding that these systems have become relatively brittle. They are difficult to maintain and modify, they do not support the kinds of user interfaces to which users of PCs have become accustomed, and they are frequently unable to support new modes of business operation. In addition, for many applications, downsizing of equipment and the introduction of client-server architectures will provide significantly lower operating costs. Under these pressures, MIS heads may find it easy to justify legacy system replacement.

There is increasing recognition that many companies have not profited adequately from their implementation of business systems. One major reason that apparently successful systems development projects have not achieved expected benefits is that the applications were based on supporting existing business processes, and when existing business processes form the foundation for the requirements definition, even anticipated gains in efficiency may be unrealized. The published experiences of a number of companies from various industries indicate that when the business processes are redesigned and information technology is viewed as an enabling tool for the redesigned processes, significant improvements become much more likely.

As a result of this observed experience, an increasing number of companies have begun using a collection of methods and tools under the general name of *business process redesign;* (BPR) or *re-engineering.* Many consulting companies have adopted BPR methods, and this book contains a description of one approach. (See Section V.)

BPR is a methodology for transforming the business processes of an enterprise to achieve breakthroughs in the quality, responsiveness, flexibility, and cost of those processes in order to compete more effectively and efficiently in the enterprise's chosen market. BPR uses a combination of industrial engineering, operations research, management theory, performance measurement, quality management, and systems analysis techniques and tools simultaneously to (1) redesign business processes, and (2) harness the power of information technology to support these restructured business processes more effectively.

The focus of BPR is first and foremost on designing an improved business process, which may then use information technology to enable its new functionality. BPR projects are designed to take a fresh look at a major business process from a *customer* perspective. The customer of a process may be the external consumer of its products or services *or* the internal recipient of the process output.

Whether the method described in this book or some modification of it is used, it is important to recognize that today's systems extend beyond the corporation to both suppliers and customers of the firm. Where new systems must interface with external parties, they must be represented on the design and development team, if only by proxy.

By using BPR or re-engineering approaches, firms work at overcoming the innate resistance to change that has plagued many attempts to introduce new technologies that affect the way employees perform their jobs.

Redesigning business processes by enabling new technology benefits the company by improving efficiency and making business processes more responsive to customer needs. In the end, this means that the company becomes more competitive, and it represents clearly the manner in which technology influences the company strategy. On the other hand, it means that there will be periods of disturbance in business processes and organizations. Success factors for business process redesign are described in Chapter 16.

SUMMARY

Businesses do not acquire technology for its own sake. They must focus on acquiring *appropriate* technology that will advance the firm's competitive position. Doing this properly requires a dedicated effort.

Acquisition of appropriate technology first requires that the technology planners understand the needs of the business and the strategic technology position that top management has adopted. Second, technology planners must maintain an awareness of technology trends to ensure the firm's ability to support its business needs and technology position. Technology planners must position MIS not only to support the firm's business directions but to influence company or business unit strategy. Third, MIS and technology planners must justify the adoption of new technology in terms of the business processes that new systems will support. This is best done through the introduction of new technology as an enabler for improving business processes.

The key to successful introduction and deployment of new information technology is business process redesign, which combines the business strategy, the process improvement justification, and the technology in a coherent approach that can be readily conveyed to senior management.

Business processes must continually be expected to evolve as business conditions and the needs of customers change and because the company needs to remain competitive. New applications of information technology will continue to be enables new products and services and for the maintenance or enhancement of business processes that underlie the competitive position of the company.

To be successful, planning technology strategy and acquiring and introducing new technology must be a continuing effort in support of business operations and strategic planning.

DISCUSSION TOPICS

- At what stage (emerging through declining) are information technologies positioned at the time you are reading this book?
- Do any emerging technologies appear to have substantial impact on the information systems of your company?
- Who should be responsible for introducing new technology into the enterprise?
- Can you describe the "technology rendezvous" for your company or for a company in an industry in which you are interested?
- Why have many "legacy" systems become unresponsive to business needs?
- What skills and experience are needed for technology planning?

REFERENCE

1. "Spending for a Rainy Day." *Information Week* (December 7, 1992): 38–48.

CHAPTER 5

Emerging Information Technologies' Impact on Business

Chapter 4 detailed technology introduction and deployment. This chapter provides some technology forecasts from the perspective of 1994 and suggests the potential impacts they will have on the way business operates. Although the technologies emerging at the time this book is read may be different than those described, the approach taken here may aid in developing the kinds of scenarios that are required for projects described in Chapters 3 and 4.

TECHNOLOGY FORECASTING

Futurist scenarios tend to stretch the planning horizon 10 to 20 years into the future. However, business has to plan for the nearer term of the next 2 to 7 years in order to survive to enjoy the long term. Considering all the factors that may affect predictions, the further we look into the future, the less success we have in prediction and the less current value our predictions have for business planning.

This is especially true for technology forecasting, which depends on projecting the current state of research into possible products of the future and the impacts of those products on their users. Such forecasts are vulnerable to market acceptance of predicted future products, the affect of competing technologies, the affects of the costs of changing to the new technologies, the market strength of the companies that introduce the new products, and a host of other nontechnological factors.

The scenarios presented here have a high probability of occurring in the period from 1995 to 2002 because they are based on technologies (or combinations of technologies) that have already reached the product development stage or are already on the market. In that sense, this chapter is not a technology forecast, since it assumes the continued penetration of business by available information technology products and services. As a result, we can be fairly confident that before the year 2000, CEOs will have to contend with most of the impacts identified here.

Most companies in advanced countries already are substantial users of information technology; as this use becomes more intensive, we can expect qualitative as well as quantitative changes to the business. These include changes to

- Relationships with customers and suppliers
- Staff work habits
- The people companies recruit
- Cost structures for products and services
- Ways managers manage.

This chapter explores the changes that can be expected as a result of information technology's impacts. More important, this chapter raises the issue of senior executives' responsibilities for including the expected impacts in their strategic planning.

Many CEOs delegate thinking about information technology to "techies" in the belief either that information technology is too technical and detailed for their attention or that specialists are needed to deal with IT issues. The message of this chapter is that the impacts of information technology over the next few years will be so far-reaching that senior executives will have to think about it.

PRODUCTS AND SERVICES WILL CHANGE

As a basis for our projections, we will examine a few of the ways in which information technology will change the products and services that companies offer. One of its greatest affects on business will result from dramatic improvements in global communications for data, voice, and video.

Global communications are enabling continuous businesses. Today we have 24-hour reservation services for travel from wherever the traveler is located. In the near future, we can expect 24-hour trading on stock and commodity exchanges around the world. We can also expect immediate funds transfer and settlement to reduce or eliminate float, and 24-hour global sales order entry and shipping information.

Information storage and retrieval systems, combined with communications, will allow distributed R&D efforts to work more closely together than ever. The pace of research and development will continue to accelerate, pushed by short product life cycles and new research tools, including cooperative groupwork systems and literature search systems that find not only what you asked for but also associated information that you may not have thought to request.

Advances in the miniaturization and durability of microprocessor chips will continue to spark their use as embedded systems to enhance the usability of manufactured products. Computer chips are already in cars and appliances. In the near future computer chips and communications devices will find their way into all kinds of products, from houses to furniture to clothing and accessories. Picture a reclining chair with the controls for the entertainment center built-in and activated by speech recognition; then add built-in heat and massage, built-in telephone connections, and built-in stereo speakers and microphones—creating the perfect relaxation environment. (The addition of a personal computer, an executive information system, and access to newswire services creates an executive control "cockpit" for business management.)

Professional and hobbyist tools will also incorporate computers. A hand drill will sense the material being drilled and adjust the torque automatically, and it will warn the operator of overheating or potential drill bit damage.

The emerging techniques of micro-electromechanical systems (MEMS) produce a miniaturized machine in combination with the intelligence on the usual silicon chip. The moving parts of the machine can be switches that activate larger devices, medical instruments, thermostats, or a host of other potential applications embedded into larger systems. MEMS holds the promise of developing an entire new industry as well as many new products.

Online information services that supply news, entertainment, trade information, R&D information, and many other information bases will be the fastest-growing business of the next decade. Intelligent "agents"—software that assists in navigating networks to find desired information or to screen out unwanted information—will be in common use by professionals and managers by 1999. Portable device access (through laptop or hand-held communicating computers) to these information sources will help business grow.

The ways to combine computers and communications with other products are limited only by the imagination.

RELATIONSHIPS WITH CUSTOMERS WILL CHANGE

One of the most rapid adopters of technology is the field of entertainment and advertising. The 1992 movie *Terminator 2* showed us a small sample of the potential for special effects developed through computer imaging technology. Advertisers have been quick to adopt this technology for their commercials, but the real change to advertising is still to come. Through the use of cable television, databases of demographic information, and computer-controlled selection of programming, mass media will give way to niche markets and highly personalized, interactive media. "Broadcasting" will give way to "narrowcasting."

Currently, companies build retail customer databases from the mailed-in warranty cards packed with their products. Retailers will also collect information when customers use their credit cards for purchases. From these sources, advertisers will be able to build customer profiles of their retail customers and use specifically directed, individually targeted advertising to sell additional goods and services. Custom catalogs of products for specific income groups, ethnic groups, and life-style groups can be assembled readily by means of computerized graphic editing techniques and even desktop printing for small volumes of high-value goods.

We can also be sure that customers will find ways to defend themselves from this onslaught of targeted advertising. For example, direct-call telephone solicitation and advertising will decline in effectiveness as middle-class targets acquire intelligent phones to screen incoming calls.

Product service will be a major differentiating factor in future competition, and such service will be increasingly automated to reduce the cost of service delivery and to speed response to the customer.

IBM and other companies, by 1993, had implemented 800-number services to provide advice to customers, but new services will go much further. We should expect 800- or 900-number service for customers' inquiries, product software maintenance, health services, and product diagnostics. For example, as an extension of the capability of the embedded computer already in a kitchen appliance, we can expect sensors connected to the microprocessor to provide on-board diagnostics. When the customer calls for repair, the service facility will ask that he or she plug the extension phone jack into the socket on the appliance. While the customer is still on the phone, the microprocessor will download the diagnostic information to the service facility's computer, which will request the necessary parts from inventory and dispatch the repair person to the customers home at a time convenient to the customer.

The next stage of development will eliminate the phone jack by embedding a short-range radio communications device with the microprocessor. This will ultimately permit the appliance to call the repair facility by itself, using the customer's telephone line. The repair facility can then call the customer and arrange a repair time *before the appliance fails.*

Speaker-independent, continuous speech recognition will allow customers to obtain information directly from computers without "pushing buttons" on their digital phones or using computers. Low-priced video phones will allow computers to respond to customers with both voice and visual presentations. You can call your bank or your broker and find out your account status, or call your favorite department store about sale items, without ever talking to a human being.

How we sell goods and services is also changing. In a movement already started, customers will specify their options for products with the assistance of computer visualization tools. Currently in the home improvement industry, customers can sit at a computer workstation with an "advisor" and plan their new kitchen, bedroom or bathroom layouts, add in the appliances and fixtures, and their choice of colors, and view their new room as it will appear after remodeling. After approval, the computer automatically generates the sales order listing for the materials and fixtures needed. These same techniques will soon be used for custom ordering of goods ranging from autos to plastic surgery to hair and makeup styles to computer try-ons of clothing in various colors and styles. Soon these tools will be packaged into reasonably priced color-screen portables for use by salespeople.

New products and services (or custom products and services) will be jointly designed with large customers by computer-linked cooperative workgroups to open new areas of sales. Already some petrochemical and plastics manufacturers are linking their computers to those of their major customers to jointly design materials that will enable the economical production of new lighter-weight, more durable, or more easily manufactured parts for products.

Manufacturing firms will increasingly link their systems directly to those of distributors and retailers, not only for inventory replenishment but for obtaining information about their customers' preferences by demographic factors. The information flood will be too much for humans to handle, so expert systems that mimic the reasoning abilities of humans in limited domains of expertise will be used to react to all but the most unusual situations.

The use of credit cards, debit cards, and other forms of payment will increase, but the "cashless society" concept is a myth. The underground economy is too strong in every country. Currency is cheaper to make and use than electronic forms of payment.

RELATIONSHIPS WITH SUPPLIERS WILL CHANGE

Gradual implementation of integrated service digital networks (ISDN), asynchronous transfer mode (ATM), and other broadband communication technologies is starting to provide concurrent transmission of voice, fax, video, and/or data over the same "telephone" line. This technology will support cooperative workgroup projects for product design, manufacture, and troubleshooting among firms and their suppliers.

Computer-aided language translation of text, already performing at better than an 80-percent level of accuracy between some languages, will make it easier to do business (or compete) in foreign markets. One world-wide manufacturer of custom heavy equipment must assemble proposals for new projects from contributors in its factories in Scandinavia and North America, from its regional sales offices and local materials suppliers, and from its field sales representatives in its customers' countries. The company has already developed the telecommunications infrastructure needed to support its global business and is anticipating its next moves to support cooperative engineering and proposal development work.

As the U.S. Department of Defense and large private-sector companies demand that their suppliers improve service by implementing electronic data interchange (EDI), increased use of EDI will naturally occur, but this is an interim step. The latter part of the decade will see direct interaction between the systems of firms and those of their suppliers in product design, engineering, R&D, inventory management, shipping information, quality assurance, and inspection, and in other areas in which the extended enterprise can operate as a single entity.

In fact, the term "extended enterprise" will increasingly characterize the manner in which businesses operate as they link more intimately with each others' systems in a process chain that reaches from raw materials through distributors to customers.

STAFF WORK HABITS WILL CHANGE

Staff work habits and the way people view their jobs will change under the new ways of operating the businesses that are enabled by information technology.

Technological unemployment (temporary or permanent skill obsolescence) will result in multiple periods of unemployment and career change during a working career. The experience of intermittent work will erode company loyalty and may bring legislation that forces employers to take greater responsibility for employee skills maintenance.

Technological unemployment will increase the number of small business ventures—"microbusinesses"—that supply to larger firms. Reduced need for particular specialty skills in one or more companies may give entrepreneurs the opportunity to provide those skills on a contract basis to a number of former employers.

Telecommuting (people working at home using computers and telecommunications) will increase, but will primarily be part-time. People are basically social animals and need the human contact provided by the office. The experiences of several firms that have adopted video-conferencing show that this technology may reduce the number of trips needed for meetings, but it does not eliminate the need for occasional face-to-face contact to build more complete understanding and rapport among people required to interact with each other.

The potential reduction in commuting time through part-time tele-commuting will mean that some employees do not have to change homes every time they change jobs. A fringe benefit to business may be more stable communities and workforces.

In most businesses today, workers are organized into relatively stable departments in which they work with the same people every day. In the near future, many workers will have to learn to work on temporary teams (computer-supported workgroups) with suppliers and customers to facili-tate design, manufacture, and delivery of products or design and delivery of new services. In fact, such temporary teams may be mode of operation increasingly used within the company.

Pressures to improve responsiveness to customers (both external cus-tomers and internal recipients of the products of business processes), com-bined with an increasing need to maintain security, will lead to better ways to stay in touch. Microprocessor employee badges may include security identification, pagers, and cellular radio. Control centers will know where employees are and be able to reach them at any time. Secure doors will rec-ognize badge wearers and permit them entry to controlled premises. Time clocks may disappear. The "communicators" worn by the crew members of the *Enterprise* in *Star Trek* are on the verge of technological reality.

The "paperless office" will continue to be myth because paper is too cheap and too convenient to be eliminated. However, personal computers and workstations will permeate the office and field environments. The ability to use a computer will become a prerequisite for most factory jobs as well as white-collar jobs. In fact, it will also be a prerequisite for field workers who make repairs and deliveries.

Field workers will never be out of touch with their office bases. Cellu-lar telephones combined with hand-held computers will relay orders and other information for immediate processing. Yet field workers will need to spend less time in their offices, may share offices with others, and may not return to base for weeks. This may reduce the need for private offices or desks at company facilities.

Nevertheless, remote personnel will create a problem for manage-ment. Alienation of these workers from the company is a potential danger. The same technology that enables them to operate remotely will have to be used to keep them up to date with company events and even to create electronic substitutes for the office water cooler.

THE KINDS OF PEOPLE RECRUITED WILL CHANGE

As products change to incorporate embedded computers and communica-tions devices, product designers will need to have the engineering skills to handle new challenges. A combination of mechanical and electronic engi-neering degrees will make a candidate for an engineering job extremely valuable. Such combined training and skills will be needed to integrate the work of design and engineering teams. Similar combinations of training and skills will be needed for product support and service personnel.

Job consolidation and computer-mediated processes will require broader employee skills resulting in a need for perennial and life-long retraining; computer-aided education (CAE) will be needed, and take-home CAE and video training will be used to supplement classroom work.

Immigrants will supplement the aging workforce in several advanced countries, but will need entry-level training. This implies more company-sponsored CAE, including speech recognition systems for improving spoken language skills.

Electronic immigrants, skilled personnel in other countries using telecommuting techniques, will increase, not just in computer-related trades but in office jobs—for example, remote inventory management, accounts payable, and accounts receivable functions.

The technological poverty of the poor and undereducated will make them less employable, and class-action suits may arise to force large employers to educate workers. On a more optimistic note, handicapped persons who would otherwise not qualify for employment will become more employable. Cyborgs (closely interfaced humans and intelligent machines) will allow the handicapped to perform physical and office tasks they might otherwise find difficult, thereby expanding the labor pool. Computer-enhanced prosthetic devices developed through research supported by the Veteran's Administration and other organizations should reach the market in the late 1990s.

THE COST STRUCTURES OF BUSINESS WILL CHANGE

Pushed by global communications capabilities, 24-hour business cycles will mean more shift work. This will lead to greater expenses for shift premium pay for employees but higher utilization of plant and capital investment. The pace of factory automation in many industries has been retarded by unfavorable tax structures that require depreciation writeoff too quickly, thus raising the direct overhead cost on products. Higher utilization of capital equipment resulting from 24-hour operation will tend to offset these overhead costs and therefore encourage greater investment in plant automation.

In addition, the continued aging of the population of most advanced countries will shrink the available workforce, also encouraging automation to reduce workforce needs.

Driven by competitive selling techniques and increasingly selective buyers, the demand for customized products will increase. Customization requires short production runs and minimum parts inventory. Computer-supported just-in-time (JIT) inventory management and flexible manufacturing automation will allow smaller firms to compete with larger ones, since the critical factor will be the cost of short runs of "customized" products rather than mass production.

Computer-mediated processes will permit increasing job consolidation. Workforce restructuring will lead to higher pay for fewer workers and a need for alternative compensation schemes.

With smaller, distributed computers providing more power for less cost, large mainframe use will gradually be confined to high-volume transaction processing systems, shared corporate databases, and computing-intensive applications. Small computers and wireless local area networks will make computing ubiquitous, and responsibility for more than half of computer costs will shift from the MIS organization to the users.

THE WAY MANAGERS MANAGE WILL CHANGE

The manner in which management decisions are made will change under the impact of new approaches enabled by information technology. Portable computing will make managers independent of time and distance, since they will be able to access company information and relay decisions and orders to their staff at any time from any place. This capability will be a mixed blessing, since 24-hour access to the business means 24-hour access to the manager. Some managers may respond by attempting to handle all the decision traffic that comes to them. Such managers will probably not last very long or will find that they need to delegate more.

Improved communications will enable managers to extend their span of control. Historically, management scientists said that a manager's effective span of control should not exceed five or six directly reporting subordinates. However, the integration of business functions in modern organizations often requires more. Such tools as electronic mail, access to corporate databases, video-conferencing, and electronic bulletin boards will enable managers to broaden their span of control, but also will require more delegation downward. Expert systems and decision support tools will be needed to handle routine business decisions, leaving exceptions to experts and to increasingly rare middle managers.

Group decision making through computer conferencing across time zones will intensify. To remain competitive, companies will have to assemble their best talents and focus them on critical decisions. Group decision making can deteriorate into decision paralysis in some companies if the computer conferencing tools are used to enable management-by-committee. To avoid such stagnation, management will be forced to adopt conference techniques in which responsibility for a decision is clearly delegated to one manager.

Specialized management for functions of the business, such as R&D, engineering design, finance, and marketing, will gradually be eroded by increases in group management through interdisciplinary teams enhanced by computer conferencing to minimize decision-delays. But, as indicated above, someone will still have to take final responsibility.

All this new availability of access and information input will flood managers with information, much of it not relevant to their needs. This flood will come not only from within the company but from online access to external sources of world and business or industry news. Under the constant pressure of information overload, executives will encourage adoption of new applications that combine graphics, expert systems, executive information systems, and other technologies to filter information and reduce data to useable form and pertinent content before they see it. Such applications, already technologically feasible in 1993, will become common before the end of the decade.

Even from this single viewpoint, it is clear that line managers must increasingly influence the way the application of IT is managed in their organizations.

New business applications for computers and communications will focus more on where the firm is going, in contrast to accounting systems that report where the firm has been. Investments will focus more on the interface with customers and suppliers to improve service and customer satisfaction, which implies applications that support a company or product strategy. For example, if a company's strategy is to produce low-priced products, its systems must, at a minimum, support cost-effective production while maintaining a level of quality sufficient to avoid customer dissatisfaction and to meet competitive requirements.

Ever closer linkages with key suppliers, such as in joint product design, JIT inventory control, joint quality assurance, and computer interfaces to distributors and retailers for resupply or custom orders, will force companies to become "extended enterprises." Executives and managers will have to co-manage the extended enterprise with their allies and "partners."

There are both benefits and dangers in the extended enterprise concept. One firm in the construction materials business, already a leader in meeting product delivery schedules, decided that it would extend its lead in this area to place competition far behind. Using business process redesign methods, the firm analyzed each process in the order-through-delivery cycle to improve speed, on the assumption that rapid delivery was the path to customer satisfaction. After some time, one manager had the temerity to ask if this basic premise was correct. In-depth interviews and analysis of customers' requirements indicated that some orders were needed as fast as possible, but for the vast majority of orders, faster delivery forced the customer to warehouse the materials and incur inventory carrying costs—a certain path to customer dissatisfaction. The project was refocused to emphasize rapid delivery *when it was wanted*. In other words, just in time.

JIT delivery is justly famous for improving service while lowering inventory carrying costs. Extremely close computer system linkages with suppliers have made JIT possible, but even this technique has its dangers. Michael Schrage[1] tells the story of how Tokyo's thousands of convenience stores, department stores, and grocery stores adopted JIT in an attempt to emulate the success of the manufacturers. Once- or twice-a-day deliveries became 10- and 12-times-a-day deliveries, with the result that literally tens of thousands of trucks and delivery vans are now congesting Tokyo's streets, and traffic has ground to a snail's pace while expensive fuel burning adds to the city's pollution. Even worse, JIT deliveries are now consistently late.

The point of these examples is that business management must manage the application of information technology or it may lead to technically correct systems that do not help the business.

The emphasis on customer satisfaction in competitive markets means that the producers of goods and services will have to improve their knowledge of their customers and of the factors that lead to satisfaction. This effort will be a continuing challenge. Collecting and organizing intelligence on markets, sales, competition, customers, trends, and technical data will be more critical to competing successfully. Those with the best market intelligence systems will have the winning card.

During the 1980s, many executives read about using computers and communications to build a "war room"—an executive conference room with large computer-driven displays on the walls and computer consoles that would allow executives to retrieve and analyze information and jointly plan the battle strategy of the company. A few companies even spent money to put in war rooms. As a concept, however, the computerized corporate war room will be obsolete before it is more extensively adopted by business. Executive information systems (EIS) based on communicating multimedia workstations will be the next wave. These workstations, supported by *groupware* (software systems that make it easier for groups to work together through networked computers) will provide far better facilities while permitting users to attend meetings from their offices, wherever they are located.

With low-cost, powerful departmental computers and increasing user knowledge leading to the demystification of computing, the responsibility for computers and applications will become dispersed throughout the company. Computers will be viewed as just another business resource (like labor, office equipment, machines, etc.) to be managed by those with departmental or strategic business unit responsibility.

Business processes will change as IT techniques already available (such as image processing) enable workflow management and concurrent sharing of information. The discipline of business process redesign will be increasingly used not only to address cost reduction but to improve the flexibility of the company to change product or service quality, style, image, functions, and features to meet customer demand. In addition, redesigned business processes will go beyond JIT to address the speed with which new products are brought to the market.

Top management must ensure that redesigned business processes enabled by IT advances are aimed at the real goals of the business and not driven by the availability of technology.

CORPORATE RISKS WILL CHANGE

Information technology will bring new or additional risks that will have to be managed by corporations.

As a direct projection of current events, increasing dependence on computers and communications will make companies more vulnerable to damage ranging from loss of information to halted business operations. Every one of us, as a customer, knows the irritation when customer-service people tell us they cannot help us because "the computer is down." A similar frustration arises when we are told, "The computer must have made a mistake."

Top management, in its drive for customer satisfaction, will have to pay more attention to the needs of the business for availability, integrity, and confidentiality of information. The domain of information security, which addresses these issues, will be of growing concern to top management. (See Section IV.)

Many corporations today operate in a global business environment, with their interfaces to customers, distributors, and suppliers enhanced by global telecommunications capabilities. The reach of telecommunications has made it easy to advertise our goods and has made third-world citizens hungry for products of the advanced nations. It enabled events in Tiananmen Square to be relayed to fax, television, and computer network users in China, and it undoubtedly contributed to the rapid collapse of the Soviet Union. Telecommunications will continue to influence the pace of change in world politics. Free information such as that which led to the Soviet Union's collapse may make doing business in some countries risky. Business intelligence for global corporations in the future will need to include political intelligence.

Finally, in the litigious climate that exists in the United States, we must consider another set of risks. If a physician or an attorney uses a procedure that may prove to be faulty or to have a high risk, he or she is required to inform the patient or client of the risk (and in many instances to obtain a signed consent form). The implication of a long history of malpractice suits is that *the availability of information mandates its use.* As corporate information bases grow and include the intelligence needed to operate the business competitively, huge stores of information will be available to management. If information is available, managers may no longer be able to effectively plead ignorance of any risk. The potential for product or service liability suits will increase dramatically in the future as customers become able to prove that "negative" information was available to the seller.

SUMMARY

Information technology will continue to affect business whether or not it is welcomed. Firms that fail to take advantage of technology advances will frequently fall to the competitive pressures of those that have adopted new techniques and tools. On the other hand, adopting technology for the sake of technology can lead to major errors and losses.

Information technology is so woven into the fabric of the firm that it not only must be responsive to the strategic directions of the company but must be considered as an influence on those strategic directions.

Top management can no longer delegate the responsibility for IT application when it has the affects described in this chapter. It is not necessary for every executive to become a computer expert, but it is necessary for every executive to insist that technologists translate the advances in information technology into potential impacts on the business so that they can be reflected in company strategy.

Note: The ideas in this chapter come from many sources, including discussions with computer professionals, consulting assignments, and news articles. However, I wish to make particular note of *The Futurist Magazine*, published by the World Future Society, as a source of ideas.

DISCUSSION TOPICS

- In each section of this chapter, predictions have been made about the impact of information technology on business. Have these predictions been realized at the time you are reading this book?
- Do you agree with the predictions? If not, why not?
- If you agree with some predictions, how will they influence your firm?
- How can you prepare yourself to take advantage of the coming changes?
- How can you prepare your company to profit from the coming changes?

REFERENCE

1. Schrage, M. "JIT in Tokyo." *San Jose Mercury News* (March 23, 1992).

IS Management Issues

Having dealt with some of the broader issues affecting information systems management, we now delve in greater detail into a few specific management issues. This section examines two types of problem: those that have occurred repeatedly with each new generation of professionals and managers, and those that are introduced by new economic or technology trends.

First, we address the problems of systems development productivity by focusing on rules for successful project management, how systems development productivity may be affected by object-oriented technologies and CASE, and how software will have to be managed in an object-oriented development environment.

Next, we focus on how to protect the company when systems development or computer/telecommunications operations are contracted to an external supplier—that is, *outsourced*.

Finally, considering the impact of client-server technology on system architecture and the delivery of information systems services, we address how to determine the appropriate time to consider adopting client-server or other new technologies to replace legacy systems.

CHAPTER 6

The Rules of Project Management

Managers and users (the "buyers" of application software) are becoming more demanding. As we pay more attention to the human interfaces and as we attempt to build increasingly comprehensive systems, projects for software development get larger and larger. If managers are not to be "condemned to repeat the past," they must take advantage of the lessons learned by others. This chapter contains rules of thumb for successful management of systems development projects. (You may find the rules to be deliberately exaggerated to get your attention.)

EIGHTEEN RULES AND SEVEN COROLLARIES FOR SUCCESSFUL PROJECTS

Rule 1: You Cannot Estimate Large Projects

Estimates are just that—approximations. However, once provided an estimate, management considers it to be a fixed budget. For this, among other, reasons, initial estimates for large projects are always overrun. As we undertake a project, we perform its various phases, and with each phase completed, we know more about the next phase. So, we are able to estimate the next phase with increasing accuracy.

Given the number of variables and unknowns in large projects, when we estimate the size of a project before starting it, we probably have a chance, based on experience, to estimate with an accuracy of no better than plus or minus 50 percent. After a requirements specification is completed, the balance of the project can probably be estimated within a tolerance of plus or minus 30 percent. When the system specification is completed, the rest of the project may be estimated within a range of plus or minus 20 percent. When the code has been written and tested, we should be able to estimate within plus or minus 10 percent for the implementation.

Our failures are often not so much in project management as they are in communicating the risks and the quality of estimates to management.

Rule 2: It Is Humanly Impossible to Control Large, Complex Projects

Project control tools are absolutely necessary for the control of large projects. Many of these tools are available today, at a relatively low cost, in a form that runs on personal computers. Project management tools are a minimum requirement. Of course, the other requirement is that you establish the appropriate reporting procedures and discipline yourself and the project team members to use the tools.

Corollary A: You cannot control people. The basic resource being controlled in project management is people. People get sick, take vacations, stand around the water cooler, and discuss the project, baseball, children, other people, and so forth. Project plans must take into account the contingencies and risks of people-related activities and the overhead time associated with communications in large projects. (See Chapter 7.)

Corollary B: Project management and control have to be built in, not added on. It is too late to implement project control after the project has started. Project estimates have to be made using the same work breakdown structure that will be used to control the project (or one as close to it as is possible). Project control methods and tools must be activated before the project begins to capture the results of all project activities. During the project, as the unexpected happens, it is advisable to update the project plans to reflect the necessary changes in order to retain control.

Rule 3: A Task Is Not Done Until It Is Done

Projects are composed of tasks, and each task must be estimated and controlled. The software industry lives continually with projects that are 95-percent completed for many weeks or months after their scheduled completion. Tasks are not done until clear evidence of their completion is available. Such evidence is a formal acceptance of the task product by the recipient of the product.

Corollary A: Most tasks depend on other tasks. This is easy to see in a PERT or CPM diagram, but it does not seem to be acceptable to many people. Every large project is composed of a series of tasks and task dependencies. In a true dependency relationship, the next task in line cannot be completed unless the first task is completed. Often, the next task cannot (or should not) be *started* before the previous task is completed. Starting the next task prematurely may result in having to do it over. Any unplanned results occurring in one task may require changes in the scope, time, and cost of other tasks, or even in the addition of new tasks to the project.

Corollary B: Tasks produce products, and products are the only real evidence of task completion. This should be self-explanatory, but what if there is no product? There is always a product, even if it is only an authorized approval that a planned task is unnecessary or a statement that a product has been accepted. Project reviews, design walkthroughs, and similar scheduled functions are all tasks. Evidence of their completion is important.

Rule 4: People Are Not Immortal

Aside from contingency planning, as I mentioned in corollary A to rule 2, do not plan a schedule on the assumption that people will continually work 80 hours a weak (misspelling intentional). Some of them may become ill. Others will quit (they may be the lucky ones). In any case, you will not complete the job on time.

Rule 5: Completion of Each Task Establishes a Requirement for the Next Task in the Sequence

Rule 5 is easy to see at the level of project phases. A requirements definition establishes the requirements for the system definition, a system definition establishes the requirements for a system specification, a systems specification establishes the requirements for coding, and so forth. It is also true that this occurs at the task level. Each completed task establishes certain parameters and constraints on the next task.

Rule 6: Sooner or Later You Have to Stop Designing the System if You Want to Complete the Project

Nothing is more destructive to the systems development process than continual change of the definition. The larger and longer the development project, the more vulnerable it is to requested changes. Little changes can creep in without associated changes being made to the specifications and estimates. Larger changes may echo throughout the system structure. In a 1993 survey report,[1] Capers Jones found that "creeping user requirements" increased the costs by an average 35 percent for the 60 projects surveyed; some large projects experienced a 200-percent increase. The answer, of course, is to have the "buyer" agree to a design freeze before the system specification is released to coding. However, Gary H. Anthes, in a 1994 Computerworld survey,[2] found that 80 percent of IS projects exceed budget and schedule because of system changes after requirements are frozen. More than 75 percent of these overruns exceeded 10 percent of the cost or schedule. The most frequently cited reasons were poor initial requirements definition, new applications were unfamiliar to users, or projects taking so long that requirements actually did change. The most recommended preventive methods to avoid "requirements creep" were joint user/developer application design (63 percent), prototyping (25 percent),thorough requirements definition (23 percent), and project management/monitoring tools (23 percent).

Not specified in the survey, but probably a better way to stop affects of requirements creep, is the use of incremental development and object-oriented design techniques.

Corollary A: In large projects, the resulting system never satisfies the buyer. The designers went by all the rules. They froze the design at the right point. The buyer agreed to the system specifications. The product delivered was exactly what the buyer wanted—three years ago. In the meantime, the business needs changed and a huge backlog of change requests accumulated. Perhaps the project was too big. With large projects we need to look for ways to compress the schedules or to implement the project incrementally.

Rule 7: Any Task That Takes More Than Ten People Cannot Be Done

It is very unlikely that a task that takes more than ten people will get done on time and within costs. Work breakdown structures need to consist of tasks that are small enough to be completed rapidly and require minimum cooperation and coordination among team members. The ideal project team consists of one person capable of doing everything—that minimizes the team coordination necessary. With a large team, the precision of communication among team members becomes critical. It is worth spending the time necessary to ensure this precision. (See Chapter 7.)

Rule 8: You Cannot Separate Data from Process

Structured design methods say that you can separate data from process. But at the implementation level, you need a knowledge of both concurrently to do the job right. In fact, some of the concepts underlying object oriented programming show that there are substantial efficiencies to be gained by unifying data and process during the system definition phase.

Rule 9: In Large Systems Development Efforts, Configuration Management Is Not Humanly Possible

As in rule 2, humans need help to juggle the number of objects, factors, and interrelationships involved in configuration management. If you are going to start a large project, acquire the necessary tools to aid in configuration management before it is too late (i.e., before you start the project).

Rule 10: There Are Always Alternatives and Risks

Whatever you are planning to do, there are always at least two alternatives. One alternative is not doing anything.

Along with each of the alternatives, there are risks, and the risks associated with each alternative are generally different. They are not simply project management risks. For example, if you break down a large project into modules to be incrementally implemented, the sequence of implementation may result in a delay of some business benefits at a cost to the user. Those delayed benefits may run the risk of adversely affecting the user's competitive position.

As described in rule 1, some of the greatest risks are in the estimating process. One mistake we frequently make in large projects is that we estimate the risks of individual tasks but do not estimate the compounded risk. That compounded risk occurs through the failure of one task affecting subsequent tasks and thus the entire project structure.

Corollary A: There are always trade-offs. More and more users and buyers of systems are becoming computer literate; however, they often do not understand the trade-offs involved in system design. On the other hand, system designers often assume that they know the answer to a trade-off question, so they do not bother to ask the buyer. In the "good old days" when machine time was expensive relative to employee time, we frequently designed systems to optimize the use of computer time and some of these systems were unfriendly to users. Now we are trying to optimize employee effectiveness, using extra machine cycles in the human interface is not a primary consideration. A successful product requires that the buyer and user like it. We need to explain the trade-offs to the buyer and let the buyer make educated business choices.

Rule 11: The Impact of Management Plans, Project Control Methods, and Development Standards Is Directly Proportional to Their Understandability and the Authority from which They Emanate

Unreadable manuals seem to be the rule for systems development organizations. Perhaps that is why so few analysts and programmers read them. We need to learn the virtue of simplicity. The intent of management controls and standards is to increase productivity. Directives or regulations that are seen as impediments to the job are quickly subverted. If standards are needed to control the job, we need to convince workers that these standards are beneficial. Even regulations emanating from the proper authority need to be "sold" to workers.

Do not promulgate a standard unless there are ways to ensure that it will be followed and unless management is willing to enforce the standard. Nothing is quite as useless as a standard that is not enforced.

Rule 12: Measurement Intervals Must Be Smaller Than Task Completion Intervals

Work breakdown structures usually contain tasks that will take several weeks or months. When the project is in trouble, we resort to "short-interval scheduling," that is, simply breaking down large tasks into smaller tasks of shorter duration. This works well for monitoring progress, but the costs of the task may already be overrun. Labor on tasks should be reported and compared to budget at least weekly in order to obtain early warning signals of cost problems. The status of project work, expected labor hours, and elapsed time to completion should be reported at biweekly or monthly intervals appropriate to the size of the task or project.

If there is anything that most managers hate on projects, it is surprises.

Rule 13: If It Is Not Documented, It Does Not Exist

We talked about documentation in relation to task completion, but this rule is really much broader. As long as information is retained in someone's head, it is vulnerable to loss. Only documented products have a real, dependable existence. The documentation may consist of text, graphics, forms, code, manuals, and so forth. It may be in either paper or electronic form. What counts is that it exists, and it must be communicated to others. The basic purpose of creating documentation is to communicate information.

Rule 14: Do Not Do Anything You Do Not Have to Do

Rule 14 would seem to be self-evident, but how many systems suffer from overdesign? How many useless communications do we produce? How many times do we send copies of documents to numerous people when only a few are interested? How often is my electronic mailbox flooded with messages that I am forced to read just in case there is something valuable? How often are new tools or standards imposed on major projects without having been tested on small projects first?

In one major multiyear development project, the project manager decided that, in order to perform the work, the team should first build a set of software development tools. Then they would use these tools to build the application. Needless to say, the project manager left the company after two years of a proposed 2.5-year effort and the application was not started because the software development tools were not completed.

A possible corollary to this rule is "Don't undertake work that you don't have the skills and experience to perform." Using this corollary may reduce your opportunities for "learning experiences," but it will surely save your company a lot of money.

Corollary A: You do have to build quality assurance into the project. Aside from the long list of things you do not have to do, there are some things that you *must* do to be successful. As each task product is completed, it must be transmitted to the next task. Each transition point represents a potential project failure point. Two things can help to reduce the risks of failure at transition points:

1. Define module interfaces as early in the project as feasible.
2. Validate completed products at each transition point through design review, walkthroughs, or acceptance testing.

Rule 15: You Can Not Get There Unless You Have a Map

The days of the Wild West are gone. The free-wheeling codeslinger no longer fits into the demands of buyers for quality products. A good part of this chapter is about project planning—creating a map to guide you from one point to another. In addition to the map, however, you need to know several very important things. First, you need to know where you are now: What is the problem? What are the skills and resources that you can bring to bear on the situation? What are the constraints within which you must work?

Second, you need to know where you want to go: What is the objective of the project? Is it realistic? How soon do you have to complete the project for the buyer to realize the benefits? What is the size of the proposed effort? Have you traveled this way before?

Third, you need to know the road conditions: What kind of problems can you anticipate during the project? What are the risks? What are the alternatives?

Rule 16: It Is Never Too Early to Plan

Even before you have a project in mind, it is valuable to plan what you will do if you receive a request for a project. It is also valuable to set guidelines for software development even before you set standards and obtain tools and methods. For example, the priorities for applications software development should observe the following sequence:

1. *Relevance.* Do not think about starting a project unless you plan a solution that is relevant to the needs of the buyer. Make sure that the ultimate user wants the product. Keep the buyer and users involved in

the project throughout the life cycle. Make sure that you and the buyer have a clear understanding of final acceptance procedures.

2. *Maintainability*. This is the key to software design. If you have established standards that emphasize the maintainability of the software, you can modify the design to obtain the required quality and functionality. If you cannot maintain the software readily, you haven't a prayer of satisfying the buyer in either the short run or the long run. This is especially true for projects of long duration because the buyer's needs will change during the course of the project. (See Corollary A to rule 6.)

3. *Quality, Validity, Accuracy*. All of these are important in software products. None of them is attainable without maintainability.

4. *Performance*. Increasingly today, performance issues can be addressed for less money through additional hardware capacity rather than through software tuning or database tuning. However, if you cannot obtain more hardware to solve the problem, maintainability again becomes a key issue.

Rule 17: Your Organization Is Not Perfect, Ever

Many software development groups approach projects with a "standard" organization for them, established according to preconceived rules. Some of these rules are healthy. For example, acceptance testing should never be done by the people who developed the system. In general, however, the organization of a project should follow its work breakdown structure. This means that the flexibility of assignment or reassignment of personnel must be anticipated by the structure as the needs of the project change.

Rule 18: The End Objective of a Software Development Project Is to Implement the Requested System

The essence of project management is to remain goal-oriented. Do not get so wrapped up in the technology, the standards, the control methods, the planning, and all the other elements of the project that you forget the real purpose. Also, do not forget that someone else is paying for the project, and they expect results.

CONCLUSION

The 18 rules of this chapter provide a foundation for good project management. These and other rules that are learned through experience can be valuable or dangerous. The greatest danger may be expressed as another rule: "Don't engrave the rules on stone tablets." One of the best ways to get into trouble is by following a single formula for success. As you continue to follow the formula, the rest of the world will keep on learning.

If you are willing to continually learn and collect new rules, you will become a "senior statesperson" in your organization and be looked up to as a fount of wisdom. Do not let it go to your head. One of the other rules is that when you are deeply involved in a project, you forget the rules.

DISCUSSION TOPICS

- To what extent are the 18 rules valid?
- What other rules have you learned in your work?
- Can you give examples that support or refute any of the rules?
- Which rules have you violated and what has it cost you or your company?

REFERENCES

1. Jones, C. "Sick Software." *Computerworld* (December 13, 1993).
2. Anthes, Gary H. "No More Creeps!" *Computerworld* (May 2, 1994): 107–110.

CHAPTER 7

Systems Development Productivity: The Impact of Team Size, CASE, and Object Technology

For years, IS managers have known intuitively that the performance of individuals in systems development groups changes under various circumstances. Psychological researchers have noticed that people often have lower performance levels in groups than their individual capabilities would indicate. This chapter examines the effect of team size on systems development productivity and overall job performance, and recommends techniques to mitigate the negative effects of large team size through such tools and techniques as CASE and object-oriented programming (OOP).

PROBLEMS ADDRESSED

Rapid advances in technology and a fast-paced business environment have made it necessary for companies to undertake increasingly complex technical projects. These projects have grown not only in complexity but in size and the number of people needed to accomplish the required tasks by a given time. Among the areas in which this phenomenon has been noticeable is the development of large computer systems.

Managers (especially those paying for these large-scale technical efforts) have become concerned with the rapid growth in the size of the development groups involved. Many managers have seen that productivity does not increase in direct proportion to the size of the project team.

Group size is often increased in a genuine effort to complete a project more quickly. The rationale for group expansion is usually expressed with such logic as

- The project must be completed before it becomes technologically or economically obsolete. This is increasingly important as systems are developed to provide strategic or competitive advantage.
- The elapsed-time goal cannot be reached if the task is performed in a linear fashion by one person.
- Dividing the work into successively smaller segments allows many people to work on the project concurrently, thus reducing the time to completion.

Through reiterative use of this logic, group size will grow at an exponential rate.

Structured design approaches, which emphasize the breakdown of projects into smaller components by defining the interfaces among components and dividing the work into compartments, do not significantly affect the growth in group size. However structured, design compartments may add to the quality of the product by increasing the clarity of the interface definition.

Assuming that the application is economically justified, it is desirable that the benefits to the organization begin to accrue as soon as possible. Speeding up the project, however, almost always increases the cost of implementation; this is a well-known cost/time trade-off problem. Sample cost/time curves are illustrated in Figure 7.1. Curve A shows the originally planned cost and time for a project. Curve B shows a reduction in project time to the point at which an increased implementation cost makes the application economically unfeasible. At the other extreme, curve C shows how the project may result in unacceptable cost increases by requiring that dedicated personnel be retained over a longer period of time and by delaying the benefits of the new system.

Figure 7.1 illustrates that cost and time cannot be treated constantly as trade-offs. In fact, the cost/time trade-off function is nonlinear (see Figure 7.2). As excessive resources (including personnel) are committed to a project, productivity and organizational efficiency decrease.[1]

NEW TOOLS AND TECHNIQUES

Although observations and some formulas and conclusions presented in this chapter were introduced during the 1970s, they have endured into the early 1990s. Since their introduction, however, new technology, including computer-aided software engineering (CASE) tools and object-oriented design and programming (OOP), has addressed these basic premises of the 1970s.

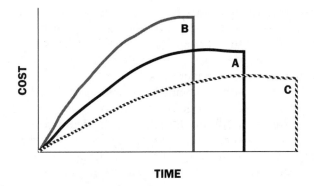

TIME

Curve A Originally planned cost and time for a project.
Curve B Reduction in project time, which increases the
         implementation cost and makes the application
         economically unfeasible.
Curve C Increased costs caused by the necessity of
         retaining personnel over a longer period of time
         and by delaying the benefits of the new system.

Figure 7.1.   Cost/Time Curves

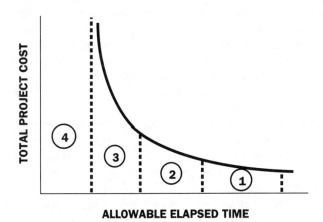

ALLOWABLE ELAPSED TIME

1 = Minimum cost
2 = Inefficient
3 = Crash project
4 = Impossible

Figure 7.2.   Cost/Time Trade-Off Function

CASE tools and their accompanying methodology promise significant improvements in productivity. But such improvements are primarily the result of improving the quality of the software developed. As discussed in a later section of this chapter, the efficiency of interactions improves as the quality of the content of communication increases.

OOP promises even greater improvements by extending the quality and efficiency of interactions through large-scale reuse of code. For example, many routines within an application that currently require individual development can be converted to reusable objects. Aside from application processing logic, these include field screening and editing, field encoding, help functions, error messages, sending and receiving screens and data, menu control, dialogue control, function key assignment, information security controls, and other commonly used routines.

In combination, CASE and OOP promise significant improvements in the quality of new applications and the reduction of costs incurred over the life of the applications. These improvements will be greater for large projects.

CALCULATING PRODUCTIVE TIME

People in formally organized groups cannot be productive 100 percent of the time for extended periods. According to general overhead estimates in the United States, in the average organization, at least 25 percent of employee time is required for vacations, sick leave, personal time off, training, coffee breaks, and administrative and organizational meetings. (These figures may be greater for some European countries.) In addition, 10 percent (a conservative estimate) of employee time is nonproductive because of late completion of activities on which the employee depends, poor work scheduling, nonwork-oriented conversation, and other forms of idle time.

Each new member of a group must communicate with the others about the task at hand. According to general experience, in groups of five or fewer members, such task-oriented communication can consume 10 percent to 30 percent of each member's time. As the number of persons in the group increases beyond five, members must spend more of their time communicating, and communication time may eventually reach an upper limit of approximately 90 percent.

The frequency of communication depends on the number of possible interactions for each member of the group. Assuming that each member may interact with every other member, the formula for computing the number of possible interactions (I) is

$$I = \frac{K(K-1)}{2}$$

where:

$$K = \text{number of people in the group}$$

The number of possible interactions increases rapidly with small increases in group size. (See Figure 7.3.)

Until group size reaches 10 members, it can be conservatively estimated that an individual spends a maximum of 10 percent of the workday communicating with others. When group size exceeds 10, however, each individual spends 0.01 percent more time communicating for each additional member of the group. This amounts to an average of less than two seconds a day per interaction—probably an impossibly conservative estimate but one that will illustrate the dimensions of the problem.

On the basis of this estimate and general experience, the nonproductive time expected for each group member is 25 percent for vacation and other authorized absences, 10 percent for idle time, and a base of 10 percent for time spent communicating—yielding a total of 45 percent. There-

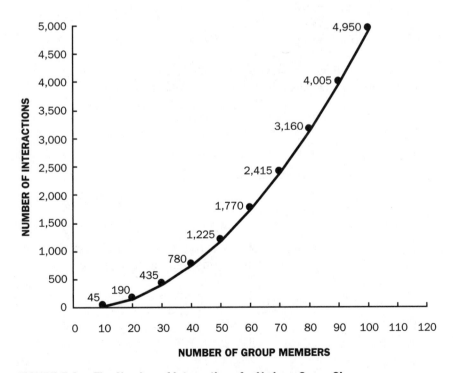

FIGURE 7.3.   The Number of Interactions for Various Group Sizes

fore, it may be estimated that 55 percent of each employee's time can be considered productive in a group of up to 10 employees.

Task-oriented communication would, at first, seem to be productive. It is, however, one of the greatest constraints on productivity. The ideal development team consists of one person, thereby eliminating the need for task-oriented communication. With every team member added, the communication load increases and the net productivity of each member decrease.

INTERNAL COMMUNICATION AND GROUP PRODUCTIVITY

The following formula can be used to compute the percentage of productive time:

$$P_t = K \left(T \left[0.55 - 0.0001 \left\{ \frac{K(K-1)}{2} \right\} \right] \right)$$

where:

P_t = productive time
K = number of people in the group
T = individual employee hours per work period

For a group of 90 people working a standard 40-hour week (a total of 3,600 available hours), the result of this formula is

$$P_t = 90 \left(40 \left[0.55 - 0.0001 \left\{ \frac{90 \times 89}{2} \right\} \right] \right)$$

P_t = 90 (40[0.55 − 0.0001 {4,005}])
P_t = 90 (40[0.1495])
P_t = 90 × 5.98
P_t = 538.2 hours

In addition, the percentage of productive time available from any specific group can be computed by use of this alternative formula:

$$P_p = 100 \left(0.55 - 0.0001 \left[\frac{K(K-1)}{2} \right] \right)$$

where:

P_p = percentage of productive time
K = number of people in the group

In the example of 90 people used above, the percentage of available time devoted to productive use would be 14.95 percent.

Because management control is limited in complex technical projects, large groups engaged in these projects are usually organized into small subgroups structured in several management layers. It may be argued that such a structure reduces the number of possible interactions among members; however, several factors inherent in this structure offset any potential reduction. For example, because more information must be communicated between groups, this new structure increases the time spent on some interactions. In addition, more managers are needed to lead the groups, and this, too, may increase the number of interactions. Finally, as organizations acquire size, depth, and formality, all communication tends to be in writing with multiple copies. Not only is communication time increased, but the resulting memos must be filed for future reference.

The premises underlying this formula are conservative; the formula assumes that all employees are honest, hardworking, competent, and present for work except for authorized absences. Factoring in dishonesty, laziness, and incompetence can result in negative production over most of the scale.

Figure 7.4 applies the formula for computing productive time to

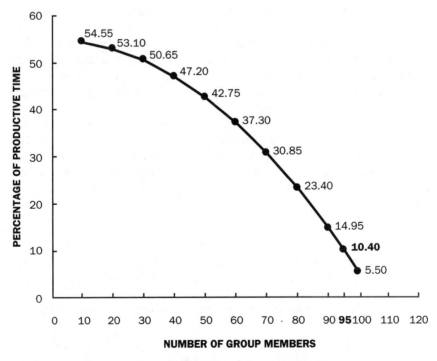

Figure 7.4.   The Percentage of Productive Time by Group Size

groups of 10 to 100 members. As indicated, a group of 95 people can be expected to spend only 10.4 percent of its time in productive effort, which is only 393.3 hours per week. Therefore, the larger group is actually less productive than a group of 20 people, which generates 424.8 productive hours a week. With groups of more than 100 members, the formula becomes less reliable, although some very large groups have been known to enter the range of negative productive output.

Several researchers have noted this decrease in efficiency as group size increases. Gerald M. Weinberg's rough rule for gauging the impact of increasing staff size on a project is that as the size of the staff is tripled, the productive capacity is doubled.[2] Louis Fried[3] and others in the early 1970s noted an inverse relationship between effectiveness (production) and group size in complex technical projects.

SENSITIVITY OF THE CURVES TO CHANGES

If systems development is still being conducted as it was during the early 1970s, no difference in the conclusions can be expected. However, the industry must seek solutions that go beyond the impact of fourth-generation languages and other similar tools that barely allow developers to keep pace with the increase in project size and user demands.

Clearly, the issue is what elements of the equation can be addressed most profitably to increase productivity. If a systems development manager can raise the productive time per employee from 55 percent to 60 percent (either through reduction of currently nonproductive time or through temporarily imposed overtime), the curves will shift evenly by that increment. But the shift is not sufficient to gain the significant advantages required for future development efforts.

On the other hand, the curves' sensitivity to changes in either the number of interactions or the duration of each interaction leads to a dramatic impact on available productive time. Figure 7.5 shows the effect of halving the number of interactions, which is achieved by changing the formula for the number of possible interactions to

$$I = \frac{K(0.5K)}{2}$$

The figure shows that in a group of 100, the number of interactions decreases approximately to that of a group of 70, as was calculated using the original equation illustrated in Figure 7.3.

This formula can be substituted into the equation for percentage of productive time:

$$P_p = 100\left(0.55 - 0.0001\left[\frac{K(0.5)}{2}\right]\right)$$

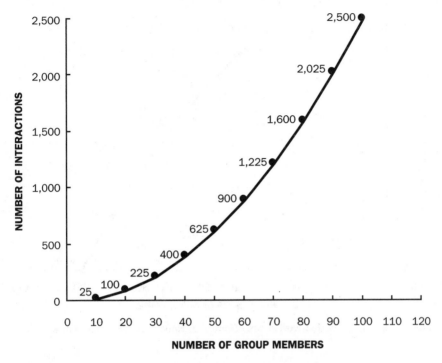

Figure 7.5.   The Effect of Halving The Number of Interactions

It results in the curve for percentage of productive time by group size shown in Figure 7.6. In a group of 100, the available productive time improves from the original 5.50 percent (shown in Figure 7.4) to 30.0 percent.

Similarly, if the time spent per interaction is halved from 0.01 percent of total standard work hours to 0.005 percent by changing the figure 0.0001 in the equation to 0.00005 and holding all other factors constant, the curve shown in Figure 7.7 is obtained. The gains in available productive time are dramatic and almost identical to those shown in Figure 7.6.

These data highlight the fact that to obtain significant improvement, both the number of interactions and the duration of the average interaction must be determined and adhered to.

SOCIAL DYNAMICS AND GROUP PRODUCTIVITY

The results cited in previous sections of this chapter are based on pragmatic experience of project management in the development of information systems. The social sciences have added pertinent observations made in experiments with people working in groups.

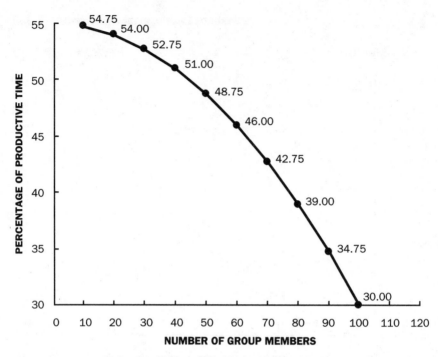

Figure 7.6. How Productive Time Is Affected by Halving the Number of Interactions

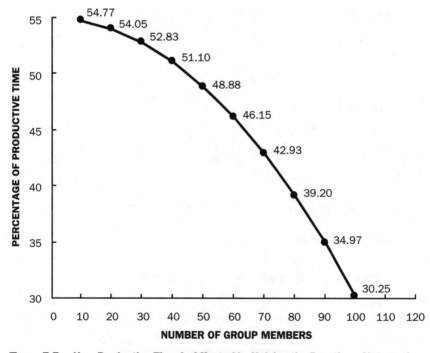

Figure 7.7. How Productive Time Is Affected by Halving the Duration of Interactions

The commons dilemma is a term coined by Robert Cass and Julian Edney for a conflict in which the needs of individuals threaten the long-term needs of the community.[4] In effect, the individual satisfies personal short-term needs or desires by taking an unequal share of a common resource; the impact of taking the extra amount is not visible to the group. Similarly, in cases calling for collective action (e.g., development projects), the individual may contribute less than the required effort when this lack of contribution is not visible.

A similar phenomenon, termed *social loafing* by B. Latane, K. Williams, and S. Harkins in 1979, was noted as early as 1927 in a study of worker performance.[5] This study measured individual and group performance by use of a strain gauge attached to a rope. Individuals pulling the rope averaged 138.6 pounds of pressure, but groups of three averaged 352 pounds—only 2.5 times the individual rate. Groups of eight averaged less than four times the individual rate.

Later experiments on this phenomenon were adapted. The environment was arranged so that the individual's perception of group size was varied even though the size of the group remained constant. Participants were blindfolded and led to believe that others were pulling with them, when in fact they always pulled alone. Output dropped substantially with increases in perceived group size: Participants pulled at 90 percent of their individual rate when they believed one other person was pulling and at only 85 percent of that rate when they believed two to six others were pulling.

Another study, by Latane, Williams, and Harkins, measured clapping and cheering by the amount of sound pressure generated. This study indicated that participants performing in pairs clapped and cheered at only 71 percent of their individual levels. Four-person groups performed at 51 percent and six-person groups at 40 percent of their individual levels. The sound of 12 hands clapping was not even three times as intense as the sound of 2.

Latane et al also measured the intensity of people shouting. Individuals in groups of two shouted at only 66 percent of individual capacity; those in groups of six, at 36 percent. The environment was then arranged so that people could not hear one another shout. Six groups of students wore headphones playing a constant 90-decibel recording of six people shouting. This was ostensibly to reduce auditory feedback and to signal each trial, but the recorded shouting actually led the students to believe that they were shouting in groups when they were actually shouting alone.

Overall, participants shouted with considerably more intensity in the second environment (perhaps as a by-product of the headphones), but the results were similar to those of the first experiment. Although the procedural changes prevented people from hearing and seeing one another, they apparently did not eliminate the feeling people had of being in a group.

In the pseudogroups, students who believed one other person was shouting shouted 82 percent as intensely as when alone; students who believed five others were shouting shouted 74 percent as intensely. The study compared the actual groups with the pseudogroups and concluded that only half of the performance loss for shouting could be attributed to lack of coordination between participants; the rest had to be ascribed to social loafing.

There are two explanations for social loafing. First, individuals in groups often compensate for perceived or anticipated inequities in the distribution of labor. Second, individuals may feel that any credit accrued to the group will be shared by all members regardless of individual contribution; therefore, they will receive credit even if they do not give their best effort.

MITIGATING THE EFFECTS OF GROUP SIZE

Managers in charge of IS projects should have a basic understanding of the concept of available productive time. This concept must be factored into project planning and estimating regardless of the size of the intended project team. To evaluate the effect of group size on the project, it is necessary to define the term *productivity*. The definition may vary according to the requirements of the organization; for general purposes, however, it can be stated as developing a system with the following characteristics:

- Maintainability—the system is well documented and modular in design.
- Effectiveness—the system meets actual corporate needs and is delivered within a reasonable time.
- Efficiency—the system uses minimal resources.

These characteristics are embedded in a system developed for the lowest possible cost consistent with quality and business objectives. Factoring in quality raises another problem, but it is assumed that the objective is to meet or improve on the estimated time and costs, which have anticipated quality factors.

Code checking by a second programmer is one of the most effective ways to improve system quality and overall programmer productivity. In conjunction with what is known about the effect of team size, this might lead to the conclusion that the most productive teams consist of two people. Each team member would be able to check on the other while minimizing time spent in communicating and reducing the opportunities for social loafing. Unfortunately, many projects cannot be developed by a team this small and still meet delivery time constraints. Improving productivity in larger teams requires methods for controlling the negative impact of internal communication management complexity, social loafing, and the commons dilemma.

EARLY TECHNIQUES FOR IMPROVING PRODUCTIVITY

During the early 1970s, the newest techniques were *structured design and programming* and the *chief programmer team*. The technique of structured design and programming has provided valuable lessons for systems development methodology and has aided in improving the quality of code. It has not, however, achieved the breakthroughs in productivity that were once envisioned.

In the chief programmer team concept, one exceptional individual is appointed chief programmer and is given a support group that performs more basic work, freeing him or her to perform more intricate tasks. The concept has not endured primarily because of the paucity of chief programmers needed for systems development. Some of the lessons learned from it are valuable for current development efforts, however.

One idea from the chief programmer team concept that can alleviate some of the problems of large teams is the assignment of specific roles to team members (e.g., programmer, reviewer, librarian). Assigning roles allows the project leader to define specific tasks and responsibilities. Moreover, the performance of individual team members can be identified and measured apart from the performance of the team. Together with a system of measuring and recognizing individual performance, this idea can reduce the effects of social loafing and the commons dilemma because the accomplishments of the individual (or lack thereof) are no longer subsumed under those of the group.

Identifying individual accomplishments seems to contradict many of the procedures in another much-discussed approach to project management—*egoless programming*. Thought by some to be a means to ensure team cooperation and increase productivity, egoless programming places all responsibility on the group to relieve the strain of criticism of each individual's work. This approach was expected to facilitate structured walkthroughs that subject designs and programs to group evaluation. Although some believe that people are never egoless, the value of the structured walkthrough can be retained by assignment of a mediator or coordinator to manage the walkthrough meeting and by use of the semantic trick of referring to the product rather than the developer (i.e., *the* program, not *your* program).[6]

Lessons learned from structured design methods can help with the issues of internal communication and management complexity. The following scenario is common:

- The project is too large for a small team to complete in a reasonable time.
- The apparent solution is to build a larger team.
- A larger team would be inefficient because of internal communication problems, social loafing, and the commons dilemma.
- The alternative solution is to divide the work among several small teams.
- Several small teams increase management complexity and coordination time.

What is needed is a method that allows small teams to work on modules of the system without increasing management complexity and coordination time. This method must also preserve the advantages gained in defining individual responsibilities and must be able to support the use of such quality control mechanisms as code review.

One of the basic concepts in structured design is *modularity*. Modularity does not mean simply writing programs in 4,000-byte blocks; a truly modular design can be segmented into a hierarchical array of functional modules that have clearly defined input, output, and boundaries. In addition, the use of reusable system design and program code can reduce the complexity and size of individual modules and the number of required staff members.

Some of these modules can be developed entirely by small teams. If the design has been properly documented and follows a structured approach to the definition of data and functions, the boundaries and interfaces of these modules are clearly defined. The modules can be developed independently and then integrated into the whole without further coordination.

During the 1970s, there were two major advancements that improved productivity: the rapidly expanding use of online programming and the introduction in many organizations of database management systems (DBMSs) and their associated data dictionaries. Online programming improved productivity by vastly accelerating the turnaround of program testing and eliminating the complex interactions between programmers and the computer operations department (i.e., by effectively reducing team size).

Developers realized the benefits of increased productivity through DBMSs and data dictionaries. First, DBMSs represented a major breakthrough in the reuse of code, freeing programmers from having to write the data access routines for each program. Second, data dictionaries standardized definitions (at least within a particular application), thereby improving the quality and efficiency of interactions among team members.

To some extent, fourth-generation languages (4GLs), introduced and established during the late 1970s and early 1980s, improved productivity.

The impact of 4GLs, however, has not been as great as that of other advancements because many organizations perceived that computer performance was adversely affected by 4GLs in online transaction-processing applications, and because 4GLs have not been as widely adopted as have DBMSs and data dictionaries. The promise of similar advancements through the use of computer-aided software engineering (CASE) and object-oriented programming (OOP) technologies was not realized until the 1990s.

THE IMPACT OF CASE AND OBJECT TECHNOLOGY

During the late 1980s, an increasing number of users and advocates of computer-aided software engineering (CASE) workstation tools appeared. As these tools improved, they permitted some of the first experiments with cooperative processing groups using workstations linked via local area networks.

The CASE concept was first extensively applied to software development for military systems, particularly embedded systems. These systems demanded large amounts of code adhering to stringent specifications and required strong version and configuration control. Although many major military contractors have developed their own tools and workstation environments since then, several new-generation software development environment tools are currently on the market. Such environments support the kinds of control and interaction among team members necessary for cooperative group work. Similar but somewhat less complex sets of tools are making increasing inroads into the CASE market for commercial applications development.

In 1989, Software Quality Research conducted a survey of commercial applications developers that use CASE tools.[7] The survey found that during the first six months after installation, users experienced as much as a 10 percent decrease in productivity, but during the second six months, productivity rose approximately 15 percent above the average rate before installation. During the last two months of the initial year, the productivity gains appeared to slow, indicating a plateau in productivity gain at about 15 percent. (Reported experiences with object technology as of this writing have shown similar changes in productivity.)

When used alone, structured design and programming techniques, data dictionaries or repositories, and other tools have not seemed to make much of a difference in productivity. When they are embedded in CASE tools, however, significant gains in productivity have been seen. It can be assumed that the reason for the gains is that an environment that permits the sharing of information relating to software development can significantly reduce the number of interactions between team members. CASE tools can accomplish this by increasing the precision of communication as compared with conversations or written notes that may require clarification. It is also probable that once team members learn to use the CASE tools, the amount of information transferred per interaction is greater and is not contaminated by the human element in the interactions. That is, the amount of social loafing is sharply reduced.

By observing the impact of CASE tools, we can make several reasonable conjectures. First, the formula must find some means of expressing the impact of increased efficiency in communication that is obtained through improved clarity and the increased density of information contained in the interactions. For this, the factor E (defined as a factor of 1 for each 50-percent improvement in interaction efficiency) is added to the formula. After the learning period in the use of CASE tools, it is realistic to expect that the number of interactions required will drop substantially, perhaps to 75 percent of the original value. Increased information density in each transaction, however, will probably double the time per interaction to 0.02 percent.

On the basis of these assumptions, the E factor can be substituted into the formula for percentage of production time:

$$P_p = 100\left(0.55 - 0.0002\left[\frac{K(0.75K)}{2(E)}\right]\right)$$

Assuming that CASE provides a 100-percent improvement in the efficiency of interactions, the formula appears as

$$P_p = 100\left(0.55 - 0.0002\left[\frac{K(0.75K)}{2(2)}\right]\right)$$

OOP; seems to promise even greater productivity gains in the future. These gains will primarily be achieved through the ability to reuse tested code and thereby reduce the amount of work to be done. It is another way of improving the information density for each interaction. As both the clarity and the density of the information in interactions are improved, it is conceivable that the number of interactions required will be further reduced.

Although currently we have insufficient experience with OOP to understand its complete value, we can assume that OOP will reduce the number of interactions even further—to 50 percent of the original amount. Furthermore, we can reasonably assume that efficiency will be improved to 150 percent of the original amount through reuse of code. However, in complex systems development projects using OOP, substantial time is devoted to identifying the appropriate objects for use; therefore, it is difficult to imagine any reduction in the time per interaction. Considering these factors, the formula for anticipating the effect of CASE and OOP is

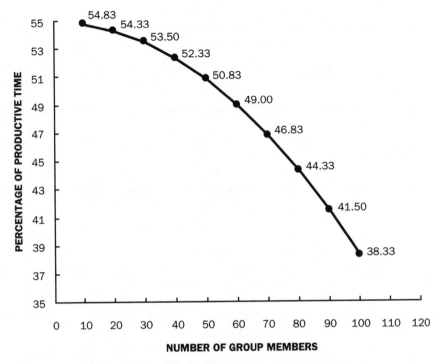

Figure 7.8. How Productive Time Is Affected by CASE and OOP

$$P_p = 100\left(0.55 - 0.0002\left[\frac{K(0.75K)}{2(3)}\right]\right)$$

The result of applying this formula to the various workgroup sizes is shown in Figure 7.8, which may be compared with Figure 7.4. With CASE tools alone or combined with OOP techniques, a significant gain in productive time can be achieved.

CONCLUSION

As information technology continues to provide increasing capacity and capability, applications have advanced to use that capacity and capability (a kind of Parkinson's Law, which states that work expands to fit the available time). This means that application size and the demands for improved productivity in systems development continue to increase. Research regarding productivity has not provided the necessary precise measurements to allow the derivation of either an accurate theory or a precise formulation.

This chapter has presented a mathematical approach that describes, to the extent possible, empirical observation. It must therefore be viewed simply as one step toward the long-term goal of improving the manner in which software development projects are designed and managed.

Empirical evidence suggests that the use of smaller teams results in greater percentages of team members' time being spent productively. Several techniques may be used to increase productive use of time, including

- Proper scheduling and task loading based on an understanding of productive time
- Clear assignment of task and product responsibility, accompanied by measurement and recognition of individual performance
- A modular design that supports clear assignment of product responsibility

In addition, such tools and techniques as CASE products and object technology that improve the clarity of communication and increase the density of information transmitted during interactions, and that reduce the number of interactions required in complex projects, can also help systems development managers achieve significant benefits.

Experiments seem to substantiate the theory that CASE tools can benefit software development significantly. A 1990 survey of systems integrators and software companies that use CASE tools indicates that the benefits of these tools are not primarily in software development productivity but rather in the quality of the software being developed.[8] By improving the quality of the software, the costs incurred over the life of the software are reduced and future modifications are easier to make. Quality is achieved through a combination of the appropriate methodology and CASE tools, which improves the efficiency of interactions among team members, including those between users and software developers.

Systems development groups must examine their needs and consider adopting appropriate CASE tools. Because these tools require a substantial investment, the systems development manager should consider several points. First, CASE tools are ineffective without an accompanying structured or object-oriented methodology for designing specifications and applications. This methodology requires that current development methods and standards be evaluated first to determine whether they need to be changed to take advantage of the benefits of CASE tools.

Second, the introduction of CASE tools and methodologies may cause a significant cultural change in the organization. As with any change, careful planning is needed to ensure the acceptance of the new technology and specific provisions must be made for training and for a pilot implementation.

Finally, in evaluating whether CASE tools will meet the specific needs of the development environment, each tool should be examined on the basis of vendor support and the tool's architecture. Tools that do not appear to support an architecture to accommodate future use of OOP should either be avoided or be viewed as short-range investments.

DISCUSSION TOPICS

- What development strategies have you used that have been successful?
- Is the analysis presented in this chapter consistent with your experience?
- What other techniques could be used to improve team productivity?
- Do you disagree with any of the premises on which this chapter is based? Why?

REFERENCES

1. Pietra Santa, A.M. "Resource Analysis of Computer Program Development." In Weinwarm, G.F. (ed.). *On the Management of Computer Programming*, Los Angeles, CA: Litton Educational Publishing, 1970.
2. Weinberg, G.M. *The Psychology of Computer Programming*. New York: Van Nostrand Reinhold, 1971.
3. Fried, L. "Don't Smother Your Project in People." *Management Advisor* (March-April 1972): 46–49.
4. Cass, R. and Edney, J. "The Commons Dilemma: A Simulation Testing the Effects of Resource Visibility and Territorial Division." *Human Ecology*, June 1978.
5. Latane, B., Williams, K., and Harkins, S. "Social Loafing." *Psychology Today* (October 1979).
6. Shoor, R. "Structured Walkthroughs: A Practical Approach in a Real Life Environment." *Computerworld* (January 21, 1980).
7. Sloat, J. "Software Productivity: The Next CASE." *Information Week* (January 8, 1990).
8. Sloat, J. *ibid.*

CHAPTER 8

The Impact of Object Technology: Managing Software Logistics

Managing purchased and internally developed software through repositories, directories, inventories, and so forth, is becoming a major effort. This chapter discusses how the problem will be exacerbated by the extensive adoption of object-oriented technology, and presents an approach to maintaining management control.

THE SOFTWARE LOGISTICS PROBLEM

The old dictionary definition of *logistics* is "that branch of military science having to do with moving, supplying, and quartering troops." In recent years, the term has been more popularly used by commercial enterprises as "managing the acquisition, inventory, and distribution of materials or services." How does this relate to software management?

The efficiency with which we make and use software is rapidly becoming a function of how well we reuse software. Reuse of software started years ago with the swapping of program routines. It then graduated to commercial sales of database management systems, telecommunications monitors, and application packages that could be reused entirely or customized to fit. Now we have spreadsheets and personal computer database management systems that can be customized by users into personal applications.

Software proliferation has led many companies to realize that if they are to minimize software development costs and ensure that ability of users to effectively communicate, they need to "manage the acquisition, inventory, and distribution" of software.

We face three basic issues in software logistics management, described in the following paragraphs.

1.   In addition to commercially available packages, companies frequently find that applications developed by one division or business unit may be reused by another, with considerable potential savings to the company as a whole. However, this transfer of applications is impeded by negotiations over transfer pricing, lack of adequate documentation for the application, lack of interest on the part of the developers, the NIH (Not Invented Here) syndrome, or the fear that attempting to generalize the application package for reuse will severely delay development and implementation.

Even if we recognize the validity of the last point, there are many responses to the other impediments. They include developing minimal corporate standards for transferable software, setting policy for transfer pricing, publicizing the availability of the software, and publicizing the benefits and financial incentives for software reuse.

2.   If communications are to be efficient and effective, people must be able to transfer their work products to others who share their work tasks or interests. A number of companies are now attempting to standardize their electronic mail to overcome the inefficiencies that developed through uncontrolled adoption of separate systems in divisions. However, there are even deeper problems. For example, employees who use different spreadsheet programs (or even different versions of the same program) cannot distribute their work to others. Furthermore, isolated purchases of software usually cost more than site licenses or "bulk" purchases. Information systems organizations that have attempted to impose standards on users have often met embarrassing failure.

But it is not necessary to impose standards (beyond those that ensure connectivity to networks) to improve the situation. First, IS managers must identify communities of users who have a need to share information and convince them that they can do so effectively only if the tools they use are compatible. Second, IS managers must demonstrate the price advantages of buying through a common pool purchase, and having done this, they must organize the purchasing activity, manage software distribution and version control (most easily done over the network), and bill the users for the service and software. This sounds very much like logistics.

3.   During the next several years, we will probably experience an explosion in the development and use of software objects. If we are to believe the fans of object-oriented software development, we will have objects for end user use, objects for programmer/analyst use, objects for departmental use, objects for business process use, standard objects for use in business units, standard objects for use throughout a corporation, permanent

objects, temporary objects, and object directories and repositories (which are, themselves, objects).

Someone will have to manage the acquisition, approval, storage, retrieval assistance, security, and distribution of objects. This is another job for software logistics management.

EXACERBATING THE LOGISTICS PROBLEM WITH OOP

The Need for Reusable Software

Software development has always been expensive. The dream of those who pay the bill has always been to obtain the results for lower cost and in less time. As previously mentioned, the search for tools to accomplish this miracle has ranged over database management systems, query systems, screen development tools, fourth-generation languages, graphic programming aids, code generators, and so forth. But the ultimate dream has always been to find ways to avoid programming altogether, and the best way to *not* program is to reuse existing code.

All of the tools previously mentioned are effective because they reuse code in some sense. For example, database management systems permit programmers to avoid developing their own access routines, which they were forced to do in the 1960s.

The developers of object-oriented programming (OOP) languages and tools promise to take the reuse of code to new levels. There has been considerable public discussion of both the benefits and the potential problems associated with OOP. For each argument there have been various responses.

One concern, for example, is that objects will require continuous maintenance and enhancement to keep up with the changing needs of the business. The response to this has been that software has always required maintenance. Another concern is that the analysis task required to identify and define appropriate objects is formidable. Advocates of OOP respond that the best software development effort results from spending more time in the definition and specification phases, and besides, companies will be able to reuse objects for long-term savings.

In fact, proponents of OOP point out that the need to define classes and subclasses of objects, the objects themselves, and the attributes, messages (function-like calls), methods (procedures), and interrelationships of objects forces the development of a better model of the system. Since many objects developed in OOP code will not be reused, isn't it enough that OOP code is usually more lucid and well organized than traditional coding methods? The process that forces analysts to define the object hierarchies makes them more familiar with the business in which the application will be used.

When these problems and objections are analyzed, many of them can be discounted; however, some remain. Viewed in isolation, OOP is nothing more than an attractive way to facilitate structured, "self-documenting," highly maintainable, and reusable code. But in the context of enterprise-wide application building, OOP presents new challenges. And for these, the solutions will require additional tools and management methods.

A Scenario of OOP Use

As the use of OOP grows, we can expect attempts to expand this use from single applications to broad application suites and from sharing of objects among a limited group of application developers to sharing by application developers (and users) throughout the company. In order to accomplish this expansion OOP will need to be used within a development framework composed of CASE tools implemented in a distributed, cooperative processing environment.

Here we construct a likely scenario of the way in which organizations will want to use OOP in the future:

- Objects will be used by decentralized application development groups to develop applications that are logically related to each other and for which common definitions (standards) for use are imposed by various levels of the organization.
- Objects will be used by end users to develop limited extensions of basic applications or to develop their own local applications in much the same way that spreadsheets and query systems are used. It is possible that the only way that users will be permitted to access corporate databases in this environment is through objects that encapsulate permitted user views of information.
- OOP will become integrated with CASE platforms not only through the inclusion of object-capable languages but through repositories of objects that contain both the objects themselves and the definitions of the objects and their permitted use. CASE tools will need improvement in their ability to manage and control versions and releases of objects as well as programs.
- Cooperative workgroup development of applications will take place among geographically separated members of a development team. This will enable telecommuters (employees working at home) and professionals working on temporary teams and contributing specialized knowledge to smoothly integrate their activities. Specialized knowledge of objects and their content will thus be more easily shared among potential object users.

This scenario envisions optimum use of and benefit from OOP through extensive reuse of proven code within a framework that allows authorized access to objects. However, under the current state of OOP, such a scenario will be difficult to implement. Effective use of OOP requires that we address two major concerns: management of the object inventory and preservation of information security in an object-oriented development environment.

Managing the Object Inventory

The first concern about OOP is object inventory management. Objects in the inventory will reside in some form of repository that presumably utilizes an *object-oriented database management system* (OODBMS). The definition of objects requires that they be identified by classes and subclasses (note that object class definitions are themselves objects). This identification provides a means of inventory management. For example, retrieving an object within a class called "Accounts Payable," will help to narrow the domain being searched for the object. A further narrowing can be done by finding a subclass called "Vendor's Invoice," and so forth. Polymorphism allows the same object name to be used in different contexts, so the object "unit price" can be used within of the "Vendor's Invoice" subclass and the "Purchase Order" subclass. (Some relational database management systems also allow polymorphism.)

Several problems develop as a result of this organizational method.

In order to take advantage of the reusability of objects, the user must be able to find the object with as little effort as possible. Within the classification scheme for a relatively straightforward application, this does not appear to present a substantial problem. However, most companies undertake the development of applications on an incremental basis. That is, they do not attempt to develop all applications at once. Furthermore, the vision of analyzing and describing the data and process flows of the entire enterprise (enterprise data modeling) has repeatedly failed. By the time all this analysis is completed, users have lost patience with information systems and a new IS director will have the opportunity to use the incremental approach. So it is feasible to limit objects to an application domain; on the other hand, limiting the objects to the narrow domain of a single application may substantially reduce the opportunities for reuse. This means that developers will have to predict, to the extent possible, the potential uses of an object to ensure its maximum utility.

It is possible to establish a class of objects that may be called "cross-application" objects. They would be the same without regard to the context within which they were to be used. For example, the treatment of data related to a specific account in the corporate chart of accounts may always be the same. On the other hand, the word *account* appears in many contexts and uses throughout a business. Another approach is to assign some objects an *attribute of* "cross-application" usability.

As applications developed with OOP proliferate, the typical data dictionary or repository will not be able to serve the needs of users for retrieving objects. Analysts and programmers who are required to move from one application to another to perform their work will find the proliferation of objects overwhelming. IS functions will need to develop taxonomies of names and definitions to permit effective retrieval.

Developing and maintaining a taxonomy is itself a massive effort. In the 1980s, a large nuclear engineering firm realized that eventually the nuclear power plants it designed would have to be decommissioned and dismantled. The dismantling would take place about 50 years after a plant was built. Whoever was faced with the task would have to know everything about the plant and its 50 years of maintenance in order to avoid contamination of the environment or injury to personnel on the job.

The company discovered that a variety of names were used for identical parts, materials, and processes (all objects) in the average plant. Furthermore, since the company designed plants for power companies throughout the world, these names were in multiple languages. Clearly, if you could not name an object, you could not find the engineering drawings or documents that described it. And if you could imagine and search for the names that appeared to be most likely, you could miss information that was stored under a name you did not think of—with potentially dangerous results.

The company decided that it had to adopt and use standard terminology for all components of the plant and all information relating to those components. A taxonomy project was started, and within two years, a massive volume was assembled; however, several problems surfaced:

- It was impossible to know when the taxonomy would be complete.
- New terms had to be created to avoid duplication.
- The taxonomy manual was so big that engineers and other employees refused to use it.

We need to learn from such examples. Here are some obvious guidelines:

- A comprehensive enterprise model at a detailed data level will never be completed because the organization changes while the model is being created.
- Design a high-level *process* and *information* model of the firm to indicate potential or existing interrelationships of data. Then choose limited domains (or business processes) for the creation of objects within an application.

- Establish object naming conventions and an object inventory system *before* you develop the first object-oriented application. In future applications development projects, use the high-level process model to identify potential data and objects that may be reusable.

The key facts to remember are that object definition (and applications development) are incremental and that objects will not be reused if they cannot be found easily.

So far, we have only discussed one dimension of the problem. Now we will examine another dimension. In a previous paragraph, we identified analysts and programmers as those who might have a problem, but in a world of increasingly distributed processing and decentralized use of computing, we must consider the following :

- Analysts and programmers will not be under centralized control in all instances.
- Other personnel, such as engineers, clerical staff, knowledge workers, and so forth, will use objects to create their own programs.

As we have learned through the proliferation of personal computers in business, the ability of end users to develop their own programs (and applications) is one of the greatest benefits that can be obtained from OOP—it cannot be ignored. Nor can the demands of an increasingly computer-literate, personal-computer-using clientele be refused. This means that the methods for retrieving objects must be available to all for a relatively small amount of effort. If not, objects will not be reused.

Once we consider end users as a component of the OOP management problem, we are led to another concern. Objects must not only cross application domains, they must exist at various levels of the corporation. For example, an object may be defined as applicable throughout the corporation in a given context (a "standard" object). Such an object may be called a "corporate object" either through being in a class of corporate objects or through having a standard attribute as a corporate object. Another object may be applicable only within a specific strategic business unit (SBU) and be called, for example, an "engine manufacturing company" object. At the next level, an object may be called a "casting division" object, and so on, down to the desktop or the computer-controlled machine tool.

Two tools may come to the (partial) rescue:

1. Text search and retrieval systems may allow users to search for objects within various contexts. But this could result in the retrieval of many possible objects from a repository for the user to evaluate before a selection is possible.

2. An approach is needed that will help the user obtain a limited number of possible objects to solve a problem and yet not force the organization to develop a taxonomy or limit the use of terms. Self-indexing of files for nonhierarchical search may help, but this may mean using the object-oriented DBMS-based repository in a manner not compatible with its inherent structure.

Regardless of the method used, there will be a clear need to establish and maintain conformance to documentation standards for objects, so that searches for objects will return meaningful results.

One possibility is to use an expert system in conjunction with a text search and retrieval system. Expert systems are very good at classification and are capable of supporting natural language interfaces. Imagine a system in which the user described the nature of the object needed and the system could find the most appropriate object. Imagine the next step, in which the user described the application at a high level and the system found and assembled all appropriate objects that fit the system context.

When objects are used throughout a large corporation, we must assume that they reside in repositories on a variety of machines in many different geographic locations. Each of these repositories need to be maintained in synchronization with the "master" repository of approved objects for the corporation, SBUs, divisions, and so forth. This implies the need to solve some other problems.

First, if objects are automatically replaced with new versions, there must be a mechanism for scheduling the recompilation or relinking of programs that used the affected objects. If objects are used in an interpretive mode (rather than being compiled into machine code), replacements will automatically affect their use in existing procedures, perhaps to the detriment of the application. Some of the methods now used to maintain distributed database concurrency and to control the distribution of personal computer programs throughout a network may be adapted to solve a part of this problem. Another approach may adapt the messaging capabilities of objects to send notification of a potential change to any subobject within the hierarchy of the object being replaced.

Second, "identical" objects may need to be developed in different languages to meet the needs of users of different computers. Even if the objects are developed in the same language, we may be faced either with using a restricted subset of the language compatible with all its potential environments, or with using a language that allows compiler flags to be placed on code and alternative versions of the code to be embedded in the object. None of these alternatives is attractive, but the first may require other classes of objects to differentiate between identical objects used on different machines (polymorphism can help here). It will certainly add some complexity to the testing process for new or replacement objects.

Third, someone in the company will be faced with the job of deciding which objects should be distributed to which of the distributed repositories. Standard corporate objects may have wide distribution, while others may have more circumscribed distribution. Object, and object class, management promises to be a major administrative role.

With sufficient market demand and increasing use of OOP, these and other problems will have to be addressed by OOP vendors and by MIS management.

Object Security

Just as data and software are the "corporate jewels" of the information infrastructure today, objects will be added to the jewel box tomorrow. When users, analysts, and programmers all have the ability to use objects in developing programs or applications, they will all need access to the jewel box. Such indiscriminate access represents a real danger to the security of objects.

Information security has been defined as consisting of three primary properties: availability, confidentiality, and integrity. As applied to the object inventory, these may be defined as

- Making objects *available* to those who need to use them when they need to use them
- Ensuring the *integrity* of objects by preventing unauthorized change
- Ensuring the *confidentiality* of objects by preventing unauthorized access

Current repositories and directories generally assume that all persons authorized to access the directory are authorized to access any item in the directory. This assumption will not do for an object inventory.

An object inventory will require an extended set of security controls to make its use safe for the firm. Such controls, required to preserve integrity, will need to be implemented at the object attribute level. In *a payroll file*, for example, the individual *salary rate* (an attribute) may be restricted to certain users. This restriction requires that this attribute have an attached attribute (sometimes called a *facet*) that specifies which programs are allowed to read the attribute. Alternatively, the salary rate attribute could have a facet that is a function that returns a blank to nonauthorized callers. In essence, each object defined in the inventory might need to be individually controlled as well as controlled within a set or class of objects.

It is clearly expected that each object in the inventory can be separately "locked" to prevent change. Once an object is accepted into inventory, the lock is enabled. A system that truly intended to protect the integrity of the objects would not permit *any* change to a locked object. If an object needed to be changed, it would have to be deleted and replaced by an approved, tested replacement, and a limited group of authorized inventory managers would be the only ones able to delete an object. Finally, a safeguard system would automatically file all deleted objects in a locked, backup repository file so that they could be retrieved in the event of incorrect removal.

It should be noted that locking logic itself is a nontrivial problem. In current database management systems, the problem of the "deadly embrace" has been solved. (This problem arises when two parties are concurrently attempting to update a record by different logical paths.) When the locking mechanism must deal with atomic objects rather than transactions or records, the solution may be more difficult.

In current security practice, the levels of security assigned to information are designated by the application owner. Each application owner has the duty to specify who may access application information, under what conditions. When objects are in common use, we will have to find new ways of designating ownership. Who will own an object that is used across many applications? Who will own an object that is a "corporate object?"

Once the ownership decision is made, how will we assign access permission? Some access permissions may be assigned by sets or classes of workers. (Please remember that in the new "alliance" mode of business operations, it is not only employees who work with a company's systems but suppliers and even customers.) Permissions may be granted by levels in the management hierarchy, by sets of people in specific functional tasks, by organizational unit, and by individual. Permissions will have to include (as they do today) the authorization to perform certain functions with an object. Functions for which authorization may need to be defined include read only, delete, add, copy, use, and lock.

Integrity may also be addressed by the attaching of rule-based logic to classes, subclasses, and objects to describe the conditions under which they may be used. This marriage of artificial intelligence techniques with object database structure may be necessary to prevent misuse of objects.

Availability of objects is partially dependent on systems availability, network availability, and so forth. However, availability may also include the concern that the object is appropriately distributed throughout the firm's processing resources so that it can be conveniently accessed by authorized personnel regardless of time or geographic location. As previously stated, in large corporations this means that objects may be distributed in repositories on a variety of machines in various geographic locations, with the potential for erroneous use multiplied.

Confidentiality may require that two levels of information access be designated for objects. One level of access may be to permit a user to determine if a desired object or reasonable facsimile exists in the inventory. This level may permit authorized personnel only to learn of the existence of objects and receive a brief description. A second level of access control may be needed to permit users to actually read the object's contents.

Confidentiality can be breached in another way. The aggregation of intelligence through repeated access to selected information databases is a threat to current systems. When the atomic level of applications is "downsized" to objects, a significant change occurs. The aggregation of objects into new relationships may permit combinations of information that would not usually be available to users, thus enabling unauthorized users to assemble intelligence to which they are not entitled. Moreover, the property of inheritance, in which an object subclass inherits the methods and structure of the superclass to which it is related, may present special concerns. We may need a classification mechanism that defines permitted relationships among objects and establishes authorization for object *relationships*, perhaps as a facet or attribute, as previously described. Alternatively, we can maintain independence between data and code that permits access controls to be placed on the data at the *user view* or *field* level within a database.

OODBMS vendors are cognizant of these problems and are attempting to develop systems that reproduce the controls available in hierarchical or relational database management systems.

Recommended Action

Many of the potential problems OOP faces are similar to those of system development tools of the past. These older problems have been addressed as a result of market pressure on vendors to supply acceptable solutions.

Object-oriented techniques may be analogous to any other important advance. For example, an automobile may be safe at 70 miles per hour but unsafe at 110 miles per hour. The potential benefits of OOP appear to be substantial, but until OOP technology enables users to manage and protect their information assets, it should be used under strictly controlled circumstances.

The following guidelines are recommended:

- Under current conditions, the lack of inventory management of objects poses a potential threat to effective widespread reusability. It is advisable to examine the inventory management capabilities of proposed OOP development systems and limit use of the tools to a scope within which available management methods will work.
- Without solving the problems related to object security, it may not be possible to ensure the protection of the company's information assets under conditions of widespread use. As with the inventory management problems, only market pressure on vendors will force them to address these problems.

- Corporations are real-world entities that expand, contract, and change according to changing business needs and strategies. A comprehensive model at a detailed data level will never be completed, since the organization changes while the model is being created. Do not attempt to build an enterprise data model. Instead, design a high-level *process* and *information* model of the firm to indicate potential or existing interrelationships of data. Then choose limited domains (or business processes) for the creation of objects within an application.
- Establish object naming conventions and an object inventory system *before* you develop the first object-oriented application. In future applications development projects, use the high-level process model to identify potential data and objects that may be reusable.
- Urge vendors to develop appropriate inventory management and security control tools. Keep tracking the market for the appearance of such tools, and adopt them as soon as they are available and proven.

CONCLUSION

The responses demanded by the three issues of software logistics management described in the beginning of this chapter have much in common. The functions required include assisting in standards setting, inventory management, version control, procurement negotiation, user coordination, service billing, "customer" service assistance, ensuring availability and integrity of controlled software, and so forth. This commonality of function implies that the same sets of skills will be needed to perform the software logistics management functions and that these functions may be performed through similar procedures under similar management structures.

Such commonality is a powerful argument for creation of a specialized organization within information systems—the software logistics management department—that will gather the functions already being performed by some IS divisions into a single organizational unit capable of selecting, implementing, and operating the tools and procedures required.

DISCUSSION TOPICS

- What specific tasks should be performed by a software logistics management department?
- Have the tools needed for object management been developed? Are they effective?
- Has the scenario of object use described in this chapter come into use?
- Do traditional information systems developers resist adopting object technology? Why?

CHAPTER 9

Outsourcing MIS Functions

*Outsourcing is the contracting of various activities or combina-
tions of activities to a business entity that specializes in managing
and operating these activities. In the outsourcing of management
information systems (MIS), the activities that may be outsourced
include applications development, applications maintenance and
enhancement, computer operations, data communications network operations, and voice communications network management. Computer operations that are closely integrated with
business processes, such as the use of personal computers, workstations, or client-server systems, are rarely outsourced; however,
selection, procurement, training, support, and maintenance of
these systems may be outsourced. This chapter discusses how to
protect your company in an outsourcing arrangement.*

THE OUTSOURCING TREND

In 1989, Eastman Kodak negotiated an agreement to outsource its data
center operations to IBM and its personal computer systems and services
to Businessland, Inc. While outsourcing, in the form of timesharing, facilities management, and contract systems development (as examples), had
been a mode of business operation since the 1960s, the Kodak deal seemed
to reawaken the market. Since 1989, a month rarely passes which some
major new outsourcing deal is not announced.

At the time of this writing, numerous examples can be found to illustrate the trend toward information systems outsourcing. For instance, in
September 1992, CSC Logic signed a contract for $39.7 million to provide
data processing and asset management to Resolution Trust, the company

set up to manage the assets of over 300 failed savings and loan banks. In June 1992, Clark Material signed a five-year agreement with IBM's Integrated Systems and Services Company (ISSC) division. In other deals, General Electric contracted EDS to manage its desktop computing consisting of over 90,000 PCs and workstations; General Dynamics signed a $3 billion agreement with Computer Sciences Corporation (CSC) for CSC to manage its information systems operations, including over 17,000 PCs and workstations at 28 sites; the FAA hired EDS for a potential $508 million over five years to manage its Computer Resources Nucleus; and United Technologies outsourced its new data center to ISSC (claiming a savings of over $100 million). Since 1989, over 35 banks with assets over $1 billion have signed major outsourcing agreements.

A 1993 analysis of outsourcing indicates that more than 25 percent of the Fortune 1000 companies outsource one or more information systems (IS) functions. However, only 22.7 percent indicate that they plan further outsourcing within the next year, and only 4 percent of these companies say they are committed to eventually outsourcing all IS functions. In fact, Kodak, which originally outsourced all its IS functions, announced in 1993 that it will gradually bring these functions back inside the company under a strategy of replacing mainframe systems with client-server systems. A survey by *Information Week* forecasted a slowdown in the outsourcing trend, as only 20 percent of the corporate MIS heads indicated any new outsourcing expectations for their data centers in 1993.[1] However, in the broader definition of outsourcing used above, it is clear that selective outsourcing of IS work will continue to be an important business strategy.

The companies that enter outsourcing agreements hope to make big gains as a result. These anticipated gains come from several sources. Some companies hope to enjoy significant savings relative to the costs of their in-house information systems; some have been able to raise cash by selling their computing equipment to an outsourcing contractor and leasing it back as a part of the agreement; some hope to gain by eliminating the distractions of IS management and allowing executives to focus on the core business of the company.

PROBLEMS FROM OUTSOURCING

With the potential to win big comes the potential to lose big. For example, two Pittsburgh banks, Integra Financial and Equimark, merged in late 1992, and each had an outsourcing agreement. When the newly merged company decided to drop one of its contracts, the losing vendor required a payment of $4.5 million for contract termination.

Some other cases illustrate the potential for major problems. EDS filed suit against Florida's Department of Health and Rehabilitative Services (HRS) in August 1992 for $46 million, claiming the money was owed for development of a new system. HRS said it was withholding payment because of system defects.

In August 1992, the project to build the Confirm reservation system collapsed, resulting in lawsuits and countersuits between Hilton Hotels, Marriott, and Budget Rent-A-Car and the outsourcing contractor, a subsidiary of AMR. Lawsuits running into the hundreds of millions of dollars were filed in an attempt to salvage something of the $125 million invested in the failed project. The failure was attributed to lack of timely disclosure of some poor technical decisions made by the development team.

Freeport-McMoRan in May 1993 paid a large penalty for canceling its 10-year, $200 million outsourcing agreement signed with EDS in 1988. In 1993 the Environmental Protection Agency accused Computer Sciences Corp. (CSC) of fraudulently billing for $13 million (about 20 percent of the contract value), and refused to renew its contract with EDS.

A General Accounting Office report issued early in 1992 charged that of the 240 banks it surveyed, between 20 percent and 30 percent had outsourcing contracts that contained some sort of "hanky-panky." The most common problem was that outsourcing contractors were paying the banks book value for their computers rather than the usually lower market value. This served to help troubled banks raise cash, but Stephen White, an electronic data processing review examiner for the Federal Deposit Insurance Corporation, asserted that the banks paid the difference to the vendors somewhere in the outsourcing agreements.

With all the early 1990s hype about outsourcing, CEOs may be included to rush into deals when they doubt the abilities of their CIOs, when they feel that their MIS people do not understand the big picture, or when they are enchanted by the glamour or by the wooing of a vendor. In one such sweetheart deal, the chairman/CEO of a major financial institution met the chairman of an outsourcing firm through political connections. After a short period of wooing, the financial firm's chairman invited the outsourcing contractor to act as an advisor to the board of directors and ordered his staff to enter an outsourcing arrangement with his friend. Despite the reluctance of the staff, a multimillion dollar agreement was soon signed. Fortunately, the staff had the foresight to include escape clauses in the contract. After the first year of dismal performance, the contract was modified to relegate the contractor to a much restricted role.

Many professionals in information systems see outsourcing as a poor management decision. They see savings evaporating through extra charges unforeseen in the contract, cash being raised as a short-term measure that will eventually imperil the company, and "focusing on the core business" as an abdication of management responsibility. With information systems an essential operating aspect of most companies today, IS professionals have voiced the opinion that information systems are an integral part of the core business, that outsourcing will impair their company's ability to respond to strategic business needs, and that the company will surrender control of functions critical to its success.

On the other hand, a number of CIOs have been instrumental in creating outsourcing agreements. Their reasons for outsourcing include

- The difficulty of managing complex functions such as communications
- Concern about buying costly technology that could rapidly become obsolete
- The difficulty of obtaining and retaining high-caliber information technology IT specialists
- Temporary outsourcing of old systems to permit concentration on migration to new-generation systems
- Internal staff without the capacity or skills to undertake a project

AVOIDING THE PITFALLS

Whatever the motivations for outsourcing, experience indicates that several areas of risk should be considered during the evaluation and contracting of outsourcing. Understanding these risks will help potential users of outsourcing improve their requests for proposal and their evaluation and contracting processes.

Escalating Costs

The most frequently noted risk of outsourcing is that of escalating costs. Many companies have complained that although the first year or two of the contract resulted in lower costs (one of the primary incentives for outsourcing), after that period the costs rapidly escalated. There are several possible reasons for this phenomenon. Contractors usually protect their profits with contract clauses that permit additional charges for increased transaction volumes beyond a baseline established in the contract. Furthermore, contractors may pass along charges for upgrading equipment or adding computer capacity. And if service requirements change, they may add charges for new or expanded services whether or not actual costs are incurred. Contractors also may fail to include such items as taxes or inflation adjustments in proposals, but they rarely fail to include them in contracts.

Buyers of services such as systems development often fail to completely specify their requirements, or they add requirements during the development project. Experienced outsourcing contractors will be certain that their contracts include provisions for additional charges incurred as a result of the buyer's failures or actions that result in additional work. The contracting firm's only protection against escalating costs is a thorough specification of the services expected and a thorough review of all contract clauses that permit the contractor to bill additional amounts over the agreed-upon price. Any contract you sign for outsourcing of computer or network operations should contain optional renewal clauses after the first year or two. Any contract for systems development or integration should be segmented by phases, with approval to continue based on satisfactory performance of each phase.

Inadequate Emergency Support

Many firms fear that they may receive poorer service from a contractor than from an in-house data center, since control over the contractor is not as easy to exercise. Under normal circumstances, this is probably not true. On the other hand, under exceptional or emergency circumstances, the response of a contractor may not be as satisfactory as that of an in-house data center. There is a basic reason for this. A contractor frequently makes a substantial part of its profit from economies of scale—that is, by combining the work of several customers into one facility that can be operated with less equipment and staff than the separate facilities of the individual customers had. As a result, in emergencies or at unexpected peak load conditions, the contractor must "balance" the needs of all its customers to meet some solution that may result in suboptimization for individual customers. Make sure that your contract specifies the minimum acceptable levels of response to your firm's needs.

Disaster Recovery

Disaster recovery and business resumption may be made more difficult by the contractor's efforts to balance the needs of clients and its need to remain profitable. To ensure that acceptable business resumption paths exist, you must contractually require that the contractor have specific capabilities and that the capabilities and facilities required are tested several times each year. This is the only way to ensure that the contractor's disaster is not also a disaster for your company.

Information Security

Backup and disaster recovery are only one aspect of information security, which consists of maintaining the *availability* of information and information processing resources, maintaining the *integrity* of information, and ensuring the *confidentiality* of information. While you can contractually bind an outsourcing contractor to meet performance specifications for maintaining availability, the burden of maintaining integrity and confidentiality will remain with your firm. If you delegate any activities that relate to the integrity and confidentiality of your firm's information to a contractor, you increase your information security risks. In the event that your firm must delegate some aspect of information security to a contractor, the responsibilities and the penalties for any security breach should be clearly spelled out in the contract. In any case, the contract should require the contractor to take appropriate precautions consistent with good business practice to safeguard your company's information. It also should spell out your firm's rights to audit the contractor's information security and facilities security practices on demand.

Financial Reliability

If a contractor encounters financial difficulties or lawsuits, you may find your data and processing capabilities unavailable through a court-ordered lockup of the contractor's facilities. In addition to carefully examining the financial condition of bidders and requiring disclosure of any pending lawsuits, you should take other precautions. Your contract should clearly state the ownership of any data, procedures, or programs on which your company depends for its operations, and you should make sure that contingency clauses exist that permit you to operate at another facility in the event of the contractor's inability to perform. Furthermore, you should ensure that current backups of data and programs are stored in one of your company's facilities. If you are outsourcing systems development or systems integration work, you should ensure that current duplicates of work in progress are stored weekly at your facility. If necessary, copies of source code or packaged software may be stored in an escrow facility to permit access in the event of the contractor's inability to operate.

Whether or not the contractor appears to be reliable, it may be dealing with information that is critical to the competitive position of your firm. Your contract should specify that the information you provide to the contractor (or bidder if such information is in the RFP) is proprietary to your company. It should also specify any penalties or damages that will be assessed against the contractor for illegal use or disclosure of your information.

Technology Change

Contractors will unhesitatingly adopt new technology if doing so will increase their profit margin. On the other hand, they may be reluctant to adopt new technology if it is perceived to threaten their profits or revenue stream. If your firm is committed to maintaining the technology edge, or if you expect to gain cost-effectiveness by adopting such newer technologies as client-server architectures, you must be very careful in delineating responsibilities under the outsourcing contract. Otherwise, there is a risk that adoption of new technology may be delayed or that total costs (including those of outsourcing) will not be reduced as anticipated by adoption of new technology, but may even increase.

Systems Architecture Change

In line with the above concern about new technology, many firms find that in order to meet the service demands of strategic business units, they must move toward increasing distribution of IS capacity. Such distribution is the antithesis of outsourcing, since it does not permit the contractor to take advantage of economies of scale. As a result, the contractor will be forced to make its profits through increased management fees or some other charges that may be related to the management and control of a distributed environment. (If the strategic business units of your firm do not feel that they are well served by a centralized IS operation, they will not be better served if the centralized operation is outsourced.)

Software License Fees

A spate of lawsuits has been engendered by the outsourcing movement, as software package suppliers have required increased license fees to move their software to the contractors' equipment. Before considering an outsourcing agreement, you should contact all software suppliers to gain a complete understanding of the cost impact of moving their systems to a contractor's facilities. Many international firms have found that a software package used in the United States costs more if acquired overseas. You should ascertain whether there are any international price differences before standardizing on software.

Contract Termination Penalties

Termination penalties in an outsourcing contract may be severe unless the contract is terminated for cause. Even in that case, the dispute may wind up in court. Contracts must contain provisions for reducing the level of service or terminating service under various circumstances (including sale or merger of your firm), with penalties limited to actual costs incurred by the termination. Furthermore, contracts should clearly indicate the ownership of information and materials, and the rights to continue use of information and information processing during a dispute, and they should require arbitration of disputes rather than litigation.

Performance Measurement

Even though it is probably impossible to envision all possible situations that may arise in an outsourcing business relationship, the essence of an outsourcing contract must be performance. The adequacy of performance can be determined only through measurement. Therefore, your contract must specify, to the extent possible, the performance expected and how it will be measured and reported. Many firms have found that once they outsourced operations, they lost the capability to monitor and measure performance against contract terms. As a result, new outsourcing contracts often contain a provision that permits the firm to employ an external consultant to evaluate the contractor's performance (either periodically or on demand).

BIDDING PRACTICES

Your company's reputation or the terms of the RFP may elicit different reactions from outsourcing bidders. H. Kent Craig gives a bidder's perspective of pricing approaches.[2] He says that his firm's pricing and terms are based on the following criteria:

- The reputation and credit history of the client. Prices are higher for a "picky" client, lower if the client is known for MIS professionalism.
- The quality of the RFP. If the bidder has to take a good deal of time and effort to figure out and document the bid, the price will be higher (or the contractor may decline to bid on a project that appears to be overly complex).
- The length of the contract. Anything over four years increases the risk to the contractor and is difficult to bid unless there are many options for adjusting costs/prices.
- Stringency of performance criteria and guarantees for compliance.

You should avoid actions or company postures that will encourage potential bidders to raise their prices for services.

Defining Requirements

To outsource systems development or integration requires that your company develop a detailed requirements definition to avoid ambiguities that may lead to increased costs or poor performance. The requirements definition must address not only the functions and features of the system but also expected performance characteristics, the business and technical environment in which the systems will operate, and the acceptance test methods and procedures. The acceptance test plans, scenarios, procedures, and test data should be independently developed by your company on the basis of the requirements specification. If the requirements are changed either by your request or by the contractor's recommendation during the course of the development project, the acceptance test should be updated to reflect the changes.

The period of the acceptance test may permit only a single "volume stress test" or may be extended to include a pilot operation and an operational period during full implementation of the system. Increased risk exposure relating to the size and scope of the system and the dependence of your company's business on successful operation should dictate the duration and conditions of the acceptance test. Many buyers require that a percentage of the contract price be withheld until final acceptance of the system. Exclusive of the warranty period, the acceptance legally signifies your satisfaction with the delivered results. Your company *must* retain the ability to perform acceptance testing or to hire an independent consultant to perform or manage such testing to be sure that it receives what it paid for.

Independent Validation and Verification

Outsourcing systems development or integration can be risky if your firm does not have the technical and management capability to carefully monitor the contractor's progress and technical decisions. If you plan to embark on a major project and have any question about your firm's ability to monitor the project, you should consider the Department of Defense's technique of independent validation and verification (I.V.& V.). The I.V.& V. approach requires that you employ an independent contractor to conduct periodic reviews of project progress and technical decisions made by the prime contractor. At your option, the independent contractor may also review requirements before the RFP is released; review design specifications and system architecture; review project control methods and system development techniques and tools to be used by the prime contractor; participate in code walkthroughs; develop interim and acceptance test plans; observe interim tests; and participate in final acceptance testing. If you cannot perform these tasks yourself, employ I.V. & V. and make sure that your prime contract contains the provision that the independent contractor will perform the tasks and report results directly to you.

Specifying Operations Needs

To outsource computer operations, you should specify, at a minimum, your performance expectations and measurement methods for

- Transaction volumes
- Critical needs for timeliness
- Critical needs for security
- Critical needs for business resumption in the event of catastrophe

- Needs for local processing (e.g., PCs, local area networks (LANs), and client-server systems)
- Anticipated new applications development
- Anticipated adoption of new technology
- Measures of performance and frequency of performance audits

Sole-Source Procurement Dangers

Sole-source procurement, the easiest way to make an outsourcing agreement, is also the most dangerous. If your company plans to examine the feasibility of outsourcing any aspect of its operations (such as a data center or telecommunications), you must first understand your present costs and levels of service. Only then should you prepare an RFP that clearly sets forth your company's expectations (but does not disclose present costs). Expectations must not only include those identified previously in this chapter, but also address such issues as the possible transfer of company employees to the contractor's staff.

Bids should always be obtained from more than one reliable firm, and the RFP should clearly state the criteria on which bids will be evaluated. The evaluation, including the comparisons to internal costs, should be performed in-house or by a consultant who is not one of the bidders. Similar rules apply to contracting for systems development or integration. If your staff lack the capacity or skills to perform the project in-house, at the least the job should be estimated internally before an RFP is released for bids.

Terms in Requests for Proposals

The RFP that you develop should include a pro forma agreement that sets forth the terms that you expect to see in the contract. These terms will include those indicated throughout this chapter. By specifying the expected agreement terms in the RFP, you have a chance to evaluate the bidders' responses to those terms as well as their technical responses. You also have a checklist of contract terms and conditions and an early warning of any potential contracting problems if bidders take issue with the proposed agreement.

Staff Management During Outsourcing

If you anticipate that your company will reduce staff as a result of outsourcing, you must plan such reductions carefully. Lawsuits have been initiated by disgruntled employees who have either been laid off or transferred to the contractor's company. The grounds for such suits may vary from improper contracting procedure (as in a 1990 suit against Nashville Electric Service), improper management of corporate assets, or claims that the employee benefits of the contractor did not equal those of the contracting firm. It is not enough to reassure employees that their jobs are secure. Your planning may have to include early retirement offers and/or extended layoff benefits. Reassurance of employees is vital during planning, evaluation, and migration, since your continued ability to provide service depends on these employees.

You should examine all the options for employees, require bidders to indicate how they will dispose of or relocate surplus employees, and require bidders to provide detailed information about their salary ranges and benefit programs. Finally, you should share as much information as possible, as early as possible, with potentially affected employees and solicit their opinions and comments so that you can deal with possible problems effectively. In 1993, a district court judge awarded damages to former employees of Blue Cross and Blue Shield of Massachusetts as a result of its 10-year, $ 800 million outsourcing deal with EDS. Blue Cross had a policy that required 60-day notice to employees and outplacement and severance benefits if it eliminated positions as a result of "workload changes, consolidations of jobs, elimination of job functions, reductions in force, or other corporate reorganization." Technically, the Blue Cross jobs were eliminated as a result of the deal, which took only five business days to be concluded.

THE CONTRACTOR IS NOT YOUR "PARTNER"

The key thing to keep in mind when outsourcing information systems is that although contractors may profess to be your "business partners," they are not. They are separate firms that must maximize profits to satisfy their shareholders, and as a result, their business interests *cannot* be congruent with those of your firm. Appropriate preparation, intelligent bidding and contracting procedures, the advice of your attorney on contracts, and strong contract performance monitoring are needed to make outsourcing a success.

CONCLUSION

The checklists in Tables 9.1 and 9.2 may be used to ensure that your firm is protected in an outsourcing arrangement. The checklist in Table 9.1 should be used in developing an RFP. Bidders should be required to respond to each paragraph in the RFP in the same sequence to make evaluation and comparison easier. Since responses to the RFP will differ, and contractors may take different exceptions to specific terms and conditions, you should also compare the responses to both the checklist and the RFP.

The checklist in Table 9.2 provides a list of actions that a prudent buyer should take in contracting for or operating with an outsourcing arrangement. This checklist can serve as the basis for developing a project plan for outsourcing.

Table 9.1.   Pitfall Avoidance Checklist 1: Items to Be Addressed by Bidders

Systems Integration or Systems Development:

- Basis for additional charges
- Phased approvals
- Storage of weekly progressive development results
- Progress reporting and monitoring
- Rights to use independent validation and verification
- System performance expectations and measurement methods
- Acceptance test methods and procedures
- Final acceptance conditions
- Warranties

Outsourcing Operations:

- Capacity or upgrade approval requirements
- New technology expectations and approvals
- Distribution of operations
- Software lease implications
- Renewal options
- Acceptable performance and measurement methods
- Disaster recovery and backup
- Disaster recovery and backup testing
- Information security provisions
- Rights to audit information security practices
- Provision for contingency operation
- Storage of information copies

All RFPs:

- Requirements specification
- Tax implications
- Inflation implications
- Proprietary information safeguards
- Termination for cause
- Partial or full termination conditions and penalties
- Rights in ownership of data and programs
- Dispute resolution
- Bid evaluation methods and parameters
- Proposed agreement terms and conditions

Table 9.2.   Pitfall Avoidance Checklist 2: Actions to Be Taken by Buyers

All Contracts:

- Develop a comprehensive requirements specification and RFP
- Obtain multiple bids for new projects
- Identify current costs (or estimate internal development costs) for comparison
- Deal openly with employment issues and employees

Operations Outsourcing:

- Store copies of data and programs at your site
- Periodically audit contractor's information security practices
- Periodically test backup and recovery capabilities
- Regularly monitor performance to contract specifications

Systems Development Outsourcing:

- Control requirements specification changes
- Regularly monitor progress, design, and technical decisions
- Plan and control acceptance testing

DISCUSSION TOPICS

- Has outsourcing remained popular?
- What are the major reasons for outsourcing?
- Are there outsourcing problems recently reported covered by the material in this chapter?
- If new outsourcing problems have been reported, what measures should be taken to eliminate or mitigate these problems?
- Has the adoption of client-server architectures changed the needs for outsourcing?

REFERENCES

1. "Spending for a Rainy Day." *Information Week* (December 7, 1992): 38–48.
2. Craig, H.K. "Outsourcing Contracts." *MIS Week* (April 9, 1990).

CHAPTER 10

The Downsizing Dilemma: Estimating Application Life

Major investments in application replacement are more frequently being considered as a result of the downsizing of systems or the migration from mainframes to client-server systems. However, replacement efforts may take substantial time and incur significant investment. Furthermore, a prudent management decision requires consideration of extending the life of the current system as long as economically feasible. One means of estimating the probable life of an application is the "scenario approach" set forth in this chapter.

CLIENT-SERVER MIGRATION STRATEGIES

As this book is written, there is a considerable amount of publicity about (and some actual accomplishment of) migration from mainframes to client-server systems. Such migration is, in most cases, a complex undertaking with considerable risk. Two substantive questions arise when a migration (or any major change of application operating environments) is considered:

1. What are the available migration strategies?
2. When should a migration effort be started?

In 1993 an IBM spokesperson presented the company's alternative strategies for migration to client-server architectures. These were the following:

- Leave mainframe databases and applications untouched while adding new logic, generally in the form of graphical user interfaces, on the workstation or PC.

- Distribute a portion of the mainframe application to the front end, leaving data security and performance optimization functions to the mainframe server.
- Distribute the data in a three-tiered computing structure, with a middle-tier server performing most of the data processes and the application divided between the front end and the mainframe.

The old IBM view of mainframe centricity continues to be reflected in these alternatives, since there is no mention of the migration strategy that many companies are adopting—that is, a gradual migration away from the mainframe by

1. Developing all new applications or major application replacements specifically for a client-server environment.
2. Moving the user interfaces from existing mainframe applications to PCs and (frequently) moving communications management to servers, leaving the mainframes as application servers (this step can take place concurrently with step 1).
3. Moving the applications to PCs or workstations and leaving the mainframe as a database server.
4. Moving mainframe databases to smaller servers or to a combination of workstations/PCs and servers.

The idea behind this increasingly popular strategy is that gradual migration will be less expensive if the mainframe is used as a server until the economics become favorable for completing the migration. Eventually, you will have offloaded enough work from the mainframe so that capacity is not an issue and you are no longer forced into annual upgrades. The old mainframe will last as long as you want it to, or until a final conversion can be cost-justified.

SEVEN PRAGMATIC RULES FOR CLIENT-SERVER ARCHITECTURE

Mainframe myopia ignores the experience of users, which has resulted in some pragmatic rules for enterprise-wide computing:

1. *Move as much processing as possible close to the user.* MIPs and disk space are cheaper, performance is better, applications are friendlier.
2. *Share as little as possible.* Run applications on PCs or workstations and share only the data. Synchronization is better, response time is better, and price/performance ratio is better with multiuser databases than with multiuser applications (e.g., PCs issuing SQL transactions against mainframe databases versus PCs logging into CICS or IMS).

3. *Build peer-to-peer networks.* User PCs communicate directly with the servers that contain the data, transaction processing monitor, or application. Three-tiered architectures (or gateways and controllers) make it difficult to synchronize data and transactions and to perform error recovery. Peer-to-peer networks should include routers or gateways only when necessary for preserving the security of the system (for example, in connecting to wide area networks that are relatively open to unauthorized users).

4. *Avoid migrating old code.* Use new technologies and techniques (e.g., business process redesign, rapid prototyping, object-oriented development, and client-server systems) to create better applications, and do not port old software or old application design to new platforms. The idea is to improve, not simply to migrate and lower the operating costs.

5. *Simplify the enterprise-wide computing environment.* This means single network protocols (TCP/IP), single-network operating systems (such as NetWare or NT Advanced Server), a common set of office applications (word processing, spreadsheets, electronic mail, etc.), and so on.

6. *Automate the management of the enterprise's information architecture.* This means proactive network and PC management, automated configuration management, automated software distribution, integrated help desk support with automated assistance, automated over-the-network backups, automated network security administration, and so on.

7. *Write as little code as possible.* Use shrink-wrapped packages on PCs with templates or macros. Develop organization-specific applications by using procedures in packaged software rather than developing programs.

Although Complementary Metal Oxide Semiconductor (CMOS)-based "mainframe" servers, such as the current Unisys 2200 Model 500 and the promised IBM machine due soon, may extend the life of legacy systems through lower-cost hardware, they do not address the basic problem of replacing legacy systems with applications and architectures that are more responsive to end users and under end users control.

Knowledge of migration strategies is a critical beginning. Next it is necessary to consider the optimum time for the migration effort to begin.

UNDERSTANDING THE "SYSTEM LIFE" PROBLEM

The concept of the "system life cycle" has received much attention over the years. Analyses and studies have been conducted showing the relative costs of development compared to the costs of maintenance and enhancement, migration planning, cost/benefit analysis, and other aspects of the life cycle. All of these studies beg the question of estimating life-cycle duration. As a result, the anticipated life of an application is usually predicated on anticipated technology changes or on the experience of the designers.

Such an approach is adequate for the cost/benefit analysis of a proposed application and for general planning, but it does not meet the needs of management decision makers who must plan for timely application replacement.

The reasons for replacing an application may include the following:

- Code and documentation have suffered from years of changes, and the system has become fragile—not trustworthy if further changes are made.
- Documentation is not up to date, and changes are costly and risky.
- Technology has provided alternatives that promise significant operating cost reduction.
- The current technology platforms (e.g., computers and operating systems) are obsolete and becoming difficult to maintain.
- Business conditions have changed so dramatically that the existing application is obsolete.
- Business processes have been redesigned and a new application is required.

Set against these reasons for replacement are a number of management concerns, including

- The high potential investment required for replacement
- Lack of skill and experience with the proposed replacement environment or new technology platforms
- Lack of availability of "packaged" solutions that could reduce replacement cost
- Doubt about the need for replacement or concerns that the need is technology-driven
- Risks associated with replacement (ranging from the trustworthiness of estimates to the retraining of users and potential business impacts)

Replacement of an application, especially when it involves concurrent replacement of the technology platform, raises sufficient management concern that a means is needed to predict the optimum replacement time. Evidence that such management hesitation exists may be seen in the extension of application life in several major businesses. For example, almost all airline reservation systems were designed in the 1960s and 1970s, and they are still running code that was written for the Sabre System in 1965. Many major banks are operating demand deposit accounting systems that were written in the 1970s and have been patched and enhanced frequently since that time.

Some corporations are able to continue operation of legacy systems for years. They lower costs by purchasing their technology platforms and using them until they (literally) fall apart or can no longer be economically maintained. Such an approach may be practical for businesses that experience little change in IS requirements. Most firms, however, must face the fact that applications will eventually reach a point where extending their life cycle becomes impractical. The management dilemma is in predicting the optimum time for replacement.

Given the costs and risks of replacement, combined with the potential requirement for a multiyear development effort and the planning that must take place well in advance of such a major effort, it is critical to know, as early as possible, when an application should be replaced. Typical means for deciding on replacement of an application include

- A cost/benefit analysis that compares the ongoing cost of maintenance and enhancement to the cost of replacement
- A make-or-buy analysis that compares the cost of new development with the cost of acquiring and modifying an application software package
- A payback analysis based on the benefits that could be obtained with the new application

These methods aid in making a decision at a specific point in time, but they do not address the issue of forecasting the optimum time for making the change. For major, mission-critical applications, a more extensive analysis is often needed.

SCENARIO-BASED PLANNING

One way to predict the optimum time for replacement of an application is to use a scenario-based approach similar to that used by many corporations in long-range business planning.

Scenario-based planning for business usually constructs two or three visions of the future business climate and then identifies how the company will respond to each vision. For example, future scenarios may include a business-as-usual environment, a business recession, or a period of inflation. Within these possible futures, a more extended scenario or vision is developed that may address regulatory changes, international competition, technological breakthroughs, and so forth. The idea is to identify possible futures that may be advantageous or disadvantageous to the company and develop rough outlines of how the company should respond. The advantage of this technique for business planners is that scenarios identify conditions and reactions for both the "upside" and "downside."

For information systems applications, this approach makes use of some of the same cost/benefit studies in the traditional approach outlined in the previous section. However, it also considers a number of other factors:

- *The kinds and frequency of business and regulatory changes that may impact the cost of maintenance and enhancement of the application.* External forces that require the company to change its business processes often require modification or enhancement to applications.
- *The expected reliability of the application as a result of expected modifications.*
- *The business risks of future maintenance activities.* Continuing change to systems eventually degrades reliability and may jeopardize business operations.
- *The service levels expected by users in application performance/reliability and in responding to requests for modification.* Compensating for degraded performance resulting from increased use of an application cannot always be accomplished by upgrading equipment; heavily modified applications become more difficult to maintain and response times to requests become longer.
- *The relative complexity of regression testing to ensure reliability after modifications are made.*
- *The continued cost of maintenance and enhancement during development and implementation of a replacement application.* The old system must continue to support business needs while the new one is being developed and implemented.
- *The overall hardware/software architecture objectives of the company's computer and network operations for the next five years and the impact on those objectives of retaining the current application.* Retaining a legacy application may force retention of obsolescent hardware and software, impeding the company's ability to justify newer platforms for other applications.
- *The primary platform vendor's hardware, software, and support trends for the key components used in operating the application.* Reduction in vendor support capabilities or elimination of support for software versions may critically affect the ability to continue operating current platforms economically.

SCENARIO DEVELOPMENT METHODOLOGY

Scenario-based planning is conducted through a series of specific tasks described below. It is expected that the study will be conducted by a small team familiar with the domains and topics involved. The extent of effort in each task depends on the familiarity of the study team with each topic area. Even when team members are familiar with an area and little investigative work is required, the conclusions of each task should be documented to contribute to the overall credibility of the conclusions presented to senior management.

Task 1: Review of Management Concerns Relating to Application Life Expectancy

The team should interview appropriate user and senior management to identify

- Known or suspected concerns and problems
- Needed, requested, or anticipated modifications to the application
- Historical and forecasted expenses for ongoing operations, maintenance, and enhancements
- Potential enhancements needed to improve business processes, such as improved human interfaces and improved query capabilities
- Changing business conditions or short- and long-term business strategies that may affect the application

The findings from these interviews form a basis for further investigation of the existing vulnerabilities of the application to change and of the potential cost impact of enhancing the application.

Task 2: Technical Audit of Application Constraints

The team should next focus on examination of attributes of the application and its operating environment that may constrain future enhancement or the expectancy. Topics to be addressed in this review include

- *Application architecture.* Is the application modular or monolithic? What computer capacities are required for programs, buffer space, user workspace, and so forth? In what language is the source code written?
- *Technology base employed.* What database access tools are used? What telecommunications monitor or tools are used? What operating system and utilities are used? Is the application dependent on other, unique software developed by the company? How is support for the technology base provided? What is the predicted future for retaining support for each element of the technology base?
- *Processing limitation.* If batch operations are required, what is the time available for completing such operations? In online operations, what are the response time requirements for users? How many concurrent users can be supported at required response time levels by the platform? What are the capacity limits of the current platform to support

these requirements now and in the future? What other applications use the platform and what limitations does this concurrent use imply?

- *Development process and history.* How frequently has the application code been modified to correct errors or to enhance functionality or performance? Roughly, what percentage of the code is from the originally released version? Has the frequency of change increased or decreased over the last three years?

- *Application documentation and maintainability.* Is application and program documentation current with the version of the application being operated? Is source code complete? Does source code contain internal documentation through comments? Is documentation complete and understandable? Have the results of tests been documented? Does a recent test data set exist? Are maintenance personnel thoroughly knowledgeable about the application? How long have current maintenance personnel been working with the application?

- *Application reliability.* How frequently has the application failed to perform correctly in the last three years? Has a failure or discrepancy log been maintained? What are the primary causes for such failures during the past three years? Has the application been unavailable to users at times during the past three years? Has the incidence of such unavailability increased? Has the duration of unavailability increased? Has recovery time increased?

- *System architecture changes.* Are major changes, unrelated to the application, being planned for the company's system architecture? For example, if other applications are being moved to new platforms or environments, will this application be forced to move also? An architectural initiative to move applications from a mainframe to a client-server environment could result in this application being the sole user of the mainframe, perhaps at a prohibitive cost.

Task 3: Investigation of Regulatory and Other External Factors

In a business environment that is increasingly subject to state, national, and international regulation and legislation, regulatory and other external pressures must be considered as potentially affecting application life. The team should conduct interviews with parties that may influence the need for change to the application, and they should explore factors that may require the company to change the application or the way it is used. Depending on the nature of the application, interviews may include organizations or groups such as

- Local, state, and federal regulating organizations—for example, environmental, health, and safety regulation may affect reporting requirements.

- The company's director of communications or legislators having interest in pending legislation that may affect the company—legislation may often affect the manner in which companies do business.
- Organizations concerned with how the application is used—for example, unions or consumer advocacy groups.
- Customers or suppliers who may interface with the application.

The comments and concerns of these parties should be recorded as potential influences on the requirements for the application in the future.

Task 4: Investigation of Vendors' Future Support Plans

Products that support the application were identified in task 2. The team must now contact the vendors of these products and determine their future plans for maintaining the products in a form that will continue to support the application as it currently exists.

Experience indicates that products go through cycles of change in which new releases may affect their ability to support existing systems. Furthermore, products have a definite life cycle of their own, after which vendors may discontinue support. The cost of maintaining obsolete products may be prohibitive, not only because of the need to employ expert assistance but because of the need to adjust other components of the overall system architecture to maintain compatibility.

The team must interview or obtain documented commitments from vendors about their plans for products and how these products will affect the maintainability of the application. Since such plans are frequently proprietary to the vendors, the company may be required to sign a confidentiality agreement with vendors in order to obtain the information. On the other hand, trade publications often speculate on product life, and in some cases the history of the vendors' support for previous products may provide reasonable insight for planning purposes.

Product plans should be obtained, to the extent possible, for existing purchased and licensed software and hardware and for anticipated new releases for the software and hardware.

Task 5: Development of Scenarios

The information gathered in previous tasks contributes to the development of the scenarios, but a key element, cost, is still required. Costs depend on the scenarios selected. Experience indicates that systems continue to require maintenance and enhancement even though replacement is planned. This is especially true when the development of the replacement system is a major undertaking involving substantial time.

At a minimum, the scenarios must include current costs of operation, anticipated costs for the application life described by the scenario, costs of enhancement and maintenance, and costs of replacement.

Part of estimating the system life is finding a point at which the cost of retaining the system exceeds the cost of replacement. This requires detailed investigation into alternative replacement scenarios and the development of cost and time estimates for them. Such alternatives include a gradual migration to a client-server-based system, the acquisition and modification of a packaged system, redesign of the business processes followed by system redevelopment, internal development of a new mainframe-based replacement system, and so forth. Other elements affecting costs include the intangible cost resulting from the opportunity loss created by retaining the old system and the utility value to the company of operating a new system that better meets business needs.

Prior to a detailed examination of costs and benefits, it is necessary to evaluate conceptual scenarios and select those that appear to be the most practical. Possible conceptual scenarios include

- *A baseline scenario,* which assumes minimal enhancements to the application in response only to external conditions that force change; no growth in the processing load (number of transactions, number of customers, etc.); and vendors' continued support for products.
- *An application enhancement scenario,* which assumes that all or most of users' desired enhancements are accommodated either at management direction or as a result of external factors forcing change; that processing load remains relatively constant; and that vendors continue support for products indefinitely.
- *An environmental change scenario,* which assumes that the company's business will change dramatically, changing the need for the application in its existing form; alternatively, that the systems architecture and the technology platforms supporting the application will change and force system replacement.
- *An aggressive change scenario,* which assumes that all or most of users' desired enhancements are accommodated either at management direction or as a result of external factors forcing change; that processing load increases dramatically; and that vendors' support for products continues indefinitely.

Obviously, other scenarios are possible depending on the situation. For example, each of the above scenarios could be dramatically modified by changing the final premise to read "vendor support is terminated in X years and costs to maintain products increase substantially."

From a list of conceptual scenarios such as those set forth above, the team should select the three or four most likely and develop full scenarios.

Generally, it is not necessary to develop scenarios in narrative form; rather, an outline or "management presentation" will usually suffice. The contents of each scenario should include

- *Section 1: Problem Description.* Briefly describe the problem faced by the company with regard to the application and the reasons for the study.
- *Section 2: Assumptions for the Business Environment.* Set forth the assumptions about business conditions that will impact the application life. These assumptions include business growth or decline and the effect on transaction volume; changing business strategies (for example, acquisition or divestiture of business units may dramatically change application needs); anticipated business process redesign initiatives that could change the application requirements; the ability of the company to invest in a major development effort; regulatory or legislative action that may force changes; interfaces with customers or suppliers that may force changes; and other external influences.
- *Section 3: Technical Considerations.* Provide a brief history of the application and address the current condition of the application in terms of maintainability and reliability, personnel skills for maintenance and enhancement, the potential loss of support for the technology platform, processing load limitations, and the maintenance and enhancement forecast for this scenario.
- *Section 4: Limitations on Application Life.* Summarize the factors that tend to limit the life of the application and draw conclusions that project a range of time (for example, five to seven years of remaining life) during which continued support of the current application will be practical. At this point, without considering cost factors, the range is based on estimates of the continued effectiveness of the application for the business, the expected continuity of product support, staffing considerations, potential platform replacement due to architecture changes not related to the application, and so forth.
- *Section 5: Current Operating Costs.* Provide a breakdown of current operating costs, including hardware, software leases, and the costs of maintenance and enhancement during the past year.
- *Section 6: Projected Operating Costs.* Project operating costs of the application for this scenario through the periods of time indicated by the range determined in Section 4. If it is anticipated that product support for critical hardware or software will be discontinued, estimate the additional costs of continuing support.
- *Section 7: Replacement Alternatives.* Identify replacement strategies for the application. These may include purchase and modification of a software package, gradual rewriting and migration of parts of the application over time, development of a new application, and out-

sourcing of the application to a specialized service. The replacement strategies should briefly describe the approach, new hardware or software required, changes to telecommunications required, impacts on users, training requirements, staff requirements, and so on. For each alternative, estimate the elapsed time required for development, implementation, and full deployment. The estimate of time for deployment or other constraints may immediately reduce the number of options available. For example, if a replacement strategy requires an elapsed time greater than the estimated life of the system, or extends beyond a time when risks become untenable, it cannot be considered.

- Section 8: *Replacement Implementation Costs.* For the selected alternative strategies, develop estimates for the cost of development and deployment (including migration or data conversion costs).
- *Section 9: Operating Costs of Replacement Alternatives.* Estimate the operating costs for each selected alternative for the first three years of operation or until the new application is fully deployed and costs are expected to be stable.
- *Section 10: Replacement Benefits.* Identify the benefits, both tangible and intangible, that will be gained by replacement.
- *Section 11: Risks.* Identify, and to the extent possible, assign probabilities to the risks of each replacement alternative and to the risks of retaining the current application. The probabilities of risks may change over time. In fact, such changes in risk probability may be a deciding factor in application life.
- *Section 12: Revised Operating Costs for the Existing Application.* Revise the projected operating costs for the current application in light of the replacement alternatives. For example, enhancement of the current application will probably be severely curtailed during development of the replacement.
- *Section 13: Financial Analysis.* Prepare a spreadsheet analysis that illustrates the annual costs for retaining the current application (Section 6) compared to those of each of the alternative replacement strategies (Section 7). The replacement alternative costs should include the revised operating costs for the existing application during replacement development (Section 12), the replacement implementation costs (Section 8), the replacement operating costs (Section 9), and the tangible benefits of the replacement (Section 10). Assuming that the replacement has a financial benefit, the payback point should appear at a time when the reduced costs plus the tangible benefits have amortized the costs of implementation.
- *Section 14: Scenario Summary.* Considering the limitations on application life (Section 4), the risks (Section 11), the elapsed time needed for replacement (Section 7), and the financial analysis (Section 13), esti-

mate the remaining life of the application and the time work on a replacement must begin.

Developing the first scenario is the most time-consuming task, since for other scenarios the cost estimates and other material developed for the first scenario may be used.

CONCLUSION

The scenario approach to estimating application life is probably the most accurate, but it will, at best, provide only a range of time within which the application must be replaced. There are too many variables and unknowns to be precise. Nevertheless, when major investments in applications are being considered and when the time for development and deployment of a replacement is substantial, scenarios provide management with the alternatives and the information they require for prudent decision making.

DISCUSSION TOPICS

- What are the difficulties in collecting information for developing scenarios?
- How similar is the information needed for estimating systems life to the information needed for competitive analysis or technology acquisition planning?
- Are shortcuts possible to reduce the cost of the scenario approach?
- What additional downsizing strategies may be applied?
- What are the external factors affecting application life? Do they differ for different businesses?

Protecting Information Assets

So far, this book has dealt with the management and business issues, at increasing levels of detail, in the processes of introducing information technology and implementing that technology to support the business of the enterprise. All such efforts may be useless unless we are able to protect the information systems that support the business.

Information security is dedicated to three major considerations:

- Ensuring that information and information processing resources are available to the business when they are needed
- Ensuring that information, once captured, remains free of unauthorized changes
- Preserving the confidentiality of information that is critical to the firm

Because the value of information security has too often been ignored by both business managers and CIOs (who should know better), this section begins by exploring the business value of information security. It then examines in some detail the impacts that emerging technologies will have on the ability to maintain information security, how to structure and manage information security in increasingly distributed information processing environments, and how to assess needs for disaster recovery.

Continuing the general theme of this book, this section relates information security to the needs of the business.

CHAPTER 11

The Business Value of Information Security

*Corporate information security managers are continually chal-
lenged to justify their positions. A 1993* **Information Week** *article
comments that "the move to flatten hierarchies, the rise of distributed computing, and the erratic on-again, off-again concern
for data protection has some high-profile users eliminating centralized security responsibility."[1] The idea underlying this attack on
corporate information security heads is that once policies have
been established, the responsibility for implementation and management should be transferred to the users of computer systems.*

  *Chris Vandenoever of Deloitte & Touche, in the same article,
said that the problem is that "Good security is invisible." But the
problem for information security managers is deeper than that.
Insurance policies are also invisible, but corporations still buy
insurance and feel comfortable with justifying the cost.*

THE PROBLEM

The root of the problem of justifying the existence of the information security function is that information security is not seen as adding value to the
business. Compounding the problem are several other factors:

- Company executives are often not aware of information security function until an incident such as a hacker intrusion or a major disaster
  jeopardizes the company's ability to do business.

I am indebted to Reinhard Schoepf of Siemens AG, Karen Worstell of Boeing Computer Services, and Pieter van Dijken of Shell Internationale Petroleum, all members
of the International Information Integrity Institute, for ideas that led to this chapter.

187

- Executives who are aware of information security tend to think of it in terms of protecting confidentiality—an unfortunate consequence of the "security" title. There is little perception that information security includes ensuring the availability and integrity of information to operate the company and planning for the recovery of the business in the event of disaster.
- Information security managers have, in general, little access to corporate executives other than the MIS director or the CIO. This means that they have minimal opportunity to convince executives of the importance of their work.
- Because the most obvious concerns for information security focus on computers and networks, management (often including information security managers) tends to forget that information is present in many other forms throughout the company. All sensitive information, regardless of media (paper documents, telephone, etc.), requires protection.
- Information security managers, as technical specialists, often do not understand the business of the company. As a result, they have difficulty making a business case for information security.

It is this set of problems that must be addressed in order to justify the cost of information security in the company. While much of the content of this chapter is familiar to information security professionals, it is provided to give context to the making of a business case for the information security function.

THE ENVIRONMENT FOR INFORMATION SECURITY

The information security function, as a distinct entity, originated in the mainframe environment of the 1960s with the introduction of network access to mainframe computers. The initial protective mechanisms and security controls were oriented to this centralized systems architecture until late in the 1980s. In fact, in many companies this orientation remains. As a result, most information security organizations reside within the management information systems (MIS) division.

It was not until the 1970s that some information security practitioners realized that information was scattered throughout the company on various media. That recognition led, in some companies, to a brief struggle among the corporate security department, the internal audit department, and the MIS division for ownership of the information security group. In most companies, MIS won the war and generally buried the usually small information security group several layers down from the top.

The first shock to this centralized viewpoint came with the advent of minicomputers and distributed computing. Suddenly, information security professionals were faced with computers that were outside the "glass house" and yet connected to networks that reached the mainframe. Frequently, the tools to implement distributed security controls were not available, and companies were reluctant to hire additional security staff for remote operations.

Next came the shock of decentralization of the MIS function as many companies pushed control of IS resources out to the business units they served, and as many users acquired PCs that were connected to corporate networks. In the early and mid-1980s, this trend was compounded by the mounting acquisition and divestiture activity of many corporations as they restructured their businesses. This rapid movement of "parts of companies" created problems for MIS and near-impossible challenges for information security.

Two more trends surfaced in the late 1980s to compound the problem. One trend was that many companies turned to outsourcing of information systems to reduce (or at least control) their costs. This resulted in the information security group either being "sold" to the outsourcing supplier or remaining in the company as a part of a substantially diminished MIS function.

The other trend, with perhaps even greater long-term impact, was that companies formed close operating relationships with both suppliers and customers to improve efficiency of operation and meet competitive threats. In the process, they opened their systems and networks to access by suppliers and customers, whose information security procedures could not be controlled by the company that established the relationships.

As if all this were not enough, two other technological/market developments have increased the vulnerability of corporate information. First, portable computers in a variety of forms are carrying corporate information into the world at large. Second, one way or another, most corporate networks are or will soon be connected to the Internet that provides freedom of exchange of technical (and often business-related) information. Internet is, for all intents, an open network that anyone can use. Connection to the Internet, without stringent means of protection, can allow any clever computer hacker to penetrate corporate computers.

In this rapidly changing environment, information security managers must find a way to convince their corporate executives that business operations may depend on the quality of their information security.

THE ROLE OF INFORMATION SECURITY

Most information security managers have a relatively clear understanding of their role in the company. In brief, it is their task to help

- Ensure the availability of valid information when users need it to run the business

- Protect the confidentiality of sensitive corporate information
- Protect the privacy of users
- Protect information assets from unauthorized modification
- Ensure the ability of the company to continue operation in the event of a disaster

In summary, the task of the information security function is to aid in protecting the company's information assets against all potential threats. (See Table 11.1.)

To carry out their duties, information security managers and the professionals on their staff usually

- Advise management on the policies and procedures needed to protect corporate information assets (including information itself and the ability to process it)
- Develop procedures and controls to conform to policy
- Assist in implementing procedures, controls, and information security tools and devices
- Assist in ensuring that managers and employees are aware of their responsibilities to protect information assets
- Plan for the recovery and continuity of the business in the event of disaster

Table 11.1   SRI International's List of Accidental and Intentional Threats to Information

• Threats to availability and usefulness	• Destroy, damage, or contaminate • Deny, prolong, or delay use or access
• Threats to integrity and authenticity	• Enter, use, or produce false data • Modify, replace, or reorder • Misrepresent • Repudiate • Misuse or fail to use as required
• Threats to confidentiality and possession	• Access • Disclose • Observe or monitor • Copy • Steal
• Exposure to threats	• Endanger by exposure to any of the above threats

Source: SRI International

- Advise management in the event of special requirements
- Advise users and systems developers on the implementation of controls for sensitive applications
- Assist in solving problems concerning information security (such as hacker penetration or virus contamination)

In addition, information security professionals may conduct periodic reviews of systems and facilities to ensure conformance to procedures, or they may assist in audits of those facilities.

Setting forth these functions concisely gives us some idea of the critical nature of the "invisible" work done by information security. However, there are some grey areas. For example, an information security specialist in a petrochemical refinery interviewed a maintenance engineer who was responsible for a part of the plant that distilled fractions of the petroleum. The engineer had been assigned to that job for about a year. The plant was over 35 years old and had been maintained by a long series of engineers who had meticulously filled out reports on any incidents and the repairs made. All these reports were filed by date in rows of file cabinets that, by this time, took up most of the office space available to the current engineer. In the event of a breakdown, the reports, filed by date, were completely useless to the engineer, who had to solve the problem as if it had never before occurred. There was no practical way to retrieve a previous report by type of incident or breakdown.

Furthermore, the maintenance engineering office, which contained all the reports and the plans for the plant, was located within 30 meters of the plant itself. In the event of a major disaster requiring access to this information (such as the location of valves) by recovery crews or firefighters, the office itself might be contaminated or destroyed.

Clearly, we are dealing here with information critical to continued operation of the plant and to disaster recovery. The information was only in paper form (within the purview of information security) and not available when needed. The information may not have been recoverable in the event of a disaster. We are also dealing with potential safety or environmental considerations.

What should be the role of an information security professional in this situation? It can vary. Consider the following options and determine which have merit:

- The information security specialist should not be in the plant in the first place. Decisions about how to manage the plant-related information are up to (a) the plant manager, (b) the maintenance engineer, (c) health and safety department, (d) the environmental engineering department, or (e) systems analysts who may be called in by the plant manager to design an information retrieval system.

- The information security specialist should report the existing and potential problems to some or all of the above, plus internal audit.
- The information security specialist should both report and advise on how to correct the problems.
- The information security specialist should ignore the problems as not a part of his or her responsibility.

The first and last options are untenable. If, in the course of usual duties, *any* employee discovers a potential hazard, that employee has a duty to the company to report it. However, the first option implies the central issue: Information assets, wherever located and in whatever form, are critical to the operation of the company, and aiding in the protection of those assets is the job of information security.

This example indicates a need in many companies for information security to coordinate activities with such departments as health and safety, environmental engineering, and corporate security, and to publicize this relationship as a part of information security awareness programs. Such publicity further serves to establish information security on at least the same plane of necessity to the corporation as the other organizations.

Instances of similar congruence between the quality assurance and information security functions also exist, and relating information security to quality management today is a clear path to recognition of information security's value.

WHAT NEEDS TO BE PROTECTED?

Not all information has the same value or the same importance to the successful operation of the company. This means that the controls exercised to protect information (and the costs of those controls) should vary commensurate with the value and importance (sensitivity) of the information. On the other hand, many system architectures are so constructed that all information processed or contained therein is either secure or insecure.

The costs of computer security include not only the costs of the security tools and processing time but also the time of information users based on the ease with which data can be accessed and the costs of administration of security. These costs are generally subsumed in the total life-cycle costs of the system. However, if they are separately identified as a component of operating costs, they should influence the systems architecture. For example, client-server technology provides the capability to implement application system and network architectures that permit segregation of applications and information on separate computers, often at a lower cost than that for combining numerous applications on a single mainframe. (The economies of scale previously attributed to mainframes are no longer true.)

The need for such segregation is obvious. For example, it is increasingly common for suppliers of retail chains to have direct access to the inventory files of the chain's stores so that they can appropriately replenish stock. This is efficient for both the supplier and the retailer. However, if the inventory application and the chain's strategic planning and payroll applications are operated on the same computer, there is little to prevent unauthorized access to them. Similar conditions may exist for entire networks if they are not adequately protected.

Client-server architectures combined with "firewall" and user authentication techniques provide a unique opportunity to assign the processing of sensitive information to separate devices, depending upon the company's requirements for protection of the information. (Firewalls typically use programs that segregate applications or entire computer systems from unauthorized access by telecommunications.) With technology and cost no longer a barrier to segregation of applications, information security should be playing a stronger role in the design of overall systems architectures and in the specification of ways to protect sensitive applications.

This stronger role will require that the initial requirements definition for applications include defining the requirements for security—a subject heretofore usually ignored until the application neared implementation. To do this, information security managers must not only create awareness of the need, but provide the policies, tools, and training to make it happen. The first of the tools needed is a means of classifying the sensitivity of information and application. It is beyond the scope of this chapter to delve into the details of checklists for sensitivity and/or applicable controls; but the basic tasks are these:

- Identify the need and importance of retaining confidentiality.
- Identify the criticality of the information to the business operation.
- Identify the criticality of integrity and authenticity to the business.
- Identify the need for availability of information and information processing resources.

These are not abstract tasks. A business unit manager should be able to roughly approximate the cost to the unit if, for example, the application were unavailable for one day, for two days, or for longer. (Many banks would be out of business if their transaction processing systems were unavailable for three days.) A manager should also be able to judge and approximate the damage if a competitor gained access to product design information or if information were corrupted and so created unusable results.

A 1993 study by the Information Systems Security Association found that information can be valued in one of three ways:

- Its value to the owners, authorized users, and unauthorized users
- Its commercial value, such as mailing lists or published references
- The cost to acquire, develop, or maintain it.

Managers must be responsible either for formally assuming the risk based on informed knowledge of the threats and the relative value of the information and application, or for approving the cost of appropriate controls and architecture. On the basis of these management judgments, information security professionals can recommend appropriate control designs and architectures for the application. Furthermore, information security will have additional means of proving its value to the corporation.

Dealing with the sensitivity issue is not confined to the initial design phase of new applications. As the operating environments of legacy systems change, they may become more vulnerable or their relative value for operations may change. Further, as desktop systems proliferate and users develop their own applications, sensitive information will move out of controlled environments. Maintaining adequate information security requires periodic reappraisal of the need for controls and the importance of applications to the business. Such reappraisals, also known as "risk screening," prioritize the need for establishing appropriate levels of control, and they communicate the nature of the issues and the scope of the problems to management.

If such reappraisals are conducted in the spirit of audits, they may encounter line management hostility. On the other hand, as Reappraisals, they provide the opportunity for a manager to make an informed decision about how the business is conducted and how it can recover from emergencies. The intent of the reappraisal is not to evaluate the controls in place—that may come later. The reappraisal is intended to redefine the requirement for controls in a changing business environment.

Reappraisals provide an excellent opportunity for demonstrating the value of information security to corporate executives. In fact, they ought to start at the top of the company, obtaining strategic direction through informing the CEO. The issues in reappraisals are well known to information security specialists. They include

- *What are the threats and risks?* How can information or information systems be harmed, and what are the potential consequences? What is the likelihood of occurrence?
- *Who or what is the enemy?* The enemy is people (employees and outsiders) and natural disasters.
- *What are the targets?* For industrial espionage, the primary targets are marketing information, product design information, and strategic

plans. For terrorists, the targets are computer centers and communications links.

- *Who "owns" the targets?* What managers and organizations own the information, and who are the custodians? Who has the managerial responsibility to protect the assets?
- *How vulnerable are the targets?* Use estimates based on current knowledge, not an audit of practices throughout the company.
- *What protective means may be used?* How can the information assets be shielded from harm? What are the approximate costs for protection?
- *What are the "corporate jewels?"* Of all the information assets, which are the most critical to continued successful operation of the company? What would the company "insure"?
- *How much loss can the company bear?* How much damage can be sustained while ensuring that the company remains viable? Which targets can be temporarily lost?
- *For which targets should we assume the risk of loss—which assets are not worth the cost of protecting?* For which applications or systems is it practical to reduce or eliminate controls? Do managers agree in this assumption of risk?

In the information security field, there are proponents of quantified risk analysis, in which cost of loss multiplied by probability of occurrence equals risk exposure, and proponents of subjective analysis, in which the probabilities are identified as "frequent," "likely," " remote," and so forth. Either method can have value if it results in appropriate management sensitivity to the issues and appropriate protective action. Since losses are frequently hidden to avoid unfavorable publicity, there are no valid statistics that support the probability of occurrence of various types of events. In the absence of reasonable measures of probability, many information security professionals prefer subjective evaluation to quantified risk analysis.

A top–down approach to reappraisals serves several purposes. It provides information security with a strategic view of the business requirement so that recommendations do not exceed the intent and expectations of the CEO. It encourages the cooperation of line management. It provides an opportunity to raise awareness at the highest level in the company. It provides a clear opportunity to demonstrate the value of information security to the company through a final report that highlights the protection gained for business assets. It provides a periodic opportunity to appraise the overall state of information security requirements and the controls in place. It offers a chance to show where money can be saved through assuming risk or changing systems architectures. Finally, it clearly positions information security as relating to the business needs of the company.

THE BUSINESS CASE—PRESERVING SHAREHOLDER VALUE

Given the previous discussion, it is now appropriate to examine how information security (or perhaps information security controls) fits into the framework of business needs.

The corporation, as a legal entity (and in the United States, the corporate officers), is responsible for the prudent management of corporate assets. This translates into a requirement for preserving and adding to shareholder value. It is therefore evident that all functions of the company must somehow be related to the shareholder value requirement.

The first derivative of this requirement is that management must create a strategy for the business(es) of the corporation. Supporting the strategy are the policies by which the business will be conducted, followed by the procedures by which the business will operate. Most businesses large enough to have an information security function long ago created the necessary strategies, policies, and procedures.

Policies and procedures for the corporation must be based on publicly accepted, sound business practices. In the United States and in many other countries, corporations are subject to an external audit that not only reviews conformance to policies and procedures, but ensures that such policies and procedures follow accepted practice. In the United States, failure to be certified by an external auditor may result in the inability of the corporation to trade its shares on the market—a severe penalty to shareholder value. Furthermore, failure to conform to accepted and legal practice may result in shareholder suits or legal penalties against corporate officers.

Information systems, whether computerized or paper-based, should conform to the policies and procedures of the company. Ultimately, corporate officers are responsible for the conduct of the business through its information systems, which represent corporate assets in several ways, among them the investments in hardware and software and the value to the business of the information itself.

In addition, for many corporations, the ability to function at all depends on the ability to manage, process, and access valid information in a timely manner. Shareholder value is clearly at stake if information processing or information is at risk.

The task of the information security function is to ensure the preservation of shareholder value (in the form of information assets) through prudent business practices consistent with the policies and procedures of the corporation. This function is carried out through the process of development and implementation of information security controls as described in the preceding sections. The chain of relationship to shareholder value is clear. It is the same chain that links corporate security, internal audit, health and safety, quality assurance, and environmental engineering to shareholder value.

Each of these organizations has a role in ensuring that proper policies and procedures are set in place and that the corporation protects shareholder value in conformance to legal requirements and prudent business practice. Similarly, each has a role at the detailed level of implementation as well as at the high level of policy setting. Each, to some extent, carries out an "invisible" task that is not recognized unless a major problem occurs, yet each makes a recognized contribution to preserving shareholder value.

ADDING TO SHAREHOLDER VALUE

The role of information security in the preservation of shareholder value is clear, but the question of adding to shareholder value must also be explored.

Previous efforts have attempted to focus on those instances in which information security adds value to the product or service of the company. Aside from computer hardware or software companies creating information security products or adding security features to products, these instances have been sparse. Some banks have attempted to attract new customers by emphasizing the "security" of their transactions and information in association with the security of customers' deposits. Some credit card issuers have touted the security features of their cards and of the supporting transaction processing system. Few of these efforts have been long-lived or have had major impact. Security is something that the customers of financial institutions take for granted. Major customer defections are related more to service considerations or the financial stability of the institution than to information security.

For the most part, information security specialists have missed the opportunity to ally themselves with the two greatest management trends of the 1990s—business process redesign and the growth of the extended enterprise or "virtual corporation."

Economic and competitive pressures on companies in the mid- to late-1980s forced many to focus on streamlining their business and operations. Initially, this streamlining led to a trend of business restructuring that resulted in concentration on the core business, often with the divesting by the corporations of subsidiaries that had been acquired or established in earlier trends toward vertical integration. The reduction in vertical integration freed the companies to choose suppliers that could provide components of the highest possible quality/cost mix.

Companies that took this route often became more competitive than they had been. However, a focus on the core business through restructuring was not enough to meet the continuing competitive pressures of a global economy. Something more was needed.

At first it appeared as if total quality management (TQM) would be the breakthrough that enhanced the competitive positions of the companies that adopted it. TQM clearly added to competitive strength by improving the quality of products and services. Unfortunately, several companies that won awards for quality as a result of TQM found that they could not take the awards to the bank. TQM addressed the satisfaction of customers, both internal and external, with the results of work (products or services), but too frequently it did not address inherent inefficiencies in the companies' operations. TQM brought into focus one fact that had been dormant since the days when industrial engineering lost its luster—that businesses are operated through processes.

Enter another trend, business process redesign (BPR). BPR is a methodology for transforming the business processes of an enterprise to achieve breakthroughs in the quality, responsiveness, flexibility, and cost of those processes in order to compete more effectively and efficiently in the market. (See Section V.)

The focus of BPR is first and foremost on designing an improved business process, which may then use information technology to enable its new functionality. When processes are redesigned with information technology used as an enabler for improved performance, they become reliant on the availability, integrity, and often the confidentiality of the information. In other words, without these key information security characteristics, the business function will not operate successfully, or may not operate at all.

Just as information systems have added shareholder value by supporting the implementation of redesigned business processes, information security also has added shareholder value by ensuring that the information systems can continue to meet their intended mission.

The consultants and analysts who supported companies' BPR efforts soon realized that, as a result of the connections in the value chain from suppliers through customers of the company, the business processes did not end at the companies' walls. The beginning step in meeting these expanded needs was the implementation of electronic data interchange (EDI) which served to speed communications and reduce paperwork (when implemented correctly). Again, although many companies now use EDI effectively, this proved to be only an interim solution.

In fact, some firms, such as the retailers and their suppliers previously mentioned, had quickly moved ahead of the EDI trend and linked their systems and users together. Similarly, major manufacturing companies moved to share product design information systems with suppliers so that the suppliers could design their components to meet the new product requirements. Plastic and polymer producers opened electronic mail links with their major customers and quickly moved beyond that to open product design specification files in an effort to speed new products to market. Generally, when a company outsources its information systems operation, it adds another supplier who may access its information for a variety of legitimate reasons. These are examples of true extension of the business process through the extended enterprise.

These examples, and the many others either implemented or in development, open up the company's information systems to the employees of other companies and the attendant risks. Information security departments have the responsibility and the challenge to enable the effective operation of the extended enterprise by ensuring that such new relationships and interconnectivity will not damage the information assets that enable the improvement.

Again, information security adds to shareholder value by enabling a safe extension of the company's environment to improve the ability of the company to meet competitive pressures.

While information security may be compared to health and safety, environmental engineering, and corporate security in terms of helping to preserve shareholder value, it is more akin to quality assurance in enabling the company to add to shareholder value.

CONCLUSION

This chapter has established a framework for thinking about ways to demonstrate the business value of information security. In part, the chapter also has addressed ways to increase the visibility of and improve the internal corporate image of the information security function.

Information security professionals need to do a better job of image building to achieve success in their mission. Awareness programs conducted by many information security groups have focused on threats, controls, and countermeasures; however, such programs have rarely (if ever) stressed the role of information security and/or the contribution it makes to the company.

Information security managers must change the way they approach their tasks if they are to gain the recognition they need to succeed. Information security managers must

- Gain a better understanding of the business of the company in order to relate their contributions to shareholder value in the minds of managers
- Gain an understanding of such techniques as business process redesign to identify the ways in which they can influence business processes and system and network architecture
- Associate information security controls with TQM so that the controls become embedded in business processes
- Develop methods for collecting and maintaining loss information from the company's experience

- Form alliances with other service groups in the company to become more effective and more visible
- Demonstrate the business case for information security as it applies to the company

Clearly, more work needs to be done in several areas. These include

- Defining clear relationships between established prudent business controls (such as accounting controls) and information security controls
- Establishing better methods for valuing information (and thus information security measures)
- Developing more accepted ways of demonstrating the value of threat avoidance
- Clarifying the cost-benefit relationship between information security costs and shareholder value
- Establishing clear relationships between information security, health and safety, environmental engineering, internal audit, quality assurance, and other corporate support activities
- Changing the image of information security to one of a conserver of and contributor to shareholder value

This chapter started with the observation that information security does not receive the recognition it deserves for its contribution to the corporation. Such recognition is not simply a matter of "proving the value" of information security. It is also a matter of access to the right levels of management, awareness on the part of corporate executives of the role that information security plays, and image. Perception is at least half of reality.

DISCUSSION TOPICS

- Do other methods exist for demonstrating the value of information security to the firm?
- How can senior management be convinced of the need for information security?
- Are there other names for the information security department that would be more illustrative of its functions and value?
- What are the roles and duties of information security?
- Consider the example of the petrochemical company given in this chapter. Are there other options than the ones described?

REFERENCE

1. Caldwell, B. "Rethinking Corporate Data Security: Security Czars Get Locked Out." *Information Week* (June 21, 1993): 16.

CHAPTER 12

Emerging Technology Impacts on Information Security

Maintaining the security of an organization's information assets becomes more difficult in this age of corporate restructuring and downsizing. Moreover, information security professionals are faced with a stream of new products and technologies that create both new threats and the potential for new defenses. This article explores the impacts of emerging technology on information security.

BACKGROUND

Information technology has changed the environment of information security

- From protecting information within the firm to protecting information in the extended enterprise
- From controlled offices and plants to a porous, multiconnected, global environment
- From limited access to intelligent devices to widespread access by increasingly computer-literate populations

And the pace of introduction of new information technology (IT) capabilities continues to create new threat possibilities. Corporate managers and their information security specialists need to be aware of these threats before adopting new technologies, so that they can take adequate countermeasures.

Information security is concerned with protecting the availability of information and information processing resources and the integrity and confidentiality of information. One or more of these functions may be threatened by the adoption of emerging technologies unless adequate protection is installed when new business applications are developed. Availability alone is a major issue. A 1993 survey of 450 Fortune 1000 IS executives by the New York research firm Find/SVP placed the cost of systems downtime in the United States at $4 billion per year with a loss of 37 million hours in worker productivity.[1] This is only part of the potential impact.

The application of information security methods has long been viewed as "insurance" against potential losses. Given that view, top management has applied the principle that one should not spend more for insurance than the potential loss might cost. When we purchase automobile insurance, we are doing the same thing, but we maintain our auto insurance continuously, knowing that another accident can occur, causing another loss.

In many cases, management is balancing information security costs against the potential for a *single* loss incident, rather than multiple incidents. This fallacious reasoning can lead to a failure to protect information assets continuously or to upgrade that protection as the technology changes and creates new opportunities for losses.

Those who intentionally damage or steal information also follow some basic economic principles. An amateur hacker may not place a specific value on his or her time and thus may be willing to put substantial effort into penetrating an information system. A professional will clearly place an implicit value on his or her time by seeking the easiest way to penetrate a system or by balancing potential profit against the time and effort necessary to carry out a crime. New technologies that create new (and possibly easier) ways to penetrate a system invite such professionals, as well as fail to deter the amateurs.

This chapter describes the potential threats and the opportunities for countermeasures that will arise during the coming years as a result of emerging information technologies.

NEW OPPORTUNITIES FOR DEFENSE

New technology holds opportunities for better means of protection and detection as well as threats. Many of the capabilities provided by technological developments will support defensive techniques for information or information processing facilities. Some of these are described in the following subsections.

Expert Systems, Neural Networks, and Mini-Supercomputers

Used individually or in combination, expert systems, neural networks, and mini-supercomputers may enable the detection of intrusion in information systems by (1) recognition of unusual behavior patterns on the part of the intruder, (2) configuration of the human interface to suit individual users and their permitted accesses, (3) detection of physical intrusion or emergencies by signal analysis of sensor input and pattern recognition, and (4) reconfiguration of networks and systems to maintain availability and circumvent failed components. In the near future, these techniques may be combined with closed-circuit video to authenticate authorized personnel by comparing digitally stored pictures to the faces of persons wishing to enter facilities. Several of these technologies may be adapted to the building of improved firewalls for systems.

Smart Cards or PCMCIA Cards

Used with card readers and carrying their own software and data, cards may enable authentication of the card owner through recognition of pressure, speed, and patterns of signatures; through questions about personal history (the answers to which are stored on the card); by comparison to a digitized picture of the owner; and/or by authentication of application access permission by cryptographic codes, access keys, and algorithms. By the late 1990s, if proven economically feasible, signature recognition or voice recognition capabilities may be used to limit access to pen-based hand-held computers to authorized users by recognition of the signature on login.

Personal Communications Numbers (PCNs)

PCNs, enabled by nationwide wireless data communications networks, permit a personal phone number to be assigned so that calls may reach an individual wherever in the United States he or she (and the instrument) is located. PCNs will permit additional authentication methods and will allow call-back techniques to work in a portable device environment.

Voice Recognition

Implementable along with continuous speech understanding, voice recognition may be used to authenticate users of voice input for inquiry systems in banking, brokerage, and other areas. By the year 2000 they may be used to limit access to hand-held computers to authorized users by recognition of the owner's voice on login.

Wireless Tokens

Wireless tokens, used as company identity badges, can enable pinpointing the location of employees on plant sites, monitoring restricted plant areas, and work check-in and check-out; they may also support paging capability for messages or hazard warnings.

Reducing Password Risks

The Obvious Password Utility System (OPUS) project at Purdue University has created a file compression technique that allows the checking of a proposed password against a list of prohibited passwords to take the same amount of time no matter how long the list. OPUS may allow prohibited password lists to be placed on small servers and improve password control so that systems are harder to crack.

Third-Party Authentication Methods

Systems like Kerberos and Sesame, available since 1992, provide a third-party authentication mechanism that operates in an open network environment, but does not permit access unless the user and the application are authenticated to each other by a separate, independent computer. ("Third-party" refers to a separate computer, not a legal entity.) Such systems may be a defense against threats caused by portable systems and open networks. Users of portable computers may call the third-party machine and request access to a specific application on the remote host. The Kerberos or the Sesame system authenticates the user to the application and the application to the user before permitting access.

NEW THREATS TO INFORMATION SECURITY

While we await new technology-based defensive measures, we must still deal with the present deployment of new technology and the threats implicit in that deployment. Some of the emerging technologies that will be deployed more extensively during the 1990s, the implicit threat potentials, and some defensive measures are described below.

Document Imaging Systems

The capabilities of document imaging systems include

- Reading and storing of images of paper documents
- Character recognition of text for abstracts or indexing
- Retrieval of stored documents by index entry
- Manipulation of stored images
- Appending notes to stored images (either text or voice)
- Workflow management tools to program the distribution of documents as action steps are needed

Workflow management is critical to taking full advantage of image processing for business process applications in which successive or parallel steps are required to process a document. Successful applications include loan processing, insurance application or claim processing, and many others that depend on moving documents through review and approval steps.

Image processing requires a mainframe or large server for processing any serious volume, but desktop and workstation versions exist for limited use. In addition, a full image processing system requires document readers (scanners), a local area network (LAN), workstations or personal computers, and laser printers for output. It is possible to operate image processing over a wide area network (WAN); however, because of the bandwidth required for reasonable response times, this is not usually done. As a result, most configurations are located within a single building or building complex.

In 1991, an insurance company installed an image processing system for processing claims. The system used a local area network attached to a minicomputer in the claims processing area. Some time later, as a result of a reorganization, one of the claims processing managers received a layoff notice. Embittered, the manager accessed the parameter-driven workflow management system and randomly realigned the processing steps into new sequences, reassigning them in an equally random fashion to the hundred or so claims processing clerks using the system. He then took the backup tapes, which were rotated weekly, and backed up the revised system files on all the tapes, replacing them in the tape cabinet. He did not steal any information, nor did he delete any information from the system. The next morning he called the personnel department and told them that he was ill and that they should send his final check to his home.

The cost to the insurance company was tens of thousands of dollars in clerical time wasted and professional and managerial time lost in finding and correcting the problem. Even worse were the weeks of delays in processing claims and handling the resultant complaint letters. No one at the company could estimate the loss of good will among its customer base.

The very techniques of workflow management that make image processing systems so effective are also their Achilles' heel. Potential threats may come from disruption of the workflow by unauthorized changes to sequence or approval levels in workflow management systems, by component failure, or by damage. Information contained on documents may be "stolen" by unauthorized copying (downloading of the image to the workstation) and release of document images by users of workstations. A more subtle threat is that it is possible to make undetectable changes to document images. This has already been done to produce digitized photographic replicas showing prominent peoples' heads united with bodies in compromising circumstances.

These threats raise issues that must be considered in the use of image processing technology. The legal status of stored images may be questioned in court because of the potential for undetectable change. In addition, there are the threats to the business from loss of confidentiality of documents; loss of availability of the system during working hours (when the business process becomes highly dependent on availability); damage to the integrity of the images and notes appended to them; and questions about the authenticity of stored documents.

Defensive measures to protect imaging systems include

- Frequent backup of the programs and data stored in secure areas
- Highly restricted access to workflow management programs combined with management review and approval of any parameter or other workflow changes prior to implementation
- Timely management of password controls and user profiles
- Periodic, unannounced audits of high-value or sensitive documents
- Restricted access to documents (some systems provide access control down to the document level)

Mini-Supercomputers

Massively parallel mini-supercomputers are capable of providing relatively inexpensive large capacity for such applications as signal processing, large-scale computation, image recognition processing, and neural network processing. They are generally designed to work as attached processors or in conjunction with workstations. Mini-supercomputers currently available can provide 4,096 processors for $85,000 or 8,192 processors for $150,000. They can interface to such devices as workstations, file servers, and local area networks.

These machines can be an inexpensive computational resource for cracking encryption codes or access codes to computers, so firms that own them are well advised to limit access control for resource use to authorized users. This is especially true if the processor is attached to a mainframe with wide area network connectivity. Such connectivity may allow unauthorized users to obtain access to the attached processor through the host machine.

Even without using a mini-supercomputer, but simply by stealing unauthorized time on conventional computers, a European hacker group in 1993 bragged that it had figured out the access codes to all the major North American telephone switches. This would allow them to make unlimited international telephones calls at no cost (or, if they were so inclined, to destroy the programming in the switches and deny service to millions of telephone users).

Defensive measures include:

- Restricted access and timely management of password controls
- Spot audits of access logs
- Firewalls

- Frequent comparisons of computer usage statistics to detect unusual increases

Neural Network Systems

Neural network systems are software (or hardware/software combinations) capable of heuristic learning within limited domains. Such systems are an outgrowth of artificial intelligence research and are currently available at different levels of capacity on systems ranging from personal computers to mainframes.

Using their heuristic learning capabilities, neural network systems can "learn" how to penetrate a network or computer system. Small systems were already in the hands of hobbyists and hackers by 1992. The capabilities of neural network programs will increase as the price/performance ratios of computers continue to improve and greater amounts of main memory and processing power become affordable for desktop machines.

Defensive measures for networks and computer systems include encrypted passwords, tokens, or other devices to make penetration more difficult, and frequent changing of passwords to increase the effort required for repetitive penetration.

Wireless Local Area Networks

Wireless LANs support connectivity of devices through radio frequency or infrared transmission between devices located in an office or an office building. Wireless LANs consist of a LAN controller and signal generators or receivers either attached to or embedded in devices. Wireless LANs have the advantage of allowing easy movement of connected devices so that office space can be reallocated or modified without regard to the constraints of hardwiring. They can connect all sizes of computers and some peripherals. As portable computers become more intensively used, wireless LANs can be easily connected to personal computers or workstations in the office for transmission of files in either direction.

Wireless LANs may be subject to signal interruption or message capture by unauthorized parties. Radio frequency LANs operate throughout the transmitting area and are therefore more vulnerable than infrared LANs which are line-of-sight only.

Major issues of concern with use of this technology pertain to retaining confidentiality and privacy of transmissions and business interruptions due to failures. But the potential also exists for other kinds of damage to wireless LAN users. For example, supermarkets have experimented with wireless terminals attached to shopping carts that detect where the shopper is located and then broadcast the specials on that aisle. As this technology is extended to inventory control and eventually to other functions in the store, it will not be long before some clever hacker finds a way to reduce his or her shopping costs and broadcasts the method over the underground networks.

Defenses against penetration of wireless systems are primarily based on the encryption of passwords and sensitive data.

Wide Area Network Radio Communications:

WAN radio communications enable hand-held or portable devices to access remote computers and exchange messages (including faxes). Wireless WANs may use satellite transmission through roof-mounted antennae or regional radio-telephone technology. Access to wireless WANs is supported by internal radio modems in notebook and hand-held computers or by wireless modems/pagers on PCMCIA cards for optional use.

Many users think that telephone land lines offer some protection from intrusion because wiretaps can often be detected and tapping into a fiber-optic line is impossible without temporarily interrupting service. Experience shows that most intrusions are logical, rather than physical, attacks on networks. Hackers typically break in through remote maintenance ports on PBXs, voice mail systems, or remote access features that permit travelers to place outgoing calls. In fact, in 1993 law enforcement officials indicted five computer hackers for breaking into the networks and computers of more than 10 firms, including Southwestern Bell, New York Telephone, Pacific Bell, U.S. West, TRW, and ITT. Damages probably amounted to millions of dollars.

The threat to information security from wireless WANs is that direct connectivity is no longer needed to "connect" to networks. Intruders may be able to fake legitimate calls once they determine access codes. Companies will need to consider such protective means as encryption for certain messages, limitations on the use of wireless WAN transmission for confidential material, and enforcement of encrypted password and user authentication controls. In most cases, protecting host systems is more critical than protecting remote or portable devices. Third-party authentication methods (described above) may be used to protect data or applications to the application level in otherwise "open" networks. In addition, where circumstances warrant, it is possible to build firewalls that, for example, permit only outbound file transfer from the host or only outbound file transfer originated internally. Firewalls may also permit host acceptance of inbound messages or file transfers only after challenge and response authentication.

Increased Use of Video-Conferencing

Travel costs for nonsales activities are of increasing concern to many companies. In many instances, the companies are not so much concerned about the costs of travel and subsistence but about the costs to the company of having key personnel away from their jobs. Crossing the United States or traveling to other countries for a one-day meeting can require a key employee to be away from his or her job for three days. Video-conferencing helps to reduce travel to trips that are essential for hands-on work. The capabilities of video-conferencing include slow-scan video for sharing documents and interactive video for conferencing.

Video-conference equipment now available sells for as little as $ 30,000 per installation. At that price, it is easy to see that saving a few trips a year can pay off quickly. However, video-conferencing is potentially vulnerable to penetration of phone switches to tap open lines and receive both ends of the conferencing transmissions.

Protection against line tapping requires additional equipment at both ends to scramble or encrypt communications during transmission. It further requires defining when to scramble communications, making users aware of the risks, and enforcing rules.

Embedded Systems

Embedding computers into mechanical devices was pioneered by the military for applications such as autopilots on aircraft and "smart" bombs and missiles. In the civil sector, process controls, robots, and automated machine tools were early applications. Now manufacturers are embedding intelligence and communications capabilities in products ranging from automobiles to microwave ovens. Computers from single-chip size to mini-size are being integrated into the equipment they direct. In factory automation systems, embedded systems are linked through local area networks to work area computers and corporate hosts.

There is increasing concern that penetration of host computers can lead to penetration of automated factory units, thereby interrupting productive capacity and creating potential hazards to workers. In the past, the need for information security controls rarely reached the factory floor or the products that were produced, since there was no connection to computers that resided on WANs. Now, however, firms must use techniques that enforce access controls and segment LANs on the factory floor to minimize the potential for unauthorized access through companies' host computers.

Furthermore, as the use of computers and communications devices in products increases, program bugs or device failure can endanger the customers who buy these products. The liability claims against maintenance mechanics and/or manufacturers can be substantial if accidents are traced to such failures. With computer-controlled medical equipment, potential liability from malfunction may be enormous.

Information security techniques must now extend to the environment in which embedded systems software is developed, to protect this software from corruption and the company from liability resulting from product failures. Security measures to ensure the integrity of embedded code must include restricted access to source and object code and periodic sample testing of products prior to shipment.

PCMCIA Cards

Personal computer memory card industry association (PCMCIA) cards are essentially small computer boards on which chips are mounted to provide memory and processing capacity. They can be inserted (docked) into slots on portable computers to add memory capacity, processing capacity, database capacity, or communications functions such as pagers, electronic mail, or fax transmission. PCMCIA cards now available contain up to 4 megabytes of storage; soon they are expected to provide up to 20 megabytes of storage in the same physical form.

Currently, removable disk drives, providing up to 20 megabytes of storage in a 1.8-inch drive, can be inserted into portable devices with double PCMCIA card slots.

The small format of PCMCIA cards and their use in portable devices such as notebook or hand-held computers makes then particularly vulnerable to theft or loss. Such theft or loss can cause business interruption or breach of confidentiality through loss of the information on the card. In addition, poor work habits such as failure to back up the data on another device can result in loss of the data if the card fails or if the host device fails in a manner that damages the card. Data recovery methods are notoriously nonexistent for small portable computers.

Security measures include

- Enforcing regular backup schedules for stored data
- Establishing procedures to store travelers' cards with valuables in hotel safety deposit boxes
- "Branding" the cards with nonremovable company logos and return addresses
- Encrypting the data and programs stored on the devices

Smart Cards

Smart cards, which consist of a computer chip mounted on a plastic card similar to a credit card, have limited intelligence and storage compared to PCMCIA cards. They are used increasingly for health records, debit cards, stored value cards, and so forth. Inserted into an access device (reader), smart cards may be used in pay telephones, transit systems, retail stores, health care offices, and ATMs, as well as used to supplement memory in hand-held computers.

The risks in this technology are the same as those in PCMCIA cards, but they may be exacerbated by the fact that smart cards can be carried in wallets along with credit cards. Since smart cards are used in stored value card systems, loss or damage to the card can deprive the owner of the value recorded.

PCMCIA cards and smart cards must contain means for authenticating users in order to protect against loss of confidentiality, privacy, or monetary value. Other protective means are the same for both for PCMCIA cards and smart cards.

Notebook and Palmtop Computers

Notebook and palmtop computers are small, portable PCs. These small computers often support wireless connection to LANs and WANs or modems providing communications capability for docking to desktop computers for up- or downloading of files (either data or programs). These devices have flat panel displays and may include microdisk storage with substantial capacity. Some models support hand writing input. Smart cards, PCMCIA cards, or flashcards may be used to add functionality or memory. By the end of the 1990s, it is expected that speech recognition capability will be available as a result of more powerful processors and greater memory capacity.

As with the cards that may be inserted in them, these machines are vulnerable to loss or theft as is the information contained in their memory. In addition, their use in public places or while visible to others (such as in air travel) may breach confidentiality or privacy.

It is vital that companies establish information security guidelines for use of these machines as they become ubiquitous. Such guidelines should include means for authentication of the user to the device before it can be used, etching or otherwise imprinting the owner's name indelibly onto the machine, and rules for protected storage of the machine when it is not in the user's possession (as in travel or at hotels). One possible problem is that most hotel safes do not have deposit boxes large enough to hold notebook computers.

Portable computers combined with communications capability may create the single largest area of information security exposure in the future. Portable computers will be ubiquitous and they will go wherever the user goes. Scenarios of business use are stressing advantages, but not security issues. Portable computers are used in many business functions, including marketing, distribution field service, public safety, health care, transportation, financial services, publishing, wholesale and retail sales, insurance sales, and others. As the use of portable computers spreads, the opportunities for information loss or damage increase. Table 12.1 presents some ways that portable computers will be used in the 1990s; these scenarios

Table 12.1.   Business Uses for Portable Computers

Industry or Function	Application	Benefits
Marketing	Track status of promotions Identify purchase influencers and imminence of decision Prepare reports on site	Better information on sales activities Reports get done more quickly
Distribution	Bill-of-lading data and calculations Delivery and field sales data collection Entering and tracking of parcel data	More timely information on field operations Better customer service
Field service	Remote access to parts catalog and availability Troubleshooting support Repair handbooks Scheduling and dispatching Service records Payment and receipt records	Better service to customer More efficient scheduling
Public safety	Dispatch instructions Police license and warrant checks Building layout information Paramedic diagnosis and treatment support	Faster emergency response Identification, apprehension of criminals Improved safety for emergency personnel Better treatment, lives saved
Transportation	Airline and train schedules Reservations Rental car check-in and receipt generation Report graffiti and damage Monitoring on-time performance	Convenience to customers Replaces paper forms and records More timely information

Table 12.1. *Continued*

Industry or Function	Application	Benefits
Financial services	Stock exchange floor trader support	More accurate records Reduced risk of fraud
Publishing	Electronic books and references (dictionaries, encyclopedias, atlases, parts catalogs, maintenance manuals)	Flexible retrieval Compact size
Travel and entertainment	Language translators, travel guides, dictionaries, and spelling checkers Hotel and restaurant reservations	Personal convenience to travelers
Wholesale sales	Recording sales results Sending results to corporate host Receiving updates on product prices and availability	More accurate and timely information both in the field and at corporate headquarters Unnecessary phone contacts eliminated Paperwork cut More productive use of staff
Retail sales	Capture sales and demographic data Update of inventory data	Assessment of promotional results Tighter control over field operations
Insurance	Access to corporate data for quotes Performing complex rate calculations	Quicker quotations to customers

show that almost every business will make use of the technology and be vulnerable to the implicit threats.

Portable computers, combined with communications that permit access to company databases, will require companies to adopt protective techniques to protect information bases from external access and to avoid the potential for aggregation of intelligence from repeated access. These techniques are in addition to those used to avoid loss of confidentiality and privacy by device theft and business interruption through device failure, loss, or theft.

New uses create new business vulnerabilities. New hospitals, for example, are being designed with "patient-centered" systems in which the services are brought to the patient (to the extent possible) rather than the patient being moved from one laboratory to another. This approach requires the installation of local area networks throughout the hospital so that specialized terminals or diagnostic devices can be connected to the computers that process the data collected. Hand-held computers may be moved with the patient or carried by attendants and plugged into the LAN to access patient records or doctors' orders. With such a system, it is easy to anticipate abuses ranging from illegal access to patient information to illegal dispensing of drugs to unauthorized persons.

Combinations of all the protective approaches described here must be applied to the use of portable devices and their connectivity to host machines.

CONCLUSION

The good guys can win, but we need to stay ahead by ensuring that information security specialists keep abreast of technology advances, anticipate the potential threats and vulnerabilities, and develop the protective measures in advance. This will only happen if top management is aware of the potential threats implicit in the use of new technology. In well-run systems development functions, information security specialists are consulted during the specification and design phases to ensure that adequate provisions are made for the security of information in applications. Information security specialists must be aware of the potential threats implicit in the adoption of new technologies, and of the defensive measures available, in order to critique the design of new applications and to inform senior management of hazards.

In fact, the information security field may itself be facing a major paradigm shift. The combination of advanced computer capabilities and communications is making information available to corporate executives and managers on an unprecedented scale. In the medical profession, malpractice suits have been won on the grounds that treatment information was available to a doctor and the doctor did not make use of it. In the same way, the availability of information mandates its use by decision makers. Corporate officers could find that they are no longer just liable for prudent protection of the company's information assets, but are liable as well for prudent use of the information available to the firm in order to protect its customers and employees. Such conditions may dramatically alter the way systems are designed and information is used. Protecting the firm from loss arising from information processing may take on a completely new dimension.

DISCUSSION TOPICS

- What other vulnerabilities may occur as a result of the introduction of new technologies?
- What other protective measures have been or can be developed?
- Have the forecasts in this chapter been realized
- What are some of the social implications of the system vulnerabilities described?
- What legislation or court decisions have influenced the manner in which new technologies are used by business?
- Has the increased use of embedded systems influenced the value of information security to the firm?

REFERENCE

1. "The True Cost of Downtime." *Information Week* (August 3, 1992): 13.

CHAPTER 13

Managing Information Security in Distributed Computing Environments

This chapter sets forth the services that must be performed to preserve information security and how responsibility for performing them should be allocated through the organization in a distributed environment or through one that is outsourcing its communications or processing facilities. The chapter also provides a basis for estimating the cost of implementing information security in these environments.

BASIC PREMISES

As information systems become increasingly distributed across organizational and geographic boundaries, the task of ensuring information security becomes more complex. In addition to the distribution of information systems, information security managers also face the challenges presented by the outsourcing of network management and operation, computer operations, and/or applications development. At the same time, many companies are reluctant to increase the size of their information security organization to offset the greater demands on its services. If information security is to be maintained at levels adequate to protect the company, information security managers must find new ways to delegate responsibility for maintaining the availability of information and information processing resources, ensuring the integrity of information, and protecting the confidentiality of information.

As techniques in information security advance, responsibilities must also include maintaining the usefulness of information (information utility) as well as its availability and ensuring the authenticity of information as well as its integrity. This chapter analyzes the required functions and suggests how the responsibility may be delegated throughout a company that has significantly decentralized its information systems resources.

The concepts in this article are founded on two corollaries to the basic premise of *assignment of accountability*. The first corollary is that control will only work if a company clearly defines the functional responsibilities of the resource providers (such as network management and computer operations) and users; explicitly assigns these responsibilities; and acquires the necessary skills or skilled personnel to implement security policies, procedures, and tools appropriate to maintain the level of information security required by the company. Furthermore, in the case of outsourcing, any delegated responsibilities must be explicitly set forth in the outsourcing contract. (See Chapter 9.)

The second corollary is that of information ownership. For all information or information processing facilities, a company must be able to identify an "owner" to whom responsibility may be assigned and who is capable of making appropriate decisions regarding information security. With outsourced information systems facilities, both the basic principle of ownership and U. S. legal requirements on corporate officers to protect corporate assets dictate that responsibility for information security cannot be divested. This means that, at most, only the responsibility for availability can be contractually delegated.

The organization of responsibility for information security may be considered as a matrix of functions arrayed against the responsible organizational units of the company. Such an array, the *security responsibility matrix*, is presented later in the chapter.

INFORMATION SECURITY SERVICES REQUIRED

The 10 services performed to develop and maintain information security are described in the following paragraphs.

1. *Policy and procedure development.* Policy and general procedure development must take place prior to detailed planning for information security, in order to provide a framework for evaluation, planning, and implementation of safeguards. Policy development includes the creation of security policy and procedures, the establishment of the necessary organizational components to support security policy, and the assignment of the responsibilities to ensure that policy is carried out.

2. *Employee security training, motivation, and awareness.* Compliance with security policy requires that the company continually make employees aware of potential threats and of their responsibilities to safeguard infor-

mation. Furthermore, specific individuals such as systems analysts, security coordinators, and computer or telecommunications operators must be trained to design or operate appropriate security controls for applications.

3.   *Establishment of security facilities and security architectures.* The computer-based tools and control systems to be used must be selected, implemented, maintained, and upgraded as necessary to meet the company's needs. In addition, those persons—such as systems analysts, programmers, and database administrators—who will use the tools, must be trained in the use of the tools provided and in any modifications to those tools.

4.   *Security development for applications.* As applications are acquired, developed, modified, or reviewed for security policy and standards conformance, the specific types of security controls must be designated and the control parameters specified. As applications evolve and are modified, and as the organizations that may access the application databases change, security requirements must be revisited to ensure that they remain consistent with application requirements. In addition, the procedures for implementing controls for applications must be developed and published, and the responsibility for control must be assigned.

5.   *Ongoing operational administration and control.* Control procedures must be implemented and managed. These procedures include password administration, access approval, file retention and backup, and similar activities that extend throughout the life of the application or system. This responsibility is divided so as to support the requirements for network availability, information confidentiality and integrity, and resource availability.

6.   *Procedural advisory services.* During every part of the application life cycle, from initial conception to ongoing operation, developers, application owners, and system operators may require advice on the appropriate use of security techniques or on potential exceptions to security policy.

7.   *Technical advisory services.* Application developers and system operators must have a reliable source of information and advice for design and operation of applications. In general, system developers do not continually work with the security aspects of applications; therefore, they will require advice when they do.

8.   *Emergency response support.* In the event of a security breach, such as penetration of computers on the network or introduction of a virus, a skilled quick-response capability is necessary. Such capability is required to limit the damage and assist with recovery.

9.   *Compliance monitoring.* Periodic audits and testing for compliance with corporate policy are necessary to ensure continual compliance. Only regular testing can ensure that the network and all connected facilities remain secure to the extent the company requires.

10. *Public relations.* In the event that public announcements relating to information security must be made, only authorized and designated personnel should be permitted to represent the company and its position to the press or other external inquirers. While this service is clearly recognized, it is not included in the matrix.

Other services. Other services may be performed by the organization that develops policies and procedures, with the assigned assistance of other organizations or individuals. These services, also not specified in the matrix, include

- Development and promulgation of information security standards
- Reporting and investigation of loss incidents or security violations
- Recommendation of penalties or awards
- Security reviews
- Liaison with human resources, insurance companies, corporate security, facilities management, and law enforcement agencies

ORGANIZATIONS RESPONSIBLE

The organizational units with responsibility for carrying out a corporate information security program span the entire company. Companies have slightly differing organizational structures; however, most will have counterparts to the organizations described below. In some cases, these organizations may be combined—for example, network and computer operations may reside in the same organization. However, since their scope of responsibility may differ and occasionally one or both may be outsourced, they are presented separately. A brief definition of each of the organizational units follows.

Network providers. These organizations manage voice and data networks and are responsible for supporting all wide area network connectivity. In some organizations, the network provider provides technical support for local area networks as well.

Application owners. These are the managers of business units and organizations that are responsible for the acquisition, development, and maintenance of applications and their databases. In cases where ownership cannot be specifically attached to an organizational unit, such as for electronic mail, an application owner must be assigned by company management. Application owners should be responsible for ensuring the integrity and confidentiality of information transmitted through the network through application-level cryptography or other technologies for appropriate applications.

Application developers. These are organizations consisting of systems analysts and programmers who acquire, develop, and maintain or enhance applications at the request of the application owner.

System operators (custodians). These are the persons or organizations responsible for the operation of the computers on which the applications reside. Where applications and databases reside on a computer operated by a functional unit within the application owner's organization, the responsibility is clear. Where applications and databases from various owners reside on a single computer or complex of computers, the system operator (or custodian) is the organization that operates the data center.

Several functions, such as access-control software administration support and the development of technical security standards and controls, should reside within the largest or most centralized system-operating organization in order to ensure company-wide coverage. (In companies that have implemented comprehensive client-server architectures and eliminated centralized mainframe-based operations, this role must be adopted by some centralized or regionalized technical support organization in order to ensure standardization and to minimize cost.) The primary focus of *technical information security function* (TISF) units is to provide security functionality to all intelligent devices connected to the network. They are responsible for

- Providing and maintaining technical security control utilities for centralized information systems resources (such as the RACF, ACF2, and Top Secret control systems now available)
- Selecting and providing security control tools for distributed computers and intelligent devices
- Supporting the security administration of user IDs, passwords, and tokens (although actual administration may be decentralized)
- Developing recommendations for technical control standards to be submitted to the information security standards process
- Developing recommendations for products that meet information security control standards and the company's operating environments
- Maintaining technical security expertise and providing consulting to other organizations requiring assistance with technical information security problems and controls (such as encryption) that are beyond the expertise of the requesting units
- Acting as the information security coordinator for the data processing organization

Corporate information security function (CISF). This organization generally resides at a corporate level. There are many variations in reporting relationships for this unit, including being a part of the overall security function or reporting to the Chief Information Officer (CIO). It has responsibility for coordinating a company-wide information security program and its manager should be responsible for overall program coordination. The unit should perform the following:

- Ensure that information security policy, procedures, and standards are complete and correct.

- Facilitate identification of information asset ownership and sensitivity classifications of applications or information by owners.
- Advise senior management of information security issues affecting the corporation.
- Establish and coordinate the process of setting information security standards by creating a corporate information security standards document that defines program elements, responsibilities, information/organizational relationships, information-sensitivity classification, and high-level control requirements. The document should have appropriate references to the information systems standards document and a section that identifies specific technical and procedural controls for information security in various types of information systems environments.
- Provide information security training and support to the group coordinators.
- Establish and sustain a corporate-wide information security awareness program.

Security coordinators. The function of security coordinator should be established for any business unit that is an application owner. Security coordinators should be responsible for

- Introducing to CISF information security issues raised within that business unit and taking positions on information security issues on behalf of that unit
- Representing the corporate information security program to that business unit (and vice versa); being familiar with information security policy, standards, and processes
- Conducting an information security awareness program within that business unit
- Reporting loss incidents and security violations
- Assisting group management in classifying information assets and identifying their ownership, reviewing security controls in the systems and application development processes, applying control standards, conducting risk acceptance procedures, acting as liaison to other information security units

Security coordinators should report to the senior managers of business units so that the unit's interests are represented and the position is recognized within the unit as having unit-wide responsibilities and authority. Each company needs to determine which business units will require this position. (For example, an information-intensive operation may require smaller units at lower organizational levels to have a security coordinator, while a less information-intensive operation may require a greater scope of operation for a security coordinator at a higher level.) When a comprehensive information security program is being implemented, this position needs to be designated through the lowest appropriate organizational levels. Once the program has been established, the position is usually part-time at lower levels and full-time in major strategic business unit.

Internal Audit. The internal audit organization is responsible for auditing all organizational units (other than itself) for compliance to corporate policy.

Computer emergency response team (CERT). This is a small, highly specialized group capable of responding to security emergencies throughout the company's network. It usually resides in the network provider's or the CIO's organization in order to serve the entire company. In addition to the permanent CERT, there may be designated emergency response teams to deal with particular types of emergencies, for example, natural disasters.

PERSONNEL COSTS

The costs associated with implementation of adequate security are a significant consideration to any business. Since security hardware and software devices vary considerably in costs, and since the focus of this article is on organization, the security responsibility matrix (Table 13.1) is annotated to estimate personnel costs associated with the performance of particular functions. Most of these costs are related either to the number of users or to the number of applications, whereas hardware and software costs are related to installed systems.

The estimates provided in the responsibility matrix are based on broad generalizations from experience and are not a substitute for detailed examination. Costs may change over time as new technologies or security tools are introduced. These estimates may be used to understand the current parameters of expected cost for distributing information security responsibility.

Costs for maintaining information security vary widely by company. The extent of this variation was illustrated in a 1990 survey by SRI International for the International Information Integrity Institute.[1] This survey showed that manufacturing companies that were members of the International Information Integrity Institute supported between 7,000 to 150,000 user IDs. Although the cost of administration and maintenance of information security is substantially a function of the number of users of the network's resources, it would seem that some cost ratios or relationships could be derived from a survey. This has not proved to be true.

The major problem in arriving at comparable costs is the difference in internal cost structures of network-using companies. These differences are illustrated by the following anecdotal observations.

As of 1992, Toyota, in Japan, used personal computers and workstations for engineering and design in a ratio of one PC or workstation for every two to four engineers. In contrast, Western companies generally have a one-to-one ratio. Access to network resources at Toyota was controlled only by login passwords as the Japanese attitude toward security was conditioned by a homogeneous population, low personnel turnover, and a culture that appears to inhibit criminal action (although some authorities believe that white collar crime in Japan has been substantially underreported). As a result, the cost of security administration was low. As Toyota and other Japanese firms move their network connections into western countries, however, they are starting to rethink their practices.

Chevron, with one of the largest networks in the United States supporting not only its internal operations but also links to every Chevron service station, operates its information systems through a wholly owned, "profit-making" subsidiary whose exclusive customer is Chevron Corporation. As a result, Chevron's cost structure includes all the general and administrative costs associated with running an independent business. In this case, the base costs against which network security costs are measured differ from those of companies that operate their information systems as a part of the internal structure.

Bank of America (like most other banks) requires a high level of security for its transaction processing systems. As these applications (and their ownership) are centralized, Bank of America is centrally administering its information security functions. The costs of centrally administered functions are naturally lower, compared to network costs, than those of decentralized ownership and administration.

THE RESPONSIBILITY MATRIX

The security responsibility matrix illustrated in Table 13.1 sets forth the services required to maintain information security throughout a network of distributed processing systems; the nominal organizations that must support these functions; and the personnel costs associated with the recommendations given in this chapter.

The matrix outlines recommended distribution of responsibilities for information security services. In many instances, an organization that bears specific responsibilities, such as an application owner, does not have all the resources or skills necessary to carry out those responsibilities. In such cases, the organization bearing primary responsibility is designated by a "P" in the appropriate matrix cell. The organizations that support the organizations with primary responsibilities are designated by an "S." Several activities require coordination among various groups. Since such coordination must be designated by policies and procedures that need to be developed by each company, the coordination activity is not shown in the matrix. The footnotes add explanatory material for the matrix cells.

Table 13.1. Security Responsibility Matrix

Services Required	Organizations Responsible						
	Network Provider	Application Owner	Application Developer	System Operator	Corporate Information Security	Security Coordinator	Internal Audit
Policy and procedure development	S[1]			S[1]	P[1] 2–3 EFTS		S[1] Advisory time only
Employee security training and awareness					P[1,2,3] 2–3 EFTS	S[4] 1.0 EFTS per 1,000–1,200 users	
Establishment of security facilities	P[5] Installation: 0.2 EFTS per system Training: 1.0 EFTS per 500 analyst/programmers		S[3] 1 day per analyst/programmer per year				S[6] Advisory time only
Security development for applications		P[6] No estimate	S[7] No estimate	S[7] No estimate	S[1,7] No estimate		

P—primary responsibility; S—support responsibility; EFTS—equivalent full-time staff.

Table 13.1. Security Responsibility Matrix *Continued*

				Organizations Responsible			
Services Required	Network Provider	Application Owner	Application Developer	System Operator	Corporate Information Security	Security Coordinator	Internal Audit

Ongoing operational administration and control:

Services Required	Network Provider	Application Owner	Application Developer	System Operator	Corporate Information Security	Security Coordinator	Internal Audit
Network availability	P[8] No additional effort			S[8] No additional effort		S[8,9] No additional effort	
Information confidentiality and integrity		P[10] 1.0 EFTS–administrator per 3,000–3,500 users 0.5 EFT–clerical per 3,000–3,500 users	S[10] 1.0 EFTS–administrator per 3,000–3,500 users 0.5 EFTS–clerical per 3,000–3,500 users	S[10] 1.0 EFTS–administrator per 3,000–3,500 users 0.5 EFTS–clerical per 3,000–3,500 users		S[4] 1.0 EFTS per 1,000–1,200 users	
Resource availability			S[11] No additional effort	P[11] No additional effort			
Procedural advisory services					P[1]	S[4,10]	

1. None of the CISF activities individually represents full-time work. In particular, if training is normally conducted by the human resources department, it may only be necessary for the CISF to develop the courseware for the regular training staff. As a result of the levels of effort involved in each of the CISF services, the combined estimates for all services have been indicated only in the primary cell and represent requirements of a major multinational company. For smaller companies, this estimate should be reduced. Network providers, system operators and internal audit provide information to the CISF or review proposed policies and procedures. For these groups, such activities consist of a few person-weeks per year on the part of existing staff. They are therefore not estimated. The establishment of policy requires corporate management approval, which is also not noted.

2. Employee security training will need to be coordinated with human resources training activities.

3. The estimate of one day per analyst/programmer devoted to training assumes that most application developers will be trained in classes of two to four hours' duration. On the other hand, database administrators may require up to one week of training if they are not currently trained on access control software use.

4. A primary security coordinator would ordinarily be dedicated full-time for a major division or strategic business unit. Most of the total effort, however, would be conducted by various existing staff members, who would be assigned part-time information security responsibility and would report indirectly to the security coordinator. As a result, the additional EFTS required might be limited to the large-business-unit coordinators. This function would be involved in password administration, access control administration, violation reporting and resolution, education and awareness training, and security coordinating activities. Most of these services have been addressed in other activities. Depending on the geographic distribution of the service and the sensitivity of the information being protected, the full-time equivalent of one security coordinator should be able to support 1,000 to 1,200 users.

5. Installation of access control software (for example, RACF, RACF or ACF2 on IBM mainframes) requires only two to three days of system programmer time per central processor. Full implementation, which entails configuration of the user and resource structure, is primarily the responsibility of access control administrative personnel and application owners. The time required for the administrative personnel depends on their skills, the administrative tools they have to use, and the complexity of the protected environment. Other than product education, not much additional system programmer time is required. The time required for installation of access control software on other than IBM systems is not significantly different from that required for RACF or ACF2 installation. Lack of familiarity, however, may require additional system programmer education for the initial installations.

For maintenance of the access control software, the system programmer's role is only the application of updates, such as new releases and program temporary fixes (PTFs), including authorized program analysis reports (APARs). One system programmer should be able to maintain RACF, for example, on two to three similar systems on a part-time basis. The other function the system programmer may carry out is the modification of RACF exits to customize the product to a specific operational environment, or to compensate for anomalies in the operating environment. The anticipated time for this effort may be from three weeks to three months of effort per exit modification. This time includes planning, testing on a test system, logging of exit effect on the system without failure, adjusting exit code, and moving to production.

For an installation that does not utilize the exits to customize the access control software, the anticipated system programmer manpower should not exceed two person-months per system per year.

Table 13.1. Security Responsibility Matrix *Continued*

	Organizations Responsible						
Services Required	Network Provider	Application Owner	Application Developer	System Operator	Corporate Information Security	Security Coordinator	Internal Audit
Technical advisory services	P[12] No additional effort						
Emergency response support	P[13]			S[14] 1.0 EFTS for the company			
Compliance monitoring	S[13]		S[15] Occasional support as required		S[1,15] Occasional support as required		P[15] 1.0 EFTS per 15–20 applications

Existing staff members knowledgeable about the access control software and access control strategy should be able to spend part of their time training and providing technical support to application programmers and analysts or computer operators. These staff members may be, but do not have to be, system programmers. Twenty percent of one EFTS per 100 supported personnel time is required.

Depending on the physical proximity of the trainer to the staff that must be trained, estimated training costs, excluding the initial time necessary to prepare training materials, is about one person-year per per 500 supported personnel. Typically this includes ad hoc technical advisory services usually provided through telephone contact or electronic mail.

When planning costs, one should remember that many computers may already have installed access control software. This estimate should be applied only to those computers that do not currently have installed access control software and to the training of analyst/programmers who have not used this software.

Information security utilities for protecting client-server systems or distributed minicomputers are immature to nonexistent. Some utilities, such as programs that protect PCs against viruses, can be distributed over networks and downloaded from a central unit to PCs attached to local area networks. This capability reduces installation time substantially.

The use of tokens and token readers on personal computers or workstations requires installation time for each unit thus protected.

Installation of third-party authentication systems for open networks, such as Kerberos or Sesame, has not been extensive enough at this writing to develop a reasonable estimate of implementation time.

6. Internal audit, in its role of ensuring compliance, may selectively choose to review installation procedures, training course material, and other aspects of installation or security training.

7. All activities relating to security for applications cannot be estimated, as they are a function of the number of applications developed or modified, the nature of those applications, and the number of databases to be accessed.

8. It is presumed that network providers support network availability as a primary function. Availability is one of the principal security aspects addressed in any strategy.

9. In the event of loss of network availability, it is assumed that the security coordinators whose groups are affected may be consulted during recovery procedures. This may be a shift in responsibility from the current recovery procedures; however, someone must provide this function.

10. In a decentralized organization where application owners are responsible for control of access to their applications, it is expected that the administration of access permissions will be managed within the user organization. Although the application owner is the responsible member of management, it is also expected that the actual authorization effort will be delegated within that organization.

Access to computing resources must be controlled on the basis of the level of sensitivity of the information in the resource being accessed. In a closed network environment, where all applications are of the same level of sensitivity and all users are permitted to access any application database, administration may be relatively simple, being limited to password control.

In an open network environment, or where sensitive applications share resources with nonsensitive applications, or in an outsourcing environment where the applications of different companies may share the same complex of equipment, security administration will be more complex. Sensitive resources or applications must be protected from unauthorized access through user profiles that restrict access or that authorize access appropriately. Such protective measures will be required, for example, as manufacturing companies' design activities (and perhaps their engineering activities) move toward collocation of their own and vendor/supplier employees to facilitate their work. This will place a heavier burden on security functions than now exists in many companies.

Creating a new user ID and setting up an access profile to the system should require 30 to 35 minutes of an administrator's time. Normally, one to two people are involved in setting up user IDs, defining resources to the system, and periodically auditing users to reconcile with authorization records. The number of high-level generic profiles that must be administered can affect the resource requirements. The application owner, also dependent on the auditing requirements, must periodically audit or have audited both the user ID and the resource access profiles. This may take from two to five person-days of effort per year if the profiles have been effectively managed during the year.

If this activity is relatively centralized, one administrator should be able to handle the work load for about 3,000 to 3,500 user IDs. Since by its nature, a substantial part of the recordkeeping for access permissions is clerical, approximately half of a clerk's time should also be allocated to this function.

If a company elects to decentralize security administration, which appears more practical from the manner in which computing, systems development, and network management is organized, the size of the application user bases or organizational constraints may restrict the range of user IDs an administrator can manage.

Table 13.1. Security Responsibility Matrix *Continued*

In addition to the above, file retention and backup require about 1.5 full-time person equivalents for each system complex. Duties involve running backup and maintaining control of offsite storage status as a part of an overall business continuity plan. It is assumed that these activities currently take place in most companies, so no additional personnel are required.

11. Resource availability means ensuring that computing facilities and application software/databases are operational as required by the using organization. This function is currently performed for each computing center by system operators and support staff. The identification of resource availability in the responsibility matrix is for completeness of the matrix. In an outsourcing environment, maintenance of specified levels of availability would normally be agreed on contractually.

12. Technical advisory services are needed only in response to requests and should usually be accommodated by telephone or electronic messaging. These duties fall within the scope of the training and installation estimates for staff unless a company has unusual requirements.

13. The emergency response team is expected to reside in the network provider's or the chief information officer's organization in order to have an overall corporate view.

14. The people responding to viruses or systems penetration are specialists in this area—but only on a part-time basis. At least one person at each major data center should be an expert on viruses or penetration or both. Because of the different environments, both a mainframe and a small-systems expert are required. Knowledgeable operations experts and system programmers should be available to provide backup and technical support when needed. Security coordinators should be knowledgeable enough about these issues to be the first line of review and reaction. Approximately three weeks of education per expert per year is needed to maintain the required level of competence. The amount of time spent on individual incidents will vary and depends on the degree and type of infection or the severity of penetration. The total personnel time expended on this activity should not exceed one person-year for most large companies.

15. One auditor should be assigned from two to four major application suites (an average of five main programs). This ratio of responsibility should result in most applications being audited approximately every two years or when major changes are made to them. In addition, each system complex should have an auditor assigned to audit the operating systems and other control software, such as CICS, DB2, communication control programs, and messaging programs. It is reasonable to estimate that one full-time information systems auditor will be able to conduct audits for each 15 to 20 applications annually.

OTHER FACTORS AFFECTING COST

In addition to the information provided in the matrix and in its notes and references, several other factors affect the cost of information security. These factors are discussed below.

Ownership. Ownership definition is a prerequisite to determining the degree of complexity of access control and administration. A major consideration in the implementation of access control software is who will be responsible for what. Clarifying ownership first can have significant benefits for the decision process required during implementation.

Administrative automation. Automation of administrative functions such as user ID and access authority reviews reduces the number of administrators required. For example, screens designed to permit easy entry of user profiles and the transfer of these profiles to the access authorization database can substantially reduce the administrative overhead associated with the authorization process. Generic profiles established for classes of workers or job functions can also aid in reducing administrative costs.

Resource definition automation. Automation of user/resource definition via interactive system productivity facility (ISPF) or similar tools also lowers administrative overhead for either centralized or decentralized administration. Conceivably, with the right kind of automation support, the input could be entered directly by the user's manager, with appropriate approvals handled online.

Naming conventions. The naming conventions used by the organization (the number of high-level qualifiers) affects the level of effort necessary for administration. Next to determination of ownership, this issue can cause the most difficulty in initial implementation if not properly addressed beforehand.

Factors: support versus demand. Estimates of cost for security administration are subject to a large number of variables and are therefore of questionable reliability without detailed examination of those variables, some of which are

- *Users:* number of groups, users, job names
- *Resources:* generic profiles, data sets, terminals, transaction names, applications, volumes
- *Security software database:* number of copies of resource access control facility (RACF), access control facility (ACF), or Top Secret security databases; level of duplication of profiles
- *Reporting:* centralized versus decentralized reporting and resolution, scope of reports
- *Geography:* locations of systems, users, resources

RISK ACCEPTANCE PROCESS

As described above, a basic premise of risk acceptance is to keep control of security in the hands of business managers. This ensures that security serves the corporation's business needs and is not arbitrarily pursued for its own sake. It is a clearly stated risk acceptance process that ensures that this principle is maintained.

Once an information asset and its owner have been identified and a control standard requirement has been identified, the information owner may legitimately decide not to implement the control, provided that he or she has documented a valid business justification for that decision. (Suppose that a control standard requires "company confidential" information to be encrypted for transmission through a network, but the cost of providing that encryption is greater than any money the corporation would lose if the confidential information were exposed to unauthorized view.) This represents the old insurance principle that it is not good business judgment to spend more to protect an asset than the asset is worth.

The decision to accept the risk and not implement the standard control must be made according to a structured process. This process ensures that the manager understands the level of risk, has a sufficient reason for accepting the risk, is the appropriate manager for the information asset in question, and has the fiscal authority for financial risk equal to that being accepted. (A manager authorized to sign for $500 purchases should not accept risks that could cost the corporation $500 million.)

Risk acceptance typically is approved only after a control review conducted according to corporate policies and procedures. It involves the business manager of the activity in which the control is to be implemented, the business manager who owns the information asset in question, and the information security coordinator of that business group. The approval of risk acceptance should be documented and reported to the approving manager's senior manager as well as to the CISF.

Correctly executed risk acceptance procedures justify variance from the standard control, yet keep the risk within the scope of company policy. They also ensure that when a decision is made against security controls, it is not made for expediency's sake but out of a sound business judgment of risks and costs, keeping security in the service of business.

INFORMATION SECURITY POLICY CONSIDERATIONS

Policies should identify the specific roles and responsibilities of organizational entities relative to applications and information assets, as described in the matrix (Table 13.1).

Under the allocation of responsibilities described, the application owner makes all the decisions about the security of the applications and information assets that support the owner's business function. However, these decisions are made within the context of an overall information security program structure that defines levels of sensitivity, organizational responsibilities, control standards, and risk acceptance procedures.

Policies also need to define classes of sensitivity by name so that control standards can be defined for them, facilitating the application owner's task of identifying controls for his or her information assets. Each company needs to determine what classes of information best meet its business environment, but the following are some suggestions that various companies have implemented:

- *Restricted*—information that is highly sensitive and should be disclosed only to persons specifically authorized by name. An example of restricted information is information pertaining to a future merger or acquisition action of the company. Patentable product design data or drawings may also be in this class.
- *Private or confidential*—information that is sensitive and should be disclosed only to those with an identified need to know it. An example of private information might be product design data. (Note that in the United States, the term "Confidential" is generally reserved for federal government use by companies that do business with the federal government.)
- *Internal*—information that, though not sensitive, is not intended for public release. Examples include corporate policy documents.
- *Public*—information, such as marketing information, that is specifically intended for release to the public.

A second type of classification that may be used in conjunction with the above categories designates integrity control. Information that should not be altered after entry (such as legal documents stored in image systems) might be classed as "Preserve" to ensure that the files that contain it are designed to lock out changes. Files that contain information that should be changed only by authorized users may be designated as "Authorized Update Only." Work files and shared work files that need to be continually modified may remain unclassified for integrity until they are in their final form.

The CISF itself should be established under a published corporate policy or directive. In a decentralized environment where security coordinators are spread throughout the company's organizational units, information security coordination may become difficult without the unifying presence of the CISF. For that reason, several companies have created an "information security council" (ISC), chaired by the head of the CISF, to manage coordination. The ISC may meet only annually or semiannually to ensure coordination of security implementation and advise on potential changes to policies or procedures. Nevertheless, its existence provides an avenue for communications at any time both vertically and laterally in the company.

CONCLUSION

In general, the structure for information security responsibility in a decentralized computing environment, or where some facilities are outsourced, follows a few basic guidelines:

- The *network provider* should be responsible for ensuring the availability of network services and for providing technical support for information security during transmission.
- *Application or information owners* should be responsible for ensuring the integrity and confidentiality (and utility and authenticity) of their information assets transmitted through the network, through use of application-level security procedures, including cryptography for appropriate applications.
- The *system operators* of computers connected to the network should be responsible for ensuring the availability of processing resources and data and for providing technical support for information security during access or processing.

The network provider does not have to identify what information requires protection; that decision is made by the application and information owners through their work with application developers and security coordinators. Application owners retain security control over their own information throughout the information's life cycle, including its transmission through the networks. Information in sensitive applications is protected for integrity and confidentiality end to end, application to application, using such tools as cryptography if appropriate.

Application owners are not likely to have the technical expertise available to handle the technical security controls required to provide end-to-end integrity and confidentiality. The lack of such expertise within the application areas may be overcome by the support provided by technical security services (in the network provider or system operator organizations) that have responsibility for establishing the security utilities and for consulting with application owners. Such support will enhance the owners' exploitation of those utilities to secure the applications' communications.

Some redundancy of controls may exist from application to application if controls are built into the applications. Technical security services should establish security utilities for all applications in a specific host environment. These security utilities will provide integrity and confidentiality control mechanisms that the applications can call when the sensitivity of the information to be transmitted by the application warrants one or more of these security controls. The primary control mechanism these utilities provide is application-level cryptography.

Some companies are beginning to build application-level cryptographic protections for sensitive information passing through primarily open networks, or they are using "third-party" authentication techniques such as Kerberos or Sesame to control access. These techniques are being adopted initially in financial areas, but are beginning to extend into nonfinancial applications that are network-intensive. Several years ago, General Motors established an extensive electronic data interchange (EDI) network between assembly plants of its different divisions, the treasurer's office, and GM's banks. GM also used ANSI X.9 cryptography to protect both the logistics information being transmitted and the financial message with which the logistics were associated. Other corporations, such as oil companies, are deploying application-level cryptography to protect sensitive proprietary seismic data passing through their networks.

The increasing distribution of information systems processing, the widespread use of wide area networks and local area networks in business, and the use of outsourcing for network management and major computer operations are demanding a response that enables companies to protect their information assets and their ability to continue normal business operations. This response can only be implemented through an appropriate organization of responsibility for information asset protection.

DISCUSSION TOPICS

- How does the assignment of responsibility described in this chapter compare to the manner in which your company manages security?
- Have costs of the various security services changed?
- What new tools can reduce the cost of security administration?
- How can you determine ownership of an application or a database?
- In what manner can managers be convinced to accept the responsibilities of ownership?

REFERENCE

1. SRI International. "Information Security Corporate Organizational Structures and Goals." Applied Research Note 10, August 1990.

CHAPTER 14

Disaster Recovery Needs Assessment

During the early 1990s, a wave of major disasters caused the destruction of computer centers and communications facilities. The 1993 bombings at the World Trade Center and the London financial district, the 1992 flooding of the Chicago business district, the 1993 Mississippi river floods, and the 1991 Florida hurricane raised awareness of the need to develop or reassess contingency and recovery plans in the event of a disaster. Corporate MIS chiefs and information security staff have long been aware of the need for such plans, but these events elevated the consciousness of senior company management in regard to the vulnerability of the information systems on which their businesses depend. With this elevated consciousness has come a related question. How much should a company spend to protect information systems from disaster and enable reasonable recovery?

FACING DISASTER RECOVERY NEEDS

Two observations are intuitively clear to most managers: (1) different businesses have different recovery needs; (2) the availability needs for different applications, databases, and communication systems also differ. For example, many banks can survive a loss of their computing capability for a day, but losing their computers and networks for three days may drive them out of business. Similarly, a stock exchange may suffer some losses if its computers or networks are down for a few hours and trades go to other exchanges; but a loss of availability for several days may be catastrophic. Network failure for a manufacturer whose operations are geared to just-in-time inventory replacement can be very costly to production and product delivery schedules. Network failure for a supermarket chain that depends on suppliers to automatically restock their shelves based on access to sales records can mean lost sales. Airlines, theaters, hotels, and others who sell services risk the loss of sales and the longer-term loss of customers if they cannot provide potential customers reservations and bookings.

Considering these different needs, methods are necessary to assist senior business management in determining how much to spend on information systems (IS) disaster recovery planning and implementation. The following paragraphs describe one method of dealing with this problem. This method is based on the premise that the "owners" of the information and information processing resources are the senior executives responsible for the business, and that these executives *must* make the business investment decisions relating to disaster recovery. All the steps in the method are described, although MIS and information security personnel may be able to carry out some of the steps more briefly based on existing knowledge and documentation of their organization's systems.

This chapter assumes that the company for which disaster recovery needs are to be assessed has multiple data centers, client-server and LAN-based systems, and distributed computing. However, it should be noted that needs assessment does not have to be done concurrently for the entire company. Disasters tend to strike in limited geographic areas. Furthermore, in most companies, strategic business units are in essentially different businesses and have different disaster recovery needs. Unless centralized data centers or communication facilities process data for more than one strategic business unit, the needs for each unit may be considered separately.

The team required to conduct the needs assessment project should include members from major computer center operations staffs and network control center staff, information security specialists with experience in disaster recovery planning, systems analysts knowledgeable in the company's mission-critical systems, and end-user support staff familiar with the company's use of personal computers, workstations, and client-server systems. The core team may often be limited to members from computer and network operations, information security, and end-user support, with other resources on call. In most companies, information security professionals are charged with the responsibility for development of information systems disaster recovery planning and often for business continuity planning. This tends to make them the "natural" leaders for the needs assessment effort.

In many instances, external consultants are brought in to lead the team. The reasons for using external consultants are these:

- Consultants who have developed many disaster recovery plans have the experience to find solutions faster and shorten the elapsed time of the project.

- Appropriate staff within the company may not have sufficient time to devote to the project.
- Management may desire the objectivity and credibility furnished by external consultants.
- Experienced consultants may have access to knowledge of industry practices not easily obtained by internal staff.

The DR needs assessment procedure is described in the following steps.

1. DEVELOPING AN UNDERSTANDING OF THE COMPANY'S CORE BUSINESS

As described above, information systems disaster recovery (DR) plans are directly related to the business of the company. This is most pertinent for mission-critical systems—those on which the company depends for its daily operation. The first tasks of DR planning are to understand the mission-critical operations of your company, identify the applications and databases that support these operations, identify the computer platforms and communications facilities that support these applications, and differentiate mission-critical applications from support applications such as accounting or administration. (Note that all following references to applications include the associated databases.) To accomplish these tasks, the DR project team must conduct interviews with management to

- Validate the team's understanding of the company's business
- Identify the owners of applications and information processing facilities
- Obtain management's perception of how critical applications are to the conduct of daily business
- Gather information regarding managements' perceptions about potential vulnerabilities
- Gather perceptions about the costs of unavailability of information and information processing resources
- Identify the impacts on business entities associated with the company's operations (such as suppliers or customers) and identify contacts in those business entities that can validate management perceptions

This information should be organized by business function or business process and documented for use in the analysis of findings. While the senior management view is clearly important, it requires validation from the customers and suppliers with whom your company does business. In today's business environment, the extended enterprise requires close relationships with other firms to carry out its functions. The perceptions of those with whom your company does business may alter the perceptions of management and the willingness to invest in DR strategies.

On the basis of the management interviews and lists of appropriate external contacts, the project team should conduct interviews with business executives from firms associated with your company's activities. (The interviews with management provide material for interview guidelines.) The purpose of these interviews is to determine the business impacts on these firms due to the inability of your company to conduct business normally. Interviewers should also attempt to determine how these firms will meet their needs if your company is not able to provide them service or information. These impacts and alternatives may be expected to vary according to how long your company's information services may be unavailable. As a result, the team should question the impacts based on unavailability or delay of a few hours, one day, and two or more days. The team should also identify the specific information used by the firms and the timing requirements for the firms' activities. To the extent possible, they should quantify the impacts in terms of operational effects and dollars.

The team should expect to find various kinds of impacts, such as a firm downgrading its image of the company, temporarily going elsewhere to transact business, suspending sales of your company's products, being forced to delay delivery of its own products or services, finding a second-source supplier, permanently discontinuing business with your company, or suspending its own operations or going out of business. These impacts, even if unquantifiable, are of particular value to your company's management in evaluating DR alternatives. For example, findings may confirm or refute management's perception of the value of maintaining your company's image with business associates.

2. DEVELOPING AN UNDERSTANDING OF THE COMPANY'S INFORMATION SYSTEMS

Most MIS groups have a reasonable understanding of the information systems within a company, but a complete disaster recovery plan also requires knowledge of the information interfaces to firms with which the company does business. The DR team should obtain

- Any documentation relating to the overall system and network architectures of the company's information systems
- Overviews of applications within the scope of this project
- Interfaces to external firms
- Documentation of MIS software management practices and procedures
- Documentation of current backup and recovery procedures and disaster recovery plans

The DR team should review all documentation before conducting interviews with MIS staff to clarify any issues or add necessary understanding.

Increasingly, critical business applications are being distributed to PCs or workstations either operating independently or connected to local area networks. The LAN or multi-LAN architecture should be documented and potential failure points or vulnerabilities identified. Users of LAN-based and PC-based applications should be interviewed to determine the criticality of these facilities and the applications they support, and to review current backup and recovery procedures. Findings should be documented so that requirements for a comprehensive DR plan are complete.

3. DEVELOPING AN UNDERSTANDING OF THE COMPANY'S CRITICAL INFORMATION FLOWS

The DR team should identify business process information flows, their content, and the timing necessary to meet business needs. It is not necessary to develop detailed process or information flowcharts for this task, but simply to record in some conveniently understandable form such as a table, the following for each mission-critical business process:

- The nature of the information (description and purpose)
- The origin of the information
- The information processing platform facility or facilities through which it flows (computers and networks)
- The recipients or users of the information (internal and external)
- The timeliness requirements
- The information previously gathered about the business impacts of unavailability

Tables should be prepared both for information flows and timing requirements from your company to external parties and for information flows that are wholly within your company. This information should be compiled in a format that describes the flows, requirements, and impacts of delayed, lost, or unavailable information.

The DR team should then work with application owners to review and ensure the correctness of findings. One way to do this efficiently is to conduct workshops with key company operations managers (application owners) to review and validate the findings to date and to identify areas in which additional information is required. Any further information required should be gathered and added to the tables prior to the conclusion of this task.

From this material it should be readily evident which applications are most critical to the continuity of the business and which platforms, data centers, or communications facilities support the most critical applications. Arranging applications in tables by platform or facility in order of cost of unavailability within critical recovery times provides an initial basis for a priority listing of disaster recovery and a schedule of disaster recovery procedures.

4. DEVELOPING AN UNDERSTANDING OF DISASTER RECOVERY PRACTICES IN THE COMPANY'S INDUSTRY

The DR team should construct an interview guide on DR practices to be used to examine and evaluate the practices of other businesses. The guide should be designed to elicit information about the key drivers for a DR plan in other companies and the actions those companies have taken to implement their plans.

Questions in the interview guide should cover such topics as the following:

- What kinds of disasters are anticipated by the disaster plan?
- What kinds of applications are considered mission critical?
- What computer/communications architectures are covered by the DR plan?
- When was the DR plan last updated?
- How much was invested in the DR plan for initial setup?
- What is the cost for annual maintenance/operation of the DR strategy?
- How often is the plan tested?
- What DR strategies are employed by the plan?
- Would the failure of any mission-critical applications potentially incur liability to other firms for failure to deliver information or the products and services of the company?

Many companies have found that surveying only firms in their own industry provides a narrow view of practices and that ideas for DR planning from other industries may be applicable (and advantageous).

Some companies are reluctant to share confidential information such as disaster recovery plans with competitors or with any other companies. There are ways to gain this information. One approach is to employ a reputable consulting firm to conduct a survey and to share the results in a "sanitized" form (deleting references to the participants) with all participants as an incentive for their participation. A second approach is to take advantage of membership in an information security association where such information is shared by specialists without disclosing sources.

One such association is the International Information Integrity Institute (I-4) operated by SRI International, in Menlo Park, California. This organization consists of the information security managers of about 60 multinational corporations who share methods and means of protecting their companies' information and information processing resources without disclosing proprietary information. One great advantage of such an organization is that members may assess their own progress every few years and keep their planning and skills up to date.

The information gathered through the survey should be compared with that of the company to establish a benchmark comparison of current position and to identify opportunities and priorities for improvement. At the conclusion of the survey task, the DR team should prepare a presentation of findings and deliver it to an audience of concerned managers and executives. This presentation will help company management to understand the measures taken by others to protect their businesses.

5. DEVELOPING AN INFORMATION UNAVAILABILITY COST MODEL

The basic principle of disaster recovery is the same as that of property insurance—one should never spend more on insurance than the potential cost of the loss being covered. To analyze the crossover between potential losses and the cost of disaster recovery methods, both the costs of potential outage and the costs of disaster recovery strategies must be compared.

The first step in this comparison is to translate the prioritized tables of application information into a cost curve (or a series of curves depending on the application platforms, data centers, and telecommunications facilities). On the basis of information gathered in earlier tasks, the DR team should develop a model showing the costs of unavailability of information and information processing or communication resources. Experience shows that the costs of unavailability can be plotted in a curve that reflects the different periods of outage. (See Figure 14.1.)

Initially, if recovery occurs quickly, there is little loss from a shutdown. But the length of the shutdown grows, costs accumulate. Often, at some point, very little added cost accrues from simply not reopening for business for the balance of the day. Should the shutdown go into a second day or more, however, one may expect costs to rise again and at some point probably reach catastrophic levels. The information gathered in the survey task should be used to plot the appropriate curve (or curves) representing the business costs of unavailability (not including recovery costs) for mission-critical systems. Note that administrative or accounting systems are not mission critical for many businesses, but for some regulated industries such as banks, accounting systems could become critical at certain reporting deadline times.

Arriving at these cost curves is an iterative procedure that involves management judgment. Once an initial set of curves is constructed, execu-

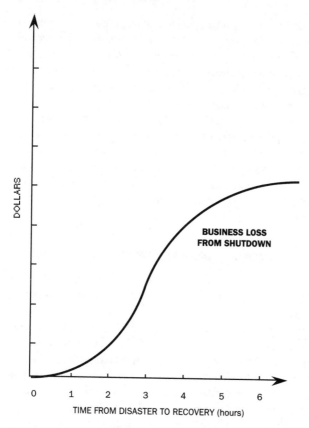

Figure 14.1.   Business Loss from Shutdown

tive management should be consulted, preferably through a workshop approach. The discussion material for this workshop should be

- The prioritized application tables
- A supplement to the tables that shows the intangible impacts of un-availability for each prioritized application
- The cost curves for each platform or other architectural element

The objective of the workshop is to provide executive management the opportunity to evaluate and set recovery priorities based on time, cost, and intangible damage to the company. At the conclusion of the work-shop, recovery priorities may be somewhat rearranged to conform to man-agements' judgment and then the final cost curves drawn.

6. DEVELOPING DISASTER SCENARIOS

Disaster scenarios are a basis for planning through analysis of the likelihood of occurrence. In most cases it is difficult to assign the probability of a catastrophe to a specific scenario. Even when there is statistical evidence of severe potential threats such as hurricanes, earthquakes, or tornadoes, it is not possible to precisely determine the probability that the company or the data center will be damaged by the event. Furthermore, quantifying risk by multiplying potential loss by the probability of events can only be misleading. Management decisions are better guided by assigning more qualitative probabilities such as "likely," "unlikely," or "rare."

The DR team should create scenarios of the types of disaster expected to occur and from which the company can reasonably expect to recover if appropriate precautions are taken. In performing this analysis, the team will usually uncover some disasters for which the cost of recovery is beyond what the business can reasonably afford.

In addition, the team should identify the types of disasters from which the company is not expected to recover. The team should expect to find that some disaster scenarios are so catastrophic that the business will either not survive or will have to be completely rebuilt. For such scenarios, business loss insurance may be the only reasonable answer, and the team should obtain insurance quotations.

Finally, as a guide for planning, the team should identify those types of disaster that are likely to also severely impact enterprises with which the company does business. This final step may lessen the need to consider some recovery measures for disasters of city-wide or regional impact when business "partners" also will be unable to transact business.

These various scenarios should be presented to management with the purpose of guiding decisions about the level of investment in disaster recovery. The team should convene a workshop of executive managers to conduct a "vulnerability analysis." Vulnerability analysis is a technique in which the executives, under the guidance of the DR team leader, jointly identify areas of greatest concern for the systems of the company. The identification process begins with a presentation and discussion listing all possible types of disasters and their impacts on high-priority applications. The discussion should aim at classifying the potential disaster scenarios according to their effect on the company's business (least expensive to most expensive) and their probability of occurring (unlikely or likely). Potentially costly events that are most likely to occur provide an instant focus for attention (see Figure 14.2).

The vulnerability analysis focuses the efforts of the needs assessment project on recovery models that respond to events representing the greatest threat.

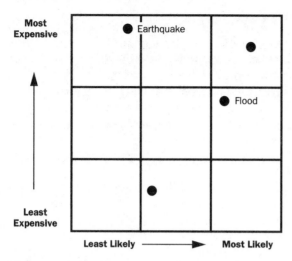

Figure 14.2.   Vulnerability Analysis Template

The information to support the vulnerability analysis varies by type of disaster and by country. In the United States, for example, information on earthquakes and floods is available from the U.S. Geological Survey (USGS). The USGS can provide maps that indicate (down to the level of specific streets) the potential for earthquake damage; however, there is no reliable means to predict earthquake frequency. Similarly, the USGS can provide potential flood maps and indicate the expected frequency of floods based on historical data. The U.S. Weather Bureau can provide information for specific areas on the frequency of hurricanes and tornadoes. There is no way to predict terrorist action, but a high-profile location is clearly more vulnerable than a remote, unmarked facility.

7. DEVELOPING RECOVERY MODELS

Many companies have acquired fault-tolerant computers for mission-critical systems. This strategy enables rapid recovery from computer failures, but does not protect the computer center or the business from disaster. Disaster plans are generally based on one or more of the following strategy models:

- *Cold site* backup through an agreement with another company or through a contract with a firm specializing in backup services.
- *Hot site* backup through building (or leasing) an alternate computer or communications management facility that is continually operational

and has the excess capacity necessary to operate the critical systems if the primary facility fails.

- *Distributed processing* backup in which critical databases are synchronously maintained and any of the sites can continue operation of critical systems if one site is lost (sometimes with slower response time).

- *Replacement*, which may be used as a DR strategy for personal computers, workstations, client-server systems, and local area networks if data and programs are properly backed up at a remote site and arrangements are made for rapid replacement in the event of a disaster.

Each of these models of DR strategy has different costs and different potentials for responding to disaster. The DR team should develop the appropriate alternatives from these models for each of the platforms or facilities identified in the previous steps.

Different business circumstances have different associated costs to the business and substantially different impacts relating to the period of unavailability. Therefore, the DR team should develop the models of recovery strategy and identify the associated disaster recovery resources and annual costs for different recovery periods. For example, given business recovery needs of one, two, or three hours, different recovery strategies required to meet these deadlines will have different costs. Figure 14.3 represents a hypothetical model of the results, showing the relationship between recovery time and incremental costs for recovery resources. Since each alternative developed provides different recovery characteristics, it is usually necessary to develop more than one curve; however, a model could be developed that shows recovery time as a continuum by means of different strategies on a single curve.

Experience shows that, depending on the company's needs and expectations, the shape of a curve of elapsed time to recovery, plotted against the incremental investment required to achieve a given target recovery period, shows an exponential decline. In some cases, instantaneous recovery is exceedingly expensive, if possible at all. As the time to recover increases, the recovery cost becomes more acceptable, but the cost of delay begins to grow.

The information gathered through a high-level design of the selected models will define this annual cost curve. These models should illustrate initial setup costs and ongoing costs. Initial setup costs should be clearly indicated to management; however, for the purposes of this analysis, they must be assumed to have a limited life based on the anticipated life of the data center or platforms in use. This life may be assumed in most cases to be between 5 and 10 years. The initial setup costs should be amortized over the anticipated life of the disaster recovery strategy and added to the annual maintenance costs to arrive at the cost curves for each model.

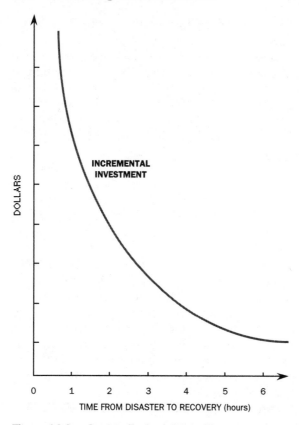

Figure 14.3.   Cost to Reduce Down Time

Certain actions and levels of investment are required in order to achieve recovery times shorter than or equal to specified times. Information acquired during earlier steps of the DR study will show what target times are reasonable for maintaining business operations and the business costs for each period of unavailability. Now the recommendations for a new strategy must be cast in terms of the requirements to reach each given level.

In addition to the initial setup costs and the ongoing costs, it is necessary to estimate the one-time costs of recovery from a disaster. These will vary according to the type of disaster (the anticipated extent of damage) and the disaster recovery strategies selected. Elements of one-time recovery cost may include

- Additional MIS labor
- Facilities cleanup, repair, or replacement

- Computer or communications hardware repair or replacement
- Additional user labor (or supplemental labor)

One-time disaster recovery costs, when added to the initial setup costs and ongoing costs, may indicate that some strategies are more costly than previously assumed. This discovery may result in a change to the strategies selected for your company. Such a change will require reevaluation and redrawing of the recovery cost curve, so this should be performed before needs assessment goes further.

One-time recovery costs for the selected strategies must now be added to the business costs of unavailability (business loss from shutdown) previously calculated, and a new cost curve must be drawn for comparison to the costs of the disaster recovery strategy.

Since several mission-critical applications often use the same data center or platform, it is possible to consolidate the curves in this comparison to show the total disaster recovery costs and the total business impact costs for each such facility. This will reduce the number of analyses necessary, and may make it possible to have a single analysis for an entire data center. However, distributed processing resources may require individual analyses.

Figure 14.4 indicates the crossover between the costs of unavailability (business loss from shutdown) during certain periods and the costs of the disaster recovery strategy (or strategies) selected. On the basic principle of insurance, the annual cost of the disaster recovery strategy should be some fraction of the potential loss. Insurance companies use a statistically sound actuarial method to set the cost of insurance, but no such statistics are generally available for information systems disaster recovery. As a result, management must use its best judgment based on the costs, the exposure, and the qualitative evaluation of the risks to decide how much the company should spend to protect itself. That amount will be in the area below the intersection.

Information presented in graphic form will assist management in choosing a level of investment that meets its willingness to sustain downtime. As management is aware, some costs are impossible to judge, as they represent opportunity costs for business lost, potential business firm failures that cannot be predicted or assessed, or losses of confidence and goodwill that are impossible to gauge. Such potential intangible losses, previously pointed out to management, have been used to establish the application recovery priorities. This contrast of estimated costs for downtime with potential investment and annual costs will permit the company's management to be better informed in its decision making.

A final workshop with company MIS managers and appropriate business operations managers is required to make the critical recommendations necessary for the needs assessment. The objective of this workshop is

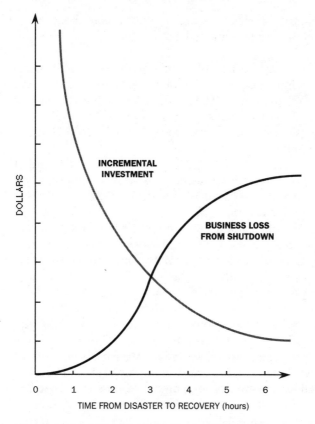

Figure 14.4.   Determining Limits for Disaster Recovery Investment

to select the levels of investment and the disaster recovery strategies to be used by the company. The materials presented should include the cost analyses performed in the preceding steps and the disaster scenarios.

8.   DEVELOPING CONCLUSIONS FOR MANAGEMENT

On the basis of the recommendations from the final workshop, the team must present its final report and recommendation to senior management. In most companies, a presentation-style report is all that is necessary. The report should contain summarized versions of the key charts and tables developed during the needs assessment and the final recommendation. It should be presented to senior management with a request to authorize the detailed planning and implementation of the recommended disaster recovery strategy.

SUMMARY

Periodic review of disaster recovery plans is an essential part of a disaster recovery strategy. Such reviews are often triggered by changes in the technological infrastructure of information systems operations. As mission-critical applications move to client-server architectures, and as business conditions change, the needs for disaster recovery may also change. Thus the first phase of any well-constructed review of disaster planning is to reassess the needs of the business. This chapter has set forth an approach to the necessary needs assessment that will ensure that the costs and strategies for information systems disaster recovery are consistent with your company's business requirements and strategy.

The approach recommended accomplishes this consistency by involving operational and executive management in the development of strategic recommendations. This approach also ensures that non-MIS management acquires an understanding of the needs and the costs of preserving the ability of the company to conduct business after a disaster.

The key deliverables of the needs assessment project are

- Tables of mission-critical information flows and the impacts of unavailability, prioritized by business cost
- Comparison of your company's disaster recovery strategies to those of other firms
- An information unavailability cost model
- A disaster vulnerability analysis
- A recovery strategies definition and cost estimates
- A recovery cost versus business disaster cost model
- A final needs assessment report and disaster recovery strategy recommendations

Keep in mind that the needs assessment must be followed by a plan for implementation, the implementation itself (including the purchase of appropriate business insurance), and periodic testing of the plan to ensure that it works.

DISCUSSION TOPICS

- Who should be responsible for making decisions about disaster recovery strategy?
- How should a disaster recovery plan be tested?

- How often should a disaster recovery plan be tested?
- What vulnerabilities exist in your geographic region?
- What disaster recovery strategies exist in your company?
- Are some companies more vulnerable to the effects of disaster than others?
- The length of time a company can survive without access to its information processing resources has been called the "time to belly-up." What is the time to belly-up for your company?

Business Process Redesign

Several chapters of this book have referred to business process redesign (BPR) as ranging from a means of introducing new information technology to a consideration in justifying information security. BPR is a combination of industrial engineering techniques, operations research methods, management theory, and information systems analysis methods that utilizes the power of information technology to transform the business processes of corporations so that they can more effectively compete in their markets.

Several 1994 surveys and reports have indicated dissatisfaction with the results of BPR projects. For example, and Arthur D. Little study found only 16 percent of the 350 executives surveyed were satisfied with project results.[1] One reason may be that many projects started under the guise of "reengineering" or BPR are not truly BPR projects, but simply traditional systems analysis under a trendy name. Another reason is the failure of many executives to commit appropriate time and resources.

This section offers both a methodology for BPR projects and a guide to avoiding the kinds of failures often experienced.

---

[1]Caldwell, Bruce, "Missteps, Miscues" *Information Week* (June 20, 1994) pp. 50–60.

CHAPTER 15

Business Process Redesign

This chapter discusses the need for business process redesign or reengineering, what it is, and how to carry out business process redesign projects.

A BRIEF BACKGROUND

John Naisbitt's *Trend Letter* of July 4, 1991, says, "In the highly competitive global marketplace of the 1990s, quality and service will be increasingly essential to business survival."[1] An increasing number of companies are boasting of their success in redesigning, or "reengineering," their business operations to achieve dramatic improvements in quality and customer satisfaction while reducing the costs of providing them to their customers.

One of the most publicized examples of business process redesign (BPR) is Cigna Corporation's reinsurance division, Cigna RE. As a result of a two-year effort, Cigna RE halved its work force, improved document turnaround time by more than 90 percent in some areas, reduced operating costs by 40 percent, and increased revenues.[2] Banc One Mortgage, a subsidiary of Banc One Corporation, implemented an image-processing-based system that permits its sequential mortgage application approval process to be handled by cooperating workgroups in which electronically connected group members can concurrently perform their tasks. The expected result is a reduction in the time needed to provide service to customers from weeks to days.[3] Hallmark Cards redesigned its operations to reduce its time-to-market by more than half for new greeting cards, gifts, and wrapping papers to keep up with changing customer preferences.[3]

Digital Equipment Corporation redesigned its internal financial functions with a focus on business issues and improved their services to the rest of the company.[4]

Other companies that have redesigned their business processes include such giants as Ford Motor Company, AT&T, Xerox, and Westinghouse.[4, 5]

Top management's interest in redesigning business processes is usually a matter of perceived threats to the business. Such threats may include tough foreign competition, deregulation of industries, mergers and acquisitions, consumer complaints, loss of market share, and poor financial performance.[6] While surveys indicate that BPR heads the list of interests of information systems (IS) executives and many claim that their companies are redesigning processes to take advantage of information technology, most senior business managers do not agree that using information technology to transform business processes is a key factor in competitive positioning.[7]

This lack of agreement indicates that the discipline of business process redesign is not well understood. Information systems executives may consider the usual systems development approaches as including business process redesign, while senior management often thinks of BPR as a new way for computer vendors to sell more products.

Since the "discipline" of business process redesign emerged only in 1989, there is little established methodology; however, certain common features in the approach to redesigning businesses are beginning to appear. The following section sets forth a framework for a methodology of business process redesign based on the experiences of several of the companies mentioned above and rooted in the need for enhancing the competitive position of the firm.

WHAT IS "BUSINESS PROCESS REDESIGN"?

Business process redesign is a combination of industrial engineering techniques, operations research methods, management theory, and information systems analysis methods that utilizes the power of information technology to transform the business processes of corporations so that they can more effectively compete in their markets.

The need for businesses to rethink their processes is driven by the pressures of modern global competition. Even though an individual company may operate regionally or locally, it cannot escape global competition because expanding national and international firms are continually invading new territories.

Companies in manufacturing, distribution, retail, and service industries have only three modes in which they can compete for the business of their customers:

- *Price.* A company may sell its products and/or services at a price lower than that of its competitors.
- *Product/service characteristics.* A company may attract customers to its products or services by emphasizing one or more of their functions, features, quality, style, image, or other characteristics.
- *Time.* A company may beat competitors by bringing new products or services to the market in advance of competitors or by ensuring that its products or services are more readily available to its customers.

Generally, most companies find that they must use a judicious mixture of the three modes for each product or service that they offer. Each of these modes has implications for the ways in which companies organize, produce, advertise, and deliver their offerings to prospective customers.

Offerings with which the company chooses to compete by selling at a lower price must be delivered at the lowest possible cost. This means managing every facet of the delivery process so that it operates at the lowest cost consistent with providing sufficient quality to the customer to retain the customer's willingness to buy.

Choosing to compete in terms of the characteristics of the offering means that the company must obtain an optimum level of flexibility in its processes so as to permit continual adjustment of those characteristics to meet changing customer demands and needs.

Competing in time-to-market requires the company to ensure that the entire process, from conception of the offering through its design, production, and eventual delivery to the marketplace, be managed to consume minimal time. Similarly, competing in delivery time means managing so that the process from receipt of the customer's order to delivery of the offering takes less time than the time consumed by the company's competitors.

The common element in these modes of competition and the means of achieving the company's objectives is that delivering the offering to customers involves a number of *processes* and that the management of the processes invariably requires *information*. (See Figure 15.1.)

Processes exist wherever one turns. There are processes to design products and services, processes to understand market and customer needs, processes to produce the offerings, processes to obtain the materials needed for production, processes to deliver the offerings, and processes to finance the production (or the customer's purchase) of the offering. These processes may exist within limited domains such as the design engineering function or the advertising department of the company; they may be cross-organizational (and most of them are to some extent); or they may involve parties outside the company such as suppliers, distributors, or customers.

Many companies have arrived at their present organization as a result of historical accident. Organizational forms have been initiated as a result

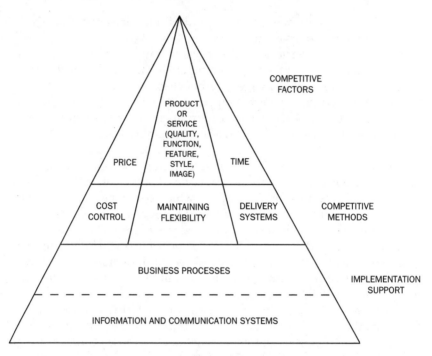

Figure 15.1. The Process-Based Pyramid

of the special skills or political strength of key individuals; as a result of functional responsibility or specialization; as a result of acquisitions or divestitures; or as a result of the available technology used by the company at some time in the past. Rarely have these forms been constructed as the result of a holistic view of the processes used by the company.

Just as many of the efforts of automating production resulted in "islands of automation," many of the organizational units of today's companies are "islands of subprocesses." As such, they have had to be linked by artificial and often expensive and time-consuming methods so that they can participate in the overall process of which they are a part. In fact, a substantial amount of the investment in information technology is devoted to supporting these linkages and the passage of information among the islands. As companies have grown to international proportions and as organizational units have become separated by time and distance, the islands have become veritable archipelagos. Automating existing business processes does not appear to result in improvement in business operations.

In fact, there is evidence to show that computerization of existing business processes alone has had disappointing results. At a conference in Copenhagen in December 1990, Erik Brynjolfsson of MIT's Sloan School of

Management presented the results of his study of a large sample of American firms from 1975 to 1985. His findings show that during that period the average number of employees per firm dropped by 20 percent, while the investments in information technology tripled. However, they also show that the companies reduced their headcounts by narrowing their focus and becoming less vertically integrated. In other words, they bought more components and services from other companies.[8] Several other sources, including Paul Strassmann's excellent book *The Business Value of Computers*, confirm the concept I posited in 1973 that "increased automation of clerical functions invariably results in increased operational costs."[9, 10]

The earliest recorded breakthrough in management occurred when Jethro, Moses' father-in-law (acting as a management consultant), advised Moses to divide his followers into tens, hundreds, and thousands and appoint leaders over each group. By improving communications, command, and control through this organizational device, Jethro helped Moses to transform the undisciplined Israelites into an effective fighting force.

But such breakthroughs have been few and far between since then. The last great breakthrough in management resulted from the work of Frederick Winslow Taylor at the beginning of this century. Taylor's work led to the creation of industrial engineering as a discipline to improve the productivity of workers. Even with substantial strides in automation, since Taylor industrial engineering has mostly been confined to production environments and rarely applied to white collar or knowledge-based work.

The first four decades of increase in the use of information technology resulted in systems that often simply supported parts of processes at best. At worst, these systems exacerbated the separation of functions by fostering the creation of new islands of white collar work.

If this is truly our current situation, what exists today that is substantially different from ninety years ago or even ten years ago? Now we have a rapidly maturing set of information technology tools, the sum of which had not previously existed. These tools have the potential to permit us finally to transform our businesses to better serve our customers and more effectively compete in the global marketplace. These tools permit us to treat business processes in a manner, and on a scale, never before possible. In fact, there is a real potential for the first breakthrough in business operations since Taylor's work.

One major limitation of business process analysis in the past was that the full scope of a process was usually beyond the capability of an analyst to describe and understand within a reasonable time. This limitation resulted in analysts segmenting the process to be able to address a part of it within the time available. Today, automated tools exist that permit a team of analysts to describe, understand, and analyze an entire process within a period consistent with the patience of senior management.

Furthermore, tools have become available for creating solutions to process problems that could not have been addressed even as recently as 1989 without high levels of technological risk to the company. Such tools include expert systems, image processing systems, and cooperative workgroup systems. During the next several years, an increasing number of these tools will be moving from the innovative and "experimental" stage to the "off-the-shelf" availability stage.

As one might expect, the current literature focuses on successes in business process redesign, just as the literature concerning systems analysis did in the early years of that discipline. We know from experience that many systems analysis projects failed to achieve their goals, so we can expect failures in BPR to occur as well. Despite the risks—and they are substantial—it is clearly time to find new approaches that may help business processes to operate in a more effective manner not only for the participants in the process but for the suppliers and customers of the firm as well.

WHAT IS THE PROCESS FOR BUSINESS PROCESS REDESIGN?

This breakthrough called BPR may be applied to business processes through a seven-step process described in Figure 15.2. This approach

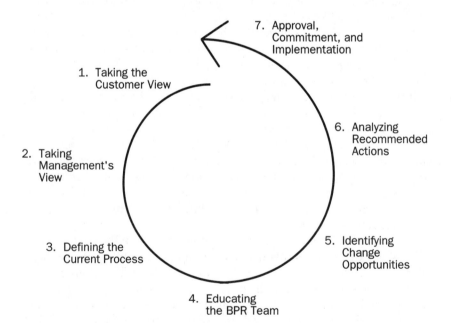

Figure 15.2.   The Seven-Step BPR Approach

makes use of four fundamental concepts as a BPR project is undertaken. These concepts are

- Maintaining a customer orientation for the business process
- Being guided by strategic management direction
- Gaining a thorough knowledge of the business process
- Using information technology as an enabling tool

As the steps are described, keep in mind the matrix in Table 15.1 that illustrates the steps in which the concepts are most prominently applied.

Step 1: Taking the Customer's View

Since the essential motivation for BPR is to improve the competitive stance of the company, it is critical to understand the company's strategic approach to its markets for the products and services being offered. Furthermore, one must understand whether or not this strategy is being effectively applied. Is the product or service gaining or losing market share? Are the results of customer surveys indicating common or consistent problems? What do marketing and sales personnel within the company think are the greatest impediments to increasing sales? What aspects of competitors' offerings make them attractive to customers? How do any identified deficiencies in products or services relate to processes within the company or between the company and its external relationships? Many large companies obtain such information through their market surveys and product satisfaction surveys.

The first step in the BPR process is to take an unbiased look at the company's products and services from a customer perspective and relate them to company processes.

Systems analysis has observed that the output of one subprocess constitutes input to the next subprocess. Similarly, quality management techniques have taught that every function in the company has "customers,"

Table 15.1. Application of Fundamental Concepts

	Steps						
Fundamental BPR Concepts	**1**	**2**	**3**	**4**	**5**	**6**	**7**
Customer orientation	•				•	•	•
Strategic management direction		•	•		•		•
Knowledge of process			•		•	•	•
Information technology as an enabler				•	•	•	

many of which are other functions within the company. As a result of this teaching, BPR recognizes that customers may be either external or internal to the company. BPR may be applied in both domains.

One approach, called *transaction analysis*, is used to survey the internal customers of specific functional units to determine their perceptions of levels of satisfaction, value received for cost, and timeliness of response. Transaction analysis provides information about internal functions (subprocesses) that is roughly equivalent to the information obtained in market surveys of external customers. These surveys serve the same purpose as a starting point for BPR. Since transaction analysis may be a key technique for analyzing business process needs, the appendix of this book describes it in more detail.

Step 2: Taking Management's View

Most top executives can respond immediately to questions about the weaknesses of their company's operations and offerings. Their knowledge of the strengths and weaknesses of their company is, of course, what permits them to guide the company's future. Interviews with top management can dramatically reduce the time necessary for analysis. In addition, the involvement of top management in the BPR process is critical because most significant business processes operate across organizational lines. Only top management can effectively guide the implementation of BPR and prevent the process from foundering as a result of parochial interests.

Furthermore, only top management can prevent the wasting of time and money to improve a business process that will make little difference to the bottom line.

The results of obtaining the customer view must be correlated with the (potentially biased) views of top management to obtain a consolidated picture of the primary competitive threats to the company. Similarly, the troubled processes identified through the analysis of customer views must be correlated with the opinions of management in order to set priorities for process improvement. The results of this step are identification of the most troubled processes and establishment of the priority with which they should be addressed.

It is important here to introduce a note of caution. Occasionally, as a result of the centralization of functions in a corporation, it is possible that a given process affects numerous products, services, and strategic business units. More often, the problems lie within strategic business units or with particular product lines or services. This factor should also be discovered in the first step of the BPR process.

As in the first step, and in all other steps of the process, BPR can be used from either an internal or external customer perspective. The essential ingredient of BPR analysis is to recognize processes as holistic rather than deal only with subprocesses and thus perpetuate islands of improvement.

On the other hand, once priorities are set for improving processes, BPR should be used to address one major process at a time. Attempting overall or comprehensive process improvement for an entire company's operations concurrently usually incurs unacceptable levels of risk. These risks result from both the process of BPR and the outcomes of the process.[11]

BPR processes require detailed definition of existing business processes; measurement of the productivity, quality, and time of existing processes; education of management in the potentials available through information technology; management workshops for identification and development of process improvements; coordination of meetings; detailed specification of systems designs; development and testing of new information systems; training of employees in new methods and procedures; and implementation of new systems. The burdens on management time may be substantial, and the anticipation of change may be disturbing to employees during the BPR process. Special training and employee information programs are needed to minimize these affects and to prevent work disturbance or employee turnover.

The outcomes of the BPR process may include reorganization of functions within the company, reduction or transfer of staff, reeducation of staff to manage and operate new systems, and new measurement methods for performance. Changes imposed on work habits and environments may be substantial in order to achieve the gains required by the company. Confining such potential disturbances to a single process reduces the risks to the company's operational capabilities.

Before proceeding into more substantive phases of the BPR process, under the direction of the highest level of management responsible for the business process to be improved, a steering committee is established that usually includes all the current managers responsible for subprocesses within the business process. The committee's responsibilities include

- Providing management direction to the BPR process
- Ensuring that adequate resources are provided for the BPR process
- Suggesting and evaluating proposed changes to the business process
- Making the final recommendations to senior management
- Guiding the implementation of changes and new systems

Under the direction of the steering committee, a BPR project team is established to perform the analysis, make recommendations, design the changes or new systems, and develop any new or modified implementations of information technology to support the modified business process.

This team consists of a project team leader, BPR analysts, and a representative from each organization currently conducting a part of the business process.

Most companies who have used BPR caution that top management commitment and involvement is essential for several reasons, including the cross-organizational nature of BPR, the likely trauma to the organization and employees, and the time (up to two years) that the project will take. For these same reasons, while the senior information systems executive may introduce BPR concepts to the company, he or she is not well positioned to lead the BPR effort. This leadership must come from line management.

Step 3: Current Process Definition and Measurement

Before any attempt to change a business process, the process should be defined and the performance of the process measured in terms consistent with the objectives for improvement.

For example, if management objectives for the process are to lower costs or improve the delivery time or response time of the process, it is important to understand the current levels of performance for these factors before change is attempted. Measurement of the existing process is important for several reasons. These reasons include the ability not only to compare results after changes are made to ensure that objectives have been achieved, but also to make appropriate design trade-offs during the BPR analysis phase. To improve an overall process, it is sometimes necessary to shift work from one subprocess to another. As a result, one subprocess may actually involve more work or time than it did before the change in order that the overall business process may realize significant improvement. This may change budgets and headcounts for specific organizations or create entirely new organizations within the company.

Steps 1 and 2 emphasize such subjective measures as customer satisfaction and customer perceptions. In step 3, the BPR process shifts to more objective measures of output that include traditional measures of production time, delivery time, productivity, cost, quality or failure rate, complaint rates, and so forth. If measurement systems are not currently in place, they will have to be developed and implemented during this phase. Measuring the outputs of current subprocesses provides the basis for diagnosis of the causes and effects of current problems, identifies specific areas requiring improvement, and helps to define specific targets to be met by an improved business process.

During this phase, performance may actually improve without change, as a result of the well-known "Hawthorne effect," in which performance often improves simply because management is paying attention to the employees involved in the process.

Concurrently with the measurement of the process outputs, the BPR project team begins definition of the current process. This definition phase is critical. The team must understand exactly what steps are now being used to conduct the process and why those steps exist. Moreover, they must understand what added value is produced (or not produced) in each step and what information is used or created and/or modified in each step.

To perform this analysis, team members must observe process activities and interview employees who perform the steps in the business process. Existing published procedures and interviews with managers and supervisors are helpful as background, but experience in systems analysis teaches that the actual work performed usually deviates from procedures (and often from management's knowledge of the process).

The BPR process takes advantage of modern information technology (IT) tools developed for computer-aided software engineering (CASE) to document the business process steps. These process and data description tools result in a graphic annotated flowchart of process steps that can be easily understood by steering committee members during the next steps. Annotations may be the elapsed time and labor hours for each step, quality measures, and other comments. In addition, it should be noted whether or not the steps add value to the product of the process—for example, steps in which documents are filed or retrieved from files normally do not add value to the product of the process. Also to be noted are whether certain steps *must* be performed before others or may be performed concurrently or in a different sequence. Computer-based project management tools such as PERT charts (available on PCs) may be used to analyze the precedence network. Such charts also aid a "cause and effect" diagnosis that can guide the specification for redesign.

Step 4: Working Group Education

The ideas that can potentially contribute to redesign of the business process are dependent on the knowledge and skills of the team. Before attempting to create redesign ideas, it is important to ensure that the team members are well armed with new ideas and concepts that they may not have had the opportunity to acquire in their present positions with the company. These ideas and concepts fall into two categories: process ideas and information technology concepts.

One of the best ways to gain process ideas is to examine the processes of other companies. Some of this knowledge can be gained by the competitive analysis described in step 1; some can be gained through membership and participation in professional associations. Another popular way of gaining ideas is by "benchmarking" processes against those of other companies. As mentioned in Chapter 14, since many companies are reluctant to share information for competitive reasons, it is common to employ a consulting firm to carry out a benchmarking project. An ethical consulting firm will perform such a project by first determining the measures for the benchmark, then selecting a list of candidates and obtaining interviews with as many as possible. The consultant will usually offer to share the results of the benchmark with all participants as an incentive for their participation. The results are, of course, sanitized to prevent disclosure of the names of participants. Experience in benchmarking shows that the interviews collect not only the information relative to the BPR measures but also insight into the manner in which processes are operated. This information can be shared with the BPR team. Experience also indicates that benchmarking should not be confined to members of the same industry in which the company does business. Some of the best ideas can come from other industries in which similar processes exist.

Julia King[12] observes that

- Before benchmarking against others, it is necessary to be familiar with your own processes and their weaknesses
- Interviewing the best "world-class" companies may be difficult, since they usually have many requests for such benchmark visits
- If your company's business processes are too far behind, interviewing "world-class" companies may be a waste of time—your company may not be able to duplicate what they do or their infrastructure for doing it.

As previously remarked, two common elements support the ability of a company to maintain and enhance its competitive posture: processes and the information relating to those processes. Where the end product of a process is a tangible product, the information flow supports the manufacture and distribution of that product. Where the end product of the process is a service, that service is supported by the information flow—in fact, the service may often consist of providing information.

Managers of functions, subprocesses and organizational units in Europe and the United States (especially middle managers) have become accustomed to using computers and data communications technology. Not only do they work with computer-produced reports, they use PCs and terminals to access and manipulate information, and they use these PCs and terminals combined with data communications networks to communicate with others. One major Scandinavian company, in the initial stages of developing a global data communications network, found that there were already over 1,000 users of electronic mail in the company and they were sending between 10,000 and 15,000 messages per month.

The introduction of PCs to the workplace created a great leap forward in the acceptance of IT tools and in the understanding of IT's potential.

Nevertheless, these tools alone have not increased productivity nor have they permitted many managers to understand the overall potential impact of information technology on company business processes. For this reason, managers and the members of the working groups need to be educated about the potential in using information technology in order to participate properly in planning changes to business processes.

It is not necessary, however, to make all managers or employees systems analysts, or to teach them the details of the technology. Instead, they must be taught the basic functions that can be performed by the combination of computers and data communications and given relevant examples of applications using information technology. It is the duty of the BPR team to identify technologies that are relevant to the process under examination, find examples of use by others, and create ideas for use of the technologies in the given business process. This material is used to develop a short course (perhaps one day) for the steering committee and for the process's supervisory personnel and key employees. This course serves as the background for analysis of the current process and for proposing changes.

Information technology provides certain specific capabilities that form the enablers for BPR. These include

- *Information storage*—the ability to store information (data, text, graphics, images, voice messages, video clips, etc.) in a form and format that permits the user or a computer application to retrieve the information when needed.
- *Information retrieval*—the ability (with appropriate approval) to access information and retrieve it from storage.
- *Information forwarding*—the ability to automatically forward information from one application or a user to another user (the basis for electronic mail and electronic data interchange).
- *Information sharing*—the ability of a number of users or applications to simultaneously access and view information.
- *Information integrity protection*—the ability to permit authorized change to information, prevent unauthorized change to information, or prevent simultaneous multiple changes to information.
- *Information modification*—the ability to permit authorized users to change or manipulate information to obtain new results.
- *Information display*—the ability to display audiovisual information in a manner that is most convenient for the functions performed by the user.
- *Information transfer*—the ability to connect computers and computer-related devices to enable the transfer of information among computers, applications, and users.

- *Computation*—the ability to combine data through algorithmic processes or formulae to obtain mathematically derived results.
- *Information comparison*—the ability to compare data and information to determine equivalence and order (the basis of sorting, retrieval, and other functions).
- *Multimedia information processing*—the ability to combine data, text, graphics, voice, and images in any of the above activities.

These capabilities support a broad range of information processes that include transaction processing, problem solving, statistical analysis, expert systems, image processing, database management, and many others. Applications of information technology can transform the way individuals work and the way managers manage by making information sharing independent of time and distance, allowing them to break the patterns that created the need for centralized or decentralized processes. Applications can replace labor-intensive work, ensure the reliable storage and retrieval of information, enable changes in the sequence in which work is performed, provide additional information needed to manage the business process, or even reduce the amount of information necessary to manage a business process.

Examples of innovative use of information technology abound in trade publications and can be used as input to the education of the company's staff members. However, it is important to note that, while new technology may be a critical enabler, it is not always necessary to introduce new technology to the firm. In fact, many solutions may be based on better use of existing technology through improving or redesigning computer applications or simply through changing the organization of work. A BPR project may result in changing office layouts, workspace arrangement, geographic location of functions, or many other factors relating to the process that are not technology-dependent.

Step 5: Identifying Change Opportunities

Armed with the knowledge of appropriate technology provided in step 4, the key participants in the BPR project are ready to become more intimately involved in changing the way things work.

The BPR team prepares material for a series of workshops to be conducted with key employees and their supervisors and with the steering committee. Presentation material consists of flip charts or slides showing

- The objectives of the BPR project
- The reasons for the project (from steps 1 and 2)
- The methods used in the BPR process
- The diagrammed description of the current business process

- Identification of how this process links to other company processes
- A diagnosis of the causes of current problems and their effects
- The expected results of the workshop (verifying the description of the current business process and obtaining ideas to change the process)

The first set of workshops should be conducted with supervisors and key employees. Several workshop sessions may be needed to cover the entire process, since individual sessions should not exceed four hours. (Experience has taught that limiting the duration of workshop sessions is important for three reasons: Key employees cannot be absent from their regular duties for too long, the concentration required by participants is exhausting, and participants will develop new ideas between sessions.) After verifying that the representation of the flow of the current process and its annotated comments are accurate, the BPR team may take the lead in suggesting some changes as a way to trigger the thoughts of the participants in the workshop.

Sessions in which change to the process is discussed should be conducted in the spirit of "brainstorming" in which no idea, however outrageous, is rejected. Ideas proposed should challenge existing organizational structures, sequences of work, geographic locations of work, management approvals for existing process results, and the unwritten assumptions that underlie the current processes. For example, the unwritten assumption in Ford Motor Company's redesign of its accounts payable process was that payment was made on delivery of an *invoice*. The new assumption, that payment should be made on delivery of the *goods*, permitted a complete redesign of their accounts payable operation and a 75 percent reduction in headcount.[13]

When the initial set of workshops has reached its conclusions, the BPR project team should document these conclusions and hold one more review session to ascertain their accuracy. After obtaining concurrence, the BPR project team should prepare a series of steering committee workshops for which, in addition to the material prepared for the previous workshops, it should prepare the following presentation:

- The changes to the business process recommended by the initial set of workshops
- Comments on the technical feasibility of suggested changes
- Comments on the roughly estimated costs of the suggested changes
- Comments on the expected benefits of the suggested changes

In the series of workshops conducted with steering committee members, the composite material developed to date is presented and discussed. Further suggestions are expected from steering committee members and from the BPR team. This series of workshops is intended to arrive at preliminary recommendations for changing the business process in a manner consistent with the objectives and with the internal environment of the company.

Step 5 results in an initial proposal for changing the business process.

Step 6: Analysis of Recommended Action

Using the conclusions of the steering committee workshops, the BPR team must now design the changed business process and specify alternatives for implementation. The output of this step will include

- A proposed new process and information flow for the business process
- The organizational changes necessary for implementation
- The technology changes or acquisitions required by alternatives
- The system changes or application replacement required by alternatives
- The estimated costs of and trade-offs available for alternatives
- The impact on other processes from alternatives
- The risks associated with alternatives
- The estimated elapsed time to implementation for alternatives
- The expected benefits from alternatives
- The recommended course of action
- A proposed action plan

Robert E. Berland of IBM, in a May 1991 lecture to the IBM Consultant's and System Integrators Conference, pointed out that evolution in computer use has taken place in a series of waves since the 1950s. In the 1960s and 1970s, the first wave was directed at saving costs. In the late 1970s to early 1990s, efforts were directed at "making money." We are now seeing the beginning of a new wave in which the emphasis must be on corporate survival—remaining in business against increasingly stiff competition. The recommendations resulting from step 6 of the BPR project must establish a new paradigm for the business process.

Step 7: Approval, Commitment, and Implementation

The output of step 6 is a proposal for business process redesign to be presented to the levels of management that must approve the investment in the new process and take responsibility for its outcome. It is assumed that this level is above that of the members of the steering committee. A presentation by the BPR team must first be made to the steering committee, whose comments or changes must be included in a final presentation to top management.

The implementation project for a major business process may take two or more years. It is vital to the success of the project that top management be committed to successful implementation and that they be kept informed of progress throughout the implementation. Other management members may need to be included in the implementation effort. These include the head of the company's human resources or personnel function, the heads of organizations that use the outputs of the business process, the public relations function, and perhaps the company's customers.

Implementation is often a major effort, of greater size than the study leading to the approved proposal. It would be trivialized by an attempt to describe the implementation tasks in one short chapter when there have been many volumes written on the subject. Even so, there are several key lessons to be learned from implementation experiences. These lessons are described in Chapter 16.

The implementation plan should include a plan to establish and measure the results of the change and periodically report on the results for at least the first few years after implementation. In fact, it is a good idea to build the measurement devices into the new process to provide continuous measurement and to form a basis for further evolution in the future. Business processes must continually evolve to remain competitive.

SUMMARY

Table 15.2 summarizes the steps, the tools, and the techniques that may be used in each step and the deliverables that may be produced from each. It is important to note that many steps indicate a variety of tools and techniques that may be applied. Those actually used for a BPR project should be selected on the basis of fit with the company or process culture, the adequacy for the task, the existing knowledge of the BPR team, and the existing documentation available to the team.

Each step of the BPR process makes a specific contribution to the redesign of the business process. These contributions are illustrated in Table 15.3.

Business process redesign sounds like a long, involved undertaking. However, many of the tools and techniques necessary to perform BPR are well known and have been applied in many industries. The development of information systems within companies has often used similar tools. The principal differences are between BPR and IS are two:

- BPR takes a *process* view of the company from the perspective of the customer that receives the output of the process.
- BPR introduces information technology as an *enabler of change* to redesign business processes to meet competitive objectives.

In many instances, the computer-based systems developed to date have failed to result in significant performance improvements in support of the competitive posture of the companies for which they were devel-

Table 15.2.   BPR Project Deliverables

BPR Project Step	Methods and Tools	Deliverables
Step 1: taking the customer's view		
Identifying factors leading to customer satisfaction from customer perspective	Customer focus groups Customer surveys Customer interviews Competitive evaluation Transaction analysis	Summary of factors leading to customer satisfaction as customer describes them Summary of satisfaction factors with competitors Evaluation of relative importance of services and satisfaction with services delivered and received (such as level, content, and timeliness), as described by customers of the process
Step 2: taking management's view		
Identifying management's perspective of factors leading to customer satisfaction and differences between two perspectives	Management interviews Management focus groups Workshop to resolve differences in views	Factors and priorities management believes lead to customer satisfaction Comparison of management's view and customers' view Resolution of differences in views between customers and management, including implications for strategy Resulting customer requirements that redesigned process should meet or exceed
Step 3: current process definition and measurement		
Documenting actual current business process and measuring outputs of process and subprocesses to develop foundation for redesign	Work flow observation Structured interview process Process flow diagramming Data and control flow diagramming CASE tools PERT tools Process cycle time analysis	

Table 15.2. *Continued*

BPR Project Step	Methods and Tools	Deliverables

Step 3: continued

	Input, intermediate, and output measurements	Overview of current work process
		Process flow description and quantitative information available on current process, including
	Statistical analysis of output production	• Material flows
		• Data and control flows
		• Work locations and operations
	Problem root-cause analysis	• Documentation
		• Measurement and test points and data obtained
	Process simplification analysis	• Percent not meeting customer requirements at each process step
		• Cycle time at each process step
		• Value-added at each process step
		• Productivity at each process step

Root causes of defects, long cycle times, and low productivity in process, covering such possible causes as

• Special causes resulting in occasional process upsets
• Process steps not capable of meeting customer requirements
• Poor definition and organization of process steps; complexity
• Inadequate documentation and training of employees
• Physical and organizational separations between process steps; problems in hand-offs
• Unevenness and delays in work and information flows
• Low-value-adding steps and support activities occurring on main process sequence

Table 15.2.   BPR Project Deliverables *Continued*

BPR Project Step	Methods and Tools	Deliverables

Step 4: working group education

Educating client's BPR participants to understand potentials of process restructuring and information technology as applicable to problem domain	Benchmark other firms processes: • Document ideas gained for evaluation Lecture slides: • Process redesign methods • Process definition and tools • IT capabilities • Business cases Workbook of articles and papers	Client BPR team participants equipped to • Engage in process redesign using systems design methods and IT tools • Help develop business case for redesign • Relate redesign effort to experiences of other successful companies

Step 5: identifying change opportunities

Workshops and brainstorming sessions with BPR team members to create new business process	Process and data/control flow diagrams CASE tools Measurement results interpretation Process walkthrough methods Alternatives evaluation methods Redesign requirements analysis and deployment Measurement and metrics design PERT tools	Summary description of alternative new business processes Process and data/control flow diagrams for alternative new processes Evaluation proposed alternative processes addresses • Business and customer requirements from step 2 • Root causes of problems from step 3 • Need for measurement and control to hold gains over previous process • Need for continuous further improvement over time Estimates of implementation and operational costs of each alternative Selection of best redesign alternative based on evaluation criteria.

Table 15.2. *Continued*

BPR Project Step	Methods and Tools	Deliverables

Step 6: analysis of recommended action

Detailed planning of new process—identifying IT implications, new technology trends, new system architectures; developing cost/benefit estimates; preparing proposal to management for business process change	Management and organizational change analysis Business case analysis System architecture Technology forecasting Project cost estimating, including training Hardware/software cost estimating Cost/benefit analysis Project planning Risk analysis Presentation preparation tools	Proposal to management for business process change, including • Description of proposed process change (overview and detailed outline) • Business case for change, including operational benefits and costs and strategic contribution to enterprise • Business systems required to support the change, including IT implications, information system architecture changes, and consistency with longer-term IT trends and forecasts • Risks associated with change, and how risks will be managed

Step 7: approval, commitment, and implementation

Obtaining management approval and detailed project planning	Presentation preparation tools Detailed implementation plan	Management approval and commitment of resources to long-range planning Detailed implementation plan

Table 15.3.   The Contribution of BPR Steps

Step	Product(s)	Contribution
1. Taking customer's view	• Definition of customer requirements and values	• Drives BPR from customer requirements
2. Taking management's view	• Process improvement needs and initial goals • Alignment of project with business strategy • BPR project structure	• Drives BPR from management strategy, needs, and priorities • Creates willingness to act and participate
3. Process definition and measurement	• Measure of current performance • Process and information flow diagrams • Documentation of current problems	• Provides objective process data • Defines actual current process • Establishes evidence of real problems
4. BPR team education	• Training of project participants	• Provides technical knowledge and external experiences needed
5. Identifying change opportunities	• Initial recommendations for process improvement	• Identifies key changes to be analyzed
6. Analyzing recommendations	• Proposal for redesign of business process	• Formalizes proposed changes and estimates costs/benefits
7. Approval, commitment, implementation	• Presentation of action plan and management approval	• Obtains commitment for the implementation of change

oped. Frequently, this failure has been the result of attempting simply to automate the existing process. Organizational management has usually resisted major change or the shifting of authority and responsibility. Instead it has opted for incremental improvements that create as little change (read "disturbance") as possible.

The objectives of BPR must be audacious. They must set targets that stretch the imagination beyond the confines of the present organization, the accepted ways of doing things, and the current sequence of the process. Only by striving for grand results can we stimulate the kinds of "breakthrough" thinking that will make a difference.[14]

The race for competitive positioning will not end with the implementation of a new business process. The new business process creates a temporary advantage that will last only until competitors make similar improvements. Then the race begins again. The most important lesson to be learned from BPR is that, like freedom, the price of staying ahead of the competition is eternal vigilance. Advances in technology and the ways in which technology can be used will continue to raise challenges for all companies.

DISCUSSION TOPICS

- What business processes in your company could benefit from BPR?
- Compare the approach described here to other approaches you have heard of.
- Do you know of any failed BPR projects? Why have they failed?
- Can you improve on any of the steps suggested?
- Are shortcuts possible in a BPR project?
- Would you rearrange the sequence of the steps? Why?

REFERENCES

1. Naisbitt, J. *John Naisbitt's Trend Letter* (July 4, 1991): 4.
2. Ryan, A.J. "Cigna Re-engineers Itself." *Computerworld* (July 8, 1991): 79.
3. "Is It Time to Junk the Way You Use Computers?." *Business Week* (July 22, 1991): 66.
4. "Building a Better Mousetrap." *Information Week* (March 25, 1991): 24.
5. Davenport, T.H., and Short, J.E., "The New Industrial Engineering: Information Technology and Business Process Redesign." *Sloan Management Review* (Summer 1990): 11.
6. Ryan, A.J. "Is Re-Engineering Right for You?" *Computerworld* (July 15, 1991): 57.
7. King, J. "Rip It Up!" *Computerworld* (July 15, 1991): 55.
8. "The Incredible Shrinking Company." *The Economist* (December 15, 1990): 65.
9. Strassmann, P. *The Business Value of Computers.* New Canaan, CT: The Information Economics Press, 1990.
10. Fried, L. "Fried's Rules." *Computer Decisions* (August 1973): 32.
11. Alter, A. E. "The Corporate Make-over." *CIO* (December 1990): 32.
12. King, J. "Benchmarking on Empty." *Computerworld* (December 20, 1993).
13. Hammer, M. "Reengineering Work: Don't Automate, Obliterate." *Harvard Business Review* (July-August 1990): 104.
14. Alter, A. E. "The Nature of the Beast." *CIO* (December 1990): 35.

CHAPTER 16

Success Factors in Business Process Redesign

After several years of industry experience with business process redesign, or "reengineering," some lessons have been learned about what makes the difference between successes and failures in BPR projects. This chapter, based on both observation and consulting experience, provides an appraisal of the key success factors that enable BPR projects to accomplish the objectives.

A FINE EXAMPLE OF A BAD BPR PROJECT

Almost everyone has heard at least one horror story about a BPR project that went wrong. One example concerns an attempt to redesign the processes of after-sale product service for a heavy equipment manufacturer. (Obviously, the story has been slightly modified to protect the guilty.)

The customers of this company purchased custom-designed heavy equipment on which their businesses relied for production. Service demands were stringent, since the customers depended on reliable operation of the machinery. With a variety of custom-designed heavy equipment to service around the world, the maintenance department was finding difficulty in maintaining and tracking spare parts inventory, identifying the configurations of custom-designed equipment, responding promptly to customer service calls, and keeping costs in line with the terms of maintenance contracts. Surveys of customer satisfaction with service continually showed that this was the company's weakest competitive aspect.

The vice president of customer service decided that drastic changes were needed. An initial survey of the problems bedeviling the organization showed a communications breakdown among the organizations that needed to cooperate to make customer service effective. The field maintenance staff did not talk to the spares master planning staff; the spares master planning staff did not talk to maintenance engineering; maintenance engineering did not talk to spares inventory control; and no one talked to accounting. Part numbers for spares were in complete disarray. Inventory overstocks of some parts were common, while other parts were chronically in short supply. Expediting of spares manufacture was the rule rather than the exception. The example could go on and on.

On the basis of the initial survey, the vice president of customer service appointed one of his managers to head a project to redesign the customer service processes. The project manager had years of experience in product maintenance, experience that led him to believe he knew the problems and the answers. However, just to make sure, he spent several weeks visiting companies with good customer service reputations in similar businesses to find out how they operated. During one visit, the project manager found that the customer service arm of that company had developed an integrated information system using a common database accessible to all interested organizations. The system supported customer order information, spares inventory, engineering change orders, spares accounting, and other necessary control functions. Users were, in effect, forced to communicate by the nature of the system. It seemed clear that this was the solution the project manager was seeking.

The project manager returned to his boss with The Answer, and before long, they had entered negotiations to purchase the system from the company that had built it. The idea was that they would buy the system, redesign their business processes to match the system functions, and modify the system where the operation could not adapt to it readily.

At this point corporate MIS was called in to assist in the system acquisition. MIS objected that the system was written in a language and used a database management system with which the company had no experience. However, the objection was overridden by the insistence of customer services that they needed the system as a solution to their problems.

The vice president of customer service requested members of engineering, MIS, inventory control, accounting, and master planning to join a task force to implement the solution and to redesign their combined processes. He set an implementation target date of one year from the formation of the task force, since he assumed that little modification to the system would be needed.

With some reluctance, these organizations agreed to furnish staff to the task force. Within a matter of weeks it became apparent that the organizations were not pleased by the idea of redesigning their processes to match the plan of customer service. Furthermore, they had their own systems for managing activities and did not wish to part with them. To add to the problem, MIS assessed the training needed for programmers to learn the language of the system and requested funds to start training immediately.

The BPR task force members examined the proposed system solution and their needs for three months and returned with a series of requests for changes to be made to the acquired system to accommodate their current processes rather than changes being made to the processes. Every suggested change appeared to be viewed by the project manager as a personal attack. The contrary positions hardened. Ultimately, some of the members went so far as to require that aspects of the acquired system be dropped and the remainder of the system interfaced to existing applications.

MIS refused to provide estimates of time and cost for the changes because it did not have enough experience with the environment and no one could agree on the changes that should be made. The project manager wrote a scathing letter to the vice presidents of the (theoretically) cooperating organizations complaining about the lack of cooperation, the lack of vision of the participants, and the lack of company loyalty shown by team members.

The accounting department withdrew from the task force, followed shortly by the engineering department. The MIS head wrote a memo to the vice president of customer services denouncing the "arrogance" of the project manager and refusing further participation in the project unless the project manager was replaced.

The project ground to a halt. The software, at a cost of several millions of dollars, was shelved until "a new attempt could be made." No one was willing to admit failure.

EIGHTEEN BPR SUCCESS FACTORS

With this painful story in mind, we can examine the factors that could have made the project a success and other success factors gained from similar experiences.

1. ENSURE MANAGEMENT COMMITMENT

Senior management must be committed to the BPR project and must make this commitment known to all employees.

When BPR projects examine processes, they typically find them existing across organization lines. Without the clear commitment of the senior management to which all involved organizations report, there is little hope that all will agree on the process transformations and the implicit reorganizations. It is not enough that senior management initiate the project; its interest and commitment must be publicized so that it is known to all employees. Indeed, some companies have found it advantageous to publicize their BPR projects to suppliers and customers who may be involved with the business processes. Such publicity demonstrates the advanced thinking and concern for the customer that management wants to show to the world. Incidentally, it also helps to ensure the continued commitment of management to the project.

---

2. ENSURE CONTINUITY AND CONSISTENCY

Stops and restarts, or chronic changes in direction, are recipes for disaster.

Once started, the BPR effort must continue to a logical conclusion. Failure to reach a conclusion demonstrates to employees (and possibly to customers) the inability of management to grapple with the tough problems of process change. One project in a Fortune 100 company started with all the right signals. Not only was the commitment of the senior executive responsible for all functions covering the process gained; he promised results to the CEO, established a steering committee for the project consisting of all the appropriate division heads, and hired a consulting team to spearhead the project.

The steering committee felt that the project's success depended on "buy-in" from the divisions' staff members, so it requested that the consultants survey over one-third of the approximately 1,200 staff members to learn their perceptions about current levels of satisfaction with the process and ideas for improvement. Furthermore, the committee requested that the consultant conduct interviews with a number of other companies that had similar processes, to "benchmark" their current process and gain more ideas for improvement.

After the investigative phases were completed, the steering committee participated with the consultants in a series of workshops to evaluate the ideas gained and to propose process improvements. The selected set of improvements was refined and further explored to determine organizational impacts, costs, and other concerns. At the end of the process improvement identification phase, the steering committee adopted 18 suggestions for recommendation to the senior executive. The senior executive was then expected to review and approve the recommendations for implementation.

Within six weeks after the recommendations were submitted, one of the recommendations was implemented. About one year later, a second recommendation was implemented, and all other recommendations were "tabled." Most of the work over a two-year period was wasted.

What were the reasons for the failure to follow through? Did the division managers who agreed to the changes in committee object to them in private discussions with the senior executive? Was the senior executive concerned about relieving some division managers close to retirement of their duties and positions? Did the "old boy" network rebel against change?

Whatever happened, the failure to follow through left employees feeling that management lacked the fortitude to make necessary changes. One employee commented later that they would have to wait for the current division heads to retire before any substantive changes could be made.

---

3. LIMIT THE SCOPE OF CHANGE

Trying to implement redesign for the whole company at once can be disastrous. Take on processes one at a time.

A few companies, such as Cigna RE, claim to have "reengineered" the company in its entirety. This may be possible when most of a company's business revolves around one major process. However, most large companies either are in a number of different businesses or have divisions so large that they are functionally separate businesses. For example, an airline may consist of a number of divisions so large and so different as to have almost independent processes. These divisions include airline operations, reservation and booking operations, aircraft maintenance, cargo operations, travel agency operations, and so forth. Attempting to reengineer all of these operations at once would obviously lead to a project beyond the means of the airline to support.

Furthermore, there are limits to the ability of employees to absorb change and learn new methods. As processes overlap, employees are forced to learn new methods of operation based on several concurrent changes. The prospect for mistakes is frightening.

Most successful BPR projects have begun by obtaining a clear definition of the scope of a major process and working within the boundaries so defined. This permits large changes to processes but incremental changes to the company as a whole.

4. MEASURE PERFORMANCE BEFORE AND AFTER THE REDESIGN

Successful redesign can only be proven by comparative performance measurement to show that objectives have been attained.

The basic question is, "How do you know you have arrived if you don't know where you are going and where you have been?"

After the early phases of a BPR project, management is expected to set improvement goals. The success of the project will be judged on the degree of attainment of those goals. Whether the goals are improved customer satisfaction, increased productivity, improved quality, faster response to the market, or something else, you cannot judge the potential for improvement or the improvement attained if the basis for measurement is lacking.

Most companies have established measures in some form for processes. Where these are lacking, metrics should be determined and measurements taken before the process design is changed. There is one note of caution here. The Hawthorne effect, in which simply paying attention to employees' work results in improvement without any changes being implemented, can influence results. Similarly, the Heisenberg effect, in which the act of measurement distorts the object being measured, must be avoided. Measurement must not be intrusive on the process being measured.

If the same business process is conducted at various places in a company by different groups of employees, each group may have developed its own work methods and found its own ways around the constraints of outdated procedures. Measurement can help to identify which team is delivering the best performance. This may provide an initial model for BPR ideas.

5. USE APPROPRIATE TOOLS AND METHODS

Adapt tools and methods from TQM, industrial engineering, and systems analysis to obtain optimum results.

The tools and methods selected for use in a BPR project depend on a number of factors. For example:

- The organizational culture may dictate that certain tools and methods are preferable to others.
- Current levels of understanding of the process may indicate that the process must be examined and flowcharted in detail or that interview

techniques alone may surface the problems and constructive suggestions for amelioration.
- If the process to be redesigned has already been determined by management, some preliminary steps may be skipped.
- Relatively small processes may use abbreviated forms of usual methods; however, large processes need more formal means of recording findings or simulating changes.

A BPR project should be approached with a conception of the overall project structure—the steps that should be performed—but with no preconception of the tools and methods that will be used. Selection of tools and methods must be based on their appropriateness for the circumstances. Therefore, it is wise to have an understanding of the variety of techniques that can be applied. Don't believe anyone who claims to have a perfect single set of tools and methods for BPR.

A BPR project structure showing potential steps, the methods and tools that can be applied, and the deliverables from each step was shown in Chapter 15.

---

6. GET THE RIGHT TEAMS FOR BPR PROJECTS

BPR teams must include employees who work in the processes. Get the best performers to join the team, not just those who have time available.

The truth is that most managers do not know the detailed operation of the processes they manage. Employees who do the work of those processes know the roadblocks and the tricks to get around them. They know the points at which they have to deviate from approved procedures to get the job done. The best producing, most conscientious employees have overcome many of the obstacles that exist. It is these employees—the best producers—whom management is often reluctant to spare from their jobs to participate in a BPR project. Nevertheless, these are the employees who have the most to contribute to a BPR team. The team should not settle for less, or take the word of the manager for the manner in which the jobs are done in a process.

BPR teams should include the following:

- Either company personnel or consultants who have experience at BPR and can provide methodology, tools knowledge, and training to the BPR team. Many companies use consultants in this role even when

company personnel may have the experience. Consultants not only provide an unbiased view of processes, but they potentially bring to the project their exposure to the solutions adopted by other clients.
- Members of the workgroups in which the process is performed.
- A member from the MIS group responsible for the computer and network applications used by the business process.

The BPR team actually performs the investigation and the analysis, not the BPR project steering committee, which guides the project and evaluates the results. The steering committee typically consists of managers of the organizations contributing to the process, led by a member of senior management.

---

7. DON'T STOP TQM FOR BPR; USE TQM TO HELP THE PROJECTS

The customer-focused efforts of TQM should not be abandoned while BPR projects are conducted. The BPR project can borrow ideas from TQM results. Employee familiarity with TQM will help with the BPR project.

Many companies have adopted total quality management (TQM) techniques in the rush to demonstrate a "quality orientation" to the world. Adopting TQM, in itself, does not guarantee that the adopter will make money. In fact, there have been some dramatic examples of award-winning companies having substantial financial problems. On the other hand, TQM has brought a customer focus to many business processes that had lost their quality orientation. Furthermore, properly conducted BPR projects will make use of the process consciousness-raising that comes from TQM. Personnel familiar with TQM will be ready candidates for assisting in BPR projects.

---

8. USE INFORMATION TECHNOLOGY AS AN ENABLER, NOT AS THE DRIVING FORCE

Start with business process improvements; then use information technology to support implementation.

Just one of the mistakes in the horror story that began this chapter is the selection of a technological solution before the problem was addressed in terms of the business process and company objectives. Too many companies have assumed that information technology is the answer to their process improvement problems and then sought applications. The old expression, "When you have a hammer, everything looks like a nail," seems to be appropriate to such thinking—or lack of thinking.

Since all business processes make use of information in some form, the potential of information technology to enable improved processes cannot be ignored. In fact, when the BPR team considers possible process changes, it should be aware of the information technologies and techniques that may be applied. The application of information technology must be considered concurrently with process redesign alternatives to take advantage of IT's potential. For this reason, in step 4 of the BPR approach discussed in Chapter 15, the BPR team is exposed to the potential uses of information technology as part of their training prior to seeking alternatives to the current process.

---

9. GET EARLY SUCCESSES WHEREVER POSSIBLE

Successes breed future successes and give confidence to BPR teams, so identify and implement "quick hits."

To quote another old expression, "Nothing succeeds like success." Earlier in this chapter, the need for approaching one process at a time was described. This approach permits the additional opportunity to select processes for redesign in which substantial gains are possible and success is very likely. If processes of relatively small scope are initially selected, it is possible to gain several successes without waiting years for results. Such early successes will boost the stock of the BPR concept and encourage other teams in the company to initiate projects.

In both large and small processes, one should seek "quick hits"—changes that can provide interim benefits before the BPR project is completed. Such quick hits usually come from changes in procedures, policies, or organization rather than from changes in information systems. Humans are more flexible and adaptable than information systems, which may need extensive work to redesign or replace.

Based on experience, there are two more reasons for seeking quick hits along the way. One is that quick hits tend to show progress and thus sustain management commitment. The other is that even if management commitment fails, the gains achieved by the quick hits will not be lost.

---

10. BE OPEN TO NEW IDEAS

Breakthrough thinking is required for dramatic advances, and breakthroughs can come from anyone involved in the process.

Selecting members of the BPR team from among the actual workers in the process is just one step in acquiring new ideas. Valuable ideas may come from others, both within the process and external to it. As in TQM, "customers" of processes may be internal (within the company) or external. These customers may often provide critical insights and suggestions. The ideas that created the current inventory supply linkages between supermarket chains and their suppliers, in which suppliers have access to store inventory data so that they can resupply more efficiently, came from the customers—the chains. The benefits have extended to both parties in the resupply process.

BRP projects that do not actively solicit ideas from the customers of processes and the suppliers to processes will not only lose potentially valuable ideas but will fail to gain the buy-in necessary to implement many of the ideas.

---

11. KEEP EMPLOYEES INFORMED

Retaining employee loyalty and commitment through the BPR project and its implementation can only be accomplished in an open environment.

A large European freight-forwarding company found that it was becoming increasingly unable to meet its customers' demands with its existing (primarily manual) methods. The CEO felt that the company needed to automate, but did not know where to start. After a meeting with his key executives, he decided to take a BPR approach to redesigning the jobs of the freight-forwarders. Immediately after employing a consultant and naming members to the BPR team, the CEO received a visit from the highly agitated union representative to the company. (In this country, almost all employees, including most of management, are union members.) The union representative threatened to call a strike if jobs were going to be affected by the changes (before any changes had even been suggested).

The CEO called in the consultant and told her about the problem. With assistance from the CEO and the head of finance, the consultant did some homework and then called a meeting of the BPR team, the union representative, and senior management.

At the meeting, the consultant laid out the steadily declining market position of the company over the last five years and projected that trend to show that the company would have to start layoffs within a year and would be out of business in five years. She made a strong case for the BPR project as saving the jobs not only of the freight-forwarders but of all the employees of the company. She then invited the union representative to become a member of the BPR team, and she offered to make the same presentation at the next union meeting. Furthermore, she promised that a monthly newsletter would be produced and distributed to all employees to inform them of the progress of the project.

At the conclusion of the meeting, the union representative withdrew his objection to the project. He declined service on the BPR team, claiming that he did not know enough about the business process or automation. He also declined the offer of a presentation by the consultant to the next union meeting. However, he did ask to borrow a copy of the slides that the consultant had used to show the company's situation.

The union representative used the slides at the next union meeting and urged employees to cooperate with the project to save their jobs with the company. The project proceeded to a successful implementation.

Another company that launched a BPR project for a major business process found that six months into the project it had lost so many employees that the existing process was foundering. Employees who were concerned about the potential loss of their jobs were actively seeking other employment. Naturally, the best and most productive were the first to find other jobs. Attempts by management to replace the lost staff with temporary help led to massive training problems, loss of quality, delays in service, and general customer dissatisfaction.

The costs in both money and company image were substantial, and almost completely avoidable. When BPR projects are initiated, all potentially affected employees should be informed honestly and openly about the intent and methods of the project. Before launching a BPR project, management must consider its possible impacts on employees and frame their responses. If employees may be laid off at the conclusion of the project, they should be informed of the possibility and of the actions the company plans to take to offset this effect. Employers may retain the cooperation of their employees in several ways, including early retirement programs, outplacement assistance, internal transfer assistance, retraining aid, and bonuses for remaining through implementation.

Employee cooperation and loyalty will almost surely evaporate if management attempts to conceal the possible threats to current jobs. A BPR project is too public to hide.

---

12. MAINTAIN PRODUCT AND SERVICE QUALITY

Ensure that proposed changes will not sacrifice quality to attain other objectives.

The objectives of BPR projects are varied and may include cost reduction, improvement in product or service characteristics (such as style, image, utility, or quality), response time, time-to-market, or combinations of these. However, the underlying purpose of BPR is to improve the competitive position of the company.

A large company in the service sector went through a period of over five years in the late 1980s and early 1990s in which it followed the then-current trend of "downsizing." A substantial percentage of the staff was offered (and accepted) early retirement packages. Limits were placed on hiring, and normal attrition was allowed to further reduce staff. As a final move, the company actively sought to reduce any staff it considered "surplus."

In the same period, the company continually surveyed its customers for satisfaction with its services. During the last two years, customer satisfaction started to erode, and along with that erosion came a noticeable erosion of business volume. Clearly, the company had cut staff in some critical processes below a level that could sustain customer satisfaction. At this point, in appraising the company's situation, the CEO initiated a thrust to establish BPR projects throughout the company.

BPR projects may ultimately help the company recover its previous competitive edge, but they should have been started sooner. As this company moves ahead in its BPR efforts, one may be sure that it will make every attempt to avoid sacrificing service quality in the interests of cost reduction.

---

13. BORROW THE BEST IDEAS YOU CAN FIND

Other companies, even those in other industries, have good ideas. Borrow the best practices from wherever you can find them. Don't put up with NIH.

Benchmarking equivalent processes in similar companies is one way to understand how well your company's current processes are performing compared to other company's. When compared to competition, your company's performance may indicate if immediate attention must be paid to a particular process.

Benchmarking similar processes in *other* industries has an added value. It may garner ideas that have not been used in the company's industry to make dramatic improvements in processes.

For BPR, the best advice is to steal ideas indiscriminately and use the best and most applicable to your company's needs and culture. Of course, this excludes patentable manufacturing processes, but all others are fair game.

Above all, do not put up with the NIH (Not-Invented-Here) syndrome.

---

14. DON'T START WITH THE SOLUTION IN MIND

Great ideas from other companies may not work in your company.

Another aspect of our initial horror story is the project manager who knew everything about the process and found the solution in advance. Borrowing ideas is fine. Buying a technological solution may also work, but only if you have first devoted the appropriate effort to gaining knowledge of the problem, identifying process solutions, and involving the participants in the process in the BPR project.

Attempting to force a solution on the business process participants can only lead to the charge of arrogance leveled at the project manager in our horror story. Since the solution was his, he viewed every suggestion as an attack on his idea.

---

15. QUESTION THE VALUE OF EVERY PART OF A BUSINESS PROCESS

Some parts of processes may not be needed at all.

In its much cited BPR project of several years ago, Ford Motor Company reportedly reduced its accounts payable staff by 75 percent. This reduction was achieved by eliminating the process of matching invoices to receivers and making payments based only on the recorded receipt of goods or services according to purchase order terms.

Another classic example comes from the Canadian government. In a process that rebated a portion of residence property tax payments to claimants over 65 years old, there were claim forms to be filed, claims to be examined, vouchers to be written, and checks to be prepared and mailed. In the interests of streamlining, a BPR team was formed to flowchart the process and examine every opportunity to speed it up and cut costs. After months of study, the team had not made significant progress.

Finally, one team member had an idea. Why not mail out checks to all claimants and then match the claimant names against the social security files after the mailing. If checks were not cashed within a certain period, it could be assumed that the claimant was dead or no longer living at the claimed residence. If claimants were not on the social security list, the claim could be examined as a potential fraud case. In any event, the losses from fraud were far less than the current cost of processing. The suggestion was adopted with obvious benefits.

The point is that in business processes that develop and change over time, it is almost certain that some parts of the process will become obsolete or unnecessary. Question the value of every part of the process.

---

16. FREEZE THE PROCESS REDESIGN BEFORE STARTING IMPLEMENTATION

Discourage midstream changes unless forced by external conditions. Implementing a moving target is costly and extends elapsed time, especially if information systems changes are involved.

Systems development managers are familiar with the impact continual changes to requirements and design have on the ability to complete development of a computer application. Not only do such changes cause projects to overrun their time and cost budgets, but the end result may be an unmaintainable agglomeration of patches.

Despite all the hype about the "learning organization" and imbuing a company culture with the need for continual change, a BPR project has to have a start and a finish. It must reach a point where you stop planning and start doing. Once the (hopefully) transforming effects of the BPR project have occurred, you may once again discuss incremental evolution of the process.

---

17. CONDUCT PILOT OPERATIONS BEFORE FULL IMPLEMENTATION

Necessary adjustments and changes are easier and less disruptive in a pilot operation (see factor 18).

This factor comes under the heading of "cutting risk." When a process is conducted at many locations in the company, the opportunity exists to try the redesigned process at only a few locations before implementing it fully at all of them. Similarly, it is frequently possible to isolate a portion of the process (such as the processing of only certain vendors' receipts in the accounts payable example) and try it before broad adoption.

The reasons for this approach are well known to systems developers. Programs may have undiscovered bugs on first release, which can be found and fixed during pilot operation with comparatively little impact on total operations. New business processes (and the computer applications that support them) may have bugs also. Confining the risk and the cost of repair to a small segment of the process until most of the bugs have been worked out makes good management sense.

---

18. ALWAYS KEEP THE CUSTOMER IN MIND

A customer focus ensures that the business will be responsive to needs after the redesign. It also encourages continued review and adaptation of processes in the future.

This success factor should probably be both the first and the last because it is pervasive throughout a BPR project. Whether the recipient of the output of a business process is another process in the company or an external party, one end objective must be to make the output attractive to the customer. Management objectives may be couched in terms of cost reduction, improved efficiency, faster time to market, or other terms. However, without delivering a product or service that satisfies the customer, no other measures may ultimately improve or sustain the company's competitive position. In fact, following the example of some Japanese manufacturers, BPR should strive not simply for customer satisfaction but for "customer delight." Customer delight surprises the customer by going beyond satisfaction to positive qualities in the product or service that the customer does not expect. It builds repeat customers to sustain the business. With internal recipients of a process, customer delight acts as a special lubricant to process interfaces that improves cooperation and the effectiveness of the entire company. (See Chapter 18.)

CONCLUSION

Revisiting the horror story in light of the above success factors shows that many of the factors were ignored:

- Management commitment was not obtained from a level high enough to cover all participants in the process.

- Appropriate methods and tools were not used to analyze the problems prior to the determination of a solution.
- The proper BPR team was not created at the start of the project.
- An information systems solution was assumed to be the driving force for the necessary changes.
- No attention was paid to obtaining early successes—the solution was all or nothing.
- The project leader was clearly opposed to ideas put forth by others.
- Employees and participants were not kept informed from the beginning of the project.
- The project manager had the solution in mind before the BPR team was created.

The project had eight strikes against it before it was well under way. Failure could have been predicted almost from the beginning.

The 18 success factors described above do not include many others that would normally be considered common sense for management (such as not writing insulting letters to participants in the process).

If your BPR project fails to use one of the 18 success factors, you had better be very careful. If two are missing, the project may be in danger. If three are ignored, start looking for another job—the project will likely fail to achieve its objectives.

DISCUSSION TOPICS

- Are the success factors described in this chapter reasonable?
- Are some of the success factors exaggerated?
- What other success factors could be added to the list?

Satisfying Users

To a great extent, perception is reality—what people perceive is acted upon as if it were real. No matter how sterling the performance of a CIO or the information systems functions of the company, they will be judged by management on the basis of perception. For this reason, the closing section of this book examines the very real problem of satisfying users and user management.

First this section looks at an application area in which the potential for exposure to top management is substantial—the implementation of executive information facilities. Next the section focuses on the broader target of users and user management, providing experience-based, practical advice on achieving a level beyond simple user satisfaction—user delight.

Without influencing the perception of information systems by users and user management, the best and most effective management techniques will not serve to enable the CIO to keep his or her job.

CHAPTER 17

Executive Information Systems

Executive information systems (EIS) may be the most visible applications in the company. The reputation of the MIS function, and perhaps its senior manager, may stand or fall depending on the results of implementing such a system. This chapter describes "executive information facilities," a step beyond the traditional EIS, and how to make sure their implementation will be successful.

TWO SHORT CASE STUDIES

In 1988 a large automobile and truck manufacturer in Japan installed an EIS in a "war room" at its headquarters. Consistent with the usual Japanese corporate culture, the requirements for the system and its displays of information were developed through progressive iterations by the information systems staff and the president's staff. These requirements were then reviewed with the president by presentation of prototypical displays and war room layouts to obtain his approval. Once approved, the facility was built and staff dedicated to supporting the information needs of the president were instructed in its use. Since packaged executive information systems are not available in Japan, a custom-built system was created. The president was actively interested in developing and using the war room and has made it a center for executive planning meetings. In addition, executives proudly display the facility and its features to visiting executives from other companies. In 1993 plans were in progress to add further communications facilities to the existing EIS.

In 1989, at a major U.S. service industry corporation, a staff assistant to the president decided to acquire an EIS to assist in the preparation of materials for executive meetings. He also hoped to convince the company's president to install the system in the corporate boardroom. After brief consultation with the information systems organization, the assistant purchased an EIS package he had seen advertised.

The data needed to supply the EIS were not readily accessible from corporate computer files because of the structure of those files. Moreover, the information systems organization was not able to fit a project into their backlog to accomplish the development work necessary to construct suitable databases and link the EIS. As a result, clerical support was utilized to enter the data into EIS databases necessary to construct reports using the EIS. The corporate executives were made aware of the existence of the EIS and its capability, but none was interested in using it directly.

To this day, the EIS is considered by management to be a costly way of preparing slides or graphic reports for distribution. The EIS workstation is located in the office of the staff assistant and is, as yet, not linked to any data resources or other display facilities in the company.

What makes the difference between success and failure in these implementations? This chapter examines the factors that lead to successful implementation of executive information facilities (EIFs). It will probably be no surprise that these factors have little to do with the technical aspects of implementation. Competent technical staff are usually available either within the user organization or through consultants. It is the management aspects of installation that create the most problems.

WHAT IS AN EXECUTIVE INFORMATION FACILITY?

The EIF has evolved from the original concept of an EIS into a broad spectrum of functionality designed to assist top management in strategic and tactical planning for the company. EIS functionality originally focused on providing an "easy" way for executives to access critical internal information relating to the operations of the firm. As a result, EISs provided easy-to-use, often object-driven access to corporate databases and a way to abstract from them. A graphical user interface is generally used to provide either touch screen or mouse controls to eliminate use of the keyboard. In addition, information was often presented in predefined graphic display form, with more sophisticated user access directly to online databases. EIS capabilities now include fourth-generation languages for support personnel and a range of tools that aid in accessing databases on various machines and/or various database management systems. With the introduction of external information access, such as input feeds from the Dow-Jones ticker, the EIS has evolved into the executive information facility.

A complete EIF may now include EIS capabilities; external feeds; access to external database services; video-conferencing; teleconferencing;

slow-speed video for document transmission; multilocation screen sharing; fax transmission; electronic mail; handwriting input to the computer; large-screen video projection; mouse, keyboard, or touch-screen controls, and laser printers. Voice-activated controls will soon be available commercially.

The purpose of constructing an EIF is to gain competitive advantage for the corporation through improving executives' access to information and decision-making aids. However, several factors have limited the speed of introduction of this technological aid:

- The reluctance of executives to learn and use computers
- The need for external information in the decision-making process
- The potential for information overload due to the inability to screen out unwanted information

In the new EIF, there is a clear trend toward solving these problems. EIF packages now provide executives the ability to search through gigabytes of information from external sources for mention of their competitors' activities and products or for mention of their own activities or products. Some packages provide geographic and demographic information in an easy-to-access graphical form. Traditional database access tools are being combined with modeling tools and spreadsheets to enhance planning capabilities. In essence, the tools to create an "executive workbench" or the information driver for a "war room" for the corporation are appearing as a stream of commercial products.

In fact, the proliferation of such products is adding a set of new problems. How does the executive decide what he or she wants and how do the corporation's professionals integrate the resulting desires into a coherent EIF?

David DeLong, in his book *Executive Support Systems: The Emergence of Top Management Computer Use*, estimates that more than half of today's executive information systems fail.[1] Observation of a number of attempts to implement executive support systems has led to guidelines for successful design and implementation of EIS and EIF. These guidelines are set forth below.

GUIDELINES FOR SUCCESSFUL IMPLEMENTATION

1. It is necessary to have a champion for the EIF at the executive level. This champion must be an "active" user to convince others of the value of the system.

The need for a champion would seem self-evident from past MIS experiences with the design of information systems. Implementation is rarely successful unless the end user champions the need for the system and the development and implementation process. Too often, however, executives have delegated the responsibility for even requirements specification to "technicians," with a resulting disappointment in the final product.

2.   In order for the champion to be an active user, the system must be easy to use. Ease of use is the result of two factors:

1. The design of the human interface must be as "intuitive" as possible.
2. The executive must have a support person *immediately* available when he or she wishes to use the system.

Executives rarely have the time or the patience to become adroit users of personal computers, much less to learn how to use sophisticated database access tools. The more successful EIS packages on the market recognize this and have carefully designed human interfaces that require little beyond a "point-and-shoot" approach. However, as additional capabilities become available and need to be added to the EIF, the task of integration often falls to the MIS group in the corporation. Such integration may often require skills beyond those available within MIS. The MIS group must be quick to recognize the need for external support and use it appropriately.

Even with the best integration, the executive should be expected to ask that information be presented in a different sequence or fashion, to request the combination of information that had been presented separately, or to request the display of new information that had not been anticipated. This is a natural part of running a business, and the typical executive is accustomed to making such requests of staff members. The EIF must not impede the executive's ability to make such requests and, in fact, must be able to respond more quickly than staff members could in the past. Essentially, this means dedicating technical or research staff to the support of the EIF as their highest-priority function. Unless the MIS organization realizes this need and anticipates it by structuring the budget for support of the EIF, the system is likely to be less responsive to executive needs than older methods. The result could be another technical success that becomes an implementation failure.

3.   Training sessions for the executive in the use of the EIF must be private.

Executives generally do not have the time or the scheduling opportunity to participate in a class. Nor do they wish to expose their ignorance to their peers or staff. In addition, private tutoring not only is more effective and a more efficient use of the executive's time, but it permits the executive to focus attention on functions he or she is most interested in performing.

4. Requirements for information regularly available through the EIF should be defined by repetitive prototyping until the user is satisfied with the presentation.

It is not reasonable to expect most executives to understand the technology underlying the EIF. As a result, one cannot expect the executive to understand the capabilities available to the developer or those in the system. Rather than ask the end user to define his or her needs, it is far more effective to provide prototype displays, or demonstrations of capabilities using prototypical information, and obtain the user's reaction to such demonstrations. It is much easier for the user to say "I like this," or "Move this column over to the left," than for the user to lay out screen formats and graphics.

5. Tools and methods for ad hoc reporting must be at two levels:

1. Tools for the executive to access the EIF files in various combinations
2. Methods and tools to rapidly follow up executive requests for detailed analyses, using support staff.

In guideline 2, the need for support personnel was noted. It should also be noted that there are two levels at which tools are needed. At the first level, for use by the executive, tools are needed in the form of "objects" that are simple for the user to identify and that will perform the required function without the user keying in entries. Such objects should be accessed through the use of icons, pull-down menus, a touch screen, or voice activation. They should not require much knowledge of the system.

At the second level, when the executive requests a report, function, or capability beyond that available through objects, rapid response requires that support personnel be provided tools that can meet special needs or construct new objects with minimal effort and maximum accuracy.

A successful EIF needs both immediate professional support and the appropriate toolkit.

6. It is essential to avoid information overload. The EIF presents an opportunity to eliminate current reports that are not used or to summarize reports (often in graphic form) that are now too detailed.

Working with the staff reporting to the executive to identify initial needs is clearly advantageous in saving executive time and in preparing prototypes. However, once a report exists, there is an inertial tendency to present it to the executive in the usual format and on the usual schedule. Creating an EIF is a marvelous opportunity to reevaluate the entire reporting structure for the executive. As the prototype is gradually presented, the following questions should be asked of the intended user:

- Is this report still needed?
- If this report is needed, with what frequency should it be generated?
- Is the presentation suitable, or should it be graphic, tabular, or in some other form?
- Is there information on other reports that should be combined with the information on this report?
- Is there information you do not now receive that you would like to have?
- How current should the information be on this report?

7.   The EIF will expand in capability through an evolutionary process. Users must be willing to assist in defining their needs progressively and must understand this evolutionary process.

The development and implementation of an EIF can be divided into phases in which increasingly complex capabilities are provided. Initial EIF implementations should be simple to establish the confidence of users in their ability to manage the tools and objects available, to keep the development costs within reason for the initial version, and to permit the implementation to take place on a schedule that is responsive to user requests.

Phase 1 might consist of providing access to existing internal files to construct executive reports or displays. Phase 2 might add displays of external information such as the stock ticker or newswires, video-conferencing, and multilocation screen sharing. Phase 3 might add manipulative capability to perform "what-if" calculations according to different scenarios or to combine information from various files into single displays of information. Phase 4 could introduce advanced technology such as voice control, artificial intelligence, and multimedia capability.

It is important to successful installation that the user understand that the EIF will evolve over time and provide increased capability, but also that the user will periodically be called upon to assist in defining these new capabilities by reviewing successive prototypes.

8.   Users must also understand the continuing development and support costs associated with maintaining the EIF capability.

The combination of the need to provide immediate support for requests and the evolutionary development of the EIF means that the user will have to anticipate an ongoing cost for the EIF, not just the initial implementation cost. Failure to obtain this understanding and agreement before the EIF development project is initiated will result in an unhappy executive at the next budget cycle. The planning and budgeting for the EIF project must clearly set forth the multiyear nature of the development and the ongoing operating costs associated with the system.

9.   Business decisions are frequently made on the basis of relationships between external and internal information. EIF support capability may be required to analyze and digest external information to present a complete decision-making picture.

Many EIF systems implemented are not completely successful because they are based on the designers' misperception that corporate decisions are made on the basis of internal information, and that all that needs to be done is to provide that internal information more quickly and in a more understandable form. Certainly, such information is necessary, but it is not sufficient. High-level corporate decision making requires external information such as the price of the corporation's stock, the price of competitors' stock, sales trends for competitors, product and market trends, and so forth. But just providing external information is not enough. Eventually, the EIF must provide the capability to display relationships between relevant external and internal information in order to adequately address the decision-making needs of the executive.

10.   A substantial part of the value of the EIF is the result of its ability to communicate (share) information among the appropriate parties. This ability must be supported by the ability to send information presentations developed through the EIF to the offices of concerned executives and by the ability to discuss such information as close to "real time" as possible. Such sharing tools may include output to fax, telephone, slowscan video with video-conferencing, or even printed output.

Information has little value unless it results in actions or is communicated to others to initiate actions. An EIF that exists in isolation in a corporate war room has limited value except when the necessary executives and managers are all assembled there. To make an effective corporatewide tool of the EIF, you must have the ability to transmit the information assembled through the EIF capabilities. Initially, this can be accomplished simply by attaching a printer to the EIF workstation to obtain paper copies of displays on command.

In the long run, for EIFs to be truly effective, communication tools that are more advanced than a printer are needed. A second step may include installing the capability to transmit a display and associated notes to the PC or workstation of selected executives and managers through electronic mail.

A third step may include multimedia cooperative processing in which executives at different locations concurrently view and manipulate common displays (multilocation screen sharing) and discuss these displays simultaneously.

11. Data manipulation and complex functions of the EIF will require support staff participation for an indefinite period into the future.

The executive user must understand that current technology will not be able to provide answers to all of his or her questions through direct interface with the EIF system. In other words, special requests will continue to require the assistance of support staff until EIF systems have the intelligence and knowledge equal to that of support staff. I have no doubt that such a capability will eventually exist, but it cannot be expected within near-term horizons.

12. Executives must feel comfortable with the security of the information contained in the EIF and with the communication of that information.

The strategic planning (and often much critical tactical planning) of the corporation takes place at the executive level toward which the EIF is directed. Such information processing, storage, and communication requires the utmost confidentiality in this competitive world. The practice of information security shows that three critical issues must be addressed: confidentiality, availability, and integrity of information. Maintaining confidentiality is insufficient to ensure the security of the EIF. Auditable controls must be built in to the system to ensure that the information cannot be accessed by unauthorized persons, that information will be available when needed by the executive, and that information will not be corrupted in any manner. Inviting the internal audit staff of the company or a qualified external consultant to examine and approve the security of the system might reassure executives that the system can be used with confidence.

13. The information in the EIF will often comprise inputs from various operating and staff executives. Secretaries and support staff of executives must be quickly linked into the EIF through office automation tools to act as information suppliers to the EIF and to abstract information from the EIF for analysis.

If an EIF is viewed as a stand-alone facility with access to corporate databases containing only operational transactions or accounting, it runs the danger of failing to include critical information not usually available in corporate databases. Such information may consist of special intelligence gained by corporate officers, information and trend analyses, or other valuable decision-making inputs from a variety of corporate sources. Eventually the EIF must reach out to the workstations of corporate officers and their staffs to gain appropriate inputs (although access to EIF files and capabilities in full may be restricted to a subset of these people). As a result, the design of the EIF must emphasize compatibility with the tools and equipment used throughout the corporate offices.

14. Functions and facilities of the EIF must work the first time they are used by the executives and must work consistently thereafter. The system must be adequately tested before installation, before changes or new displays are implemented, and periodically when not in use by the executive staff.

In guideline 12, concerns about availability and information integrity were addressed. The present concern is with initial and continuing reliability and consistency of operation. Creating an EIF exposes the system's developers to the toughest client in the corporation, the one with the least patience with failure or tolerance for error. Thus, rigorous quality assurance in installation and upgrading of the EIF is essential. In fact, it would be wise to adopt the techniques used by some military systems integrators in which the system is completely constructed and tested at a "manufacturing" site first, then disassembled, shipped, reassembled, and retested at the delivery point.

Do not expose the executive to your mistakes. For example, a copy of the EIF should be maintained in the development facility (to the extent possible and consistent with security). New or prototype displays should be developed "off-line" and out of view of the executive, then presented for successive evaluation and comment.

CONCLUSION

An EIF can be of significant value as an aid to corporate planning and control, but it can realize its full potential only if the users understand the power of its tools and its limitations. "Overselling" an EIF by permitting unwarranted expectations will result in disappointment of the most important client system developers can have. It will probably also result in the installation of an expensive facility that is underutilized. The guidelines stated in this chapter can aid in avoiding such failures.

DISCUSSION TOPICS

- Do you know of any EIFs in use? How and by whom are they used? Have they successfully met their original intent?
- What features could be added to an EIF to make it easier for an executive to learn and use?
- What factors motivate an executive to learn and use an EIF?

REFERENCE

1. Rockart, J.F., and Delong, D.W., "Executive Support Systems: The Emergence of Top Management Computer Use," Irwin, Homewood, IL, 1988.

CHAPTER 18

Beyond Satisfaction

Being a successful CIO requires ensuring the satisfaction of your customers. This chapter describes methods and techniques that can lead beyond the usual levels of customer satisfaction. It is fitting that this book end with a chapter on ways to ensure that you keep your job and become a candidate for the next major opportunity.

THE CHALLENGE: USER DELIGHT

In early 1993, Deloitte & Touche surveyed 534 North American CIOs[1] and found that CIO turnover amounted to 25 percent in companies with over $5 billion in revenue. In fact, turnover was not far behind that figure for companies with over $300 million in revenue. Deloitte & Touche also found that in 1991 and 1992, over a third of CIOs who left their positions were dismissed or demoted and that the average tenure for new CIOs was between 18 and 24 months.

During this same period, several surveys indicated that the top issues commanding the attention of CIOs were aligning IS strategy with corporate strategy and redesigning business processes. If one is to believe the turnover rates in the early 1990s, the issues chosen by CIOs must have been somewhat off the mark.

Trying to play the political game and stay current with the continual power shifts in corporate management probably does not help either. After all, the political game has been going on for millennia—certainly longer than the last few years of CIO turnover statistics. It seems that the core issue for preserving job tenure is related to the satisfaction of those to whom the CIO and the MIS function provide their services. In MIS parlance, the recipients of their services are called "users." (In some more perceptive MIS organizations, they are called "customers.")

In this increasingly competitive world, many firms are finding that "customer satisfaction" simply is not enough to retain customer loyalty. These firms are now taking a lesson from Tom Peters' book *Liberation Management* and striving for "customer delight."[2] Customer delight may be defined as surprising the customer with enhanced product or service qualities that go beyond customer expectations. In a similar fashion, CIOs and their MIS groups must strive for "user delight" beyond user satisfaction.

Adopting a mission to create user delight means answering three fundamental questions:

- How can user delight be defined?
- How can user delight be achieved?
- How can MIS be made to adopt the right attitudes?

DEFINING USER DELIGHT

A major Japanese auto manufacturer took several paths in the early 1990s to design a car from the ground up. The intention was to create a car that would achieve customer delight and a strong foothold in the market from the day it was introduced. First, the engineering team identified the two target cars in their chosen price range that had the greatest reputations for customer satisfaction. They examined every facet of these cars. In fact, they dismantled them to determine how they were engineered and built.

Next, they obtained demographic studies of the target cars' owners, identifying the incomes, the professions, the commuting habits, the life styles, the family sizes, the number of cars owned, and any other statistics that might add to their knowledge of the potential buyers for the new car. Based on the first two studies, they envisioned features for the new car that might be desired by or delight the potential buyers. Following this, they surveyed a sample of owners of the target cars in person to find out what the owners liked or disliked about the cars and the service provided by dealers. This survey asked owners what other features they would like to have that were not provided by their current cars. However, realizing that the owners might have difficulty visualizing potential improvements, the engineers prepared a list. After the owners provided their suggestions, they were asked to rank the improvements visualized by the engineers.

At the end of the study, the designers and engineers had insights into the manufacturing processes that contributed to satisfaction, the features of ownership that provided satisfaction, and the features that would enhance the product to create customer delight. The car was a success from the start.

CIOs can learn several lessons from this automaker's approach:

- Know your customers.
- Know your customers' needs.
- Know how the competition works.
- Identify satisfaction factors.
- Create customer delight ideas.
- Validate customer delight ideas.
- Implement customer delight ideas.

These are complex lessons for designing and building a successful car. They are no less complex for MIS, but they are different.

The Lessons in Defining User Delight

Know your customers. An auto manufacturer must consider primary buyers and secondary buyers (generally spouses), but for volume sales they must consider classes of buyers and use generalizations from demographic information supplemented by individual interviews. For MIS there are generally several "buyers" or customers to consider—the end user, first-line supervision, middle management, and the executive level. Each successive level is further away from the actual business process work supported by the information system. On the other hand, each successive level has more "clout" in the organization and is able to exert more influence on management decisions and/or more political pressure. This creates an inverse relationship between knowledge of the work (and the ability to judge the satisfaction with the information systems) and the ability to influence the design of the information systems. (See Figure 18.1.)

Executive	Clout		Job knowledge
Middle manager	Clout		Job knowledge
Supervisor	Clout		Job knowledge
End user	Clout	Job knowledge	

Figure 18.1. Relative job knowledge compared to clout

On the other hand, end users have some hidden clout. That is, the views of top management are influenced by opinions that filter up the chain and responses to executive concerns about workgroup performance. In plain English, if MIS is getting in the way of workers doing their jobs, top management will hear about it sooner or later.

For a single application, you need to know the goals, desires, habits, and prejudices of the four levels concerned, which is clearly difficult if not impossible. Fortunately for the CIO, this does not mean the he or she must know everyone in the company. What it does mean is that part of the CIO's job is to establish regular communications with other executives in the company and to make sure that members of the MIS staff establish such channels at other levels. It also means that in the process of application design or business process redesign, the membership of the design team must represent the end users who will use the system.

Know your customers' needs. Step 1 of this process is knowing your customers' business. That corporations are recognizing this requirement is evidenced by the increasing number of non-MIS executives who are being named to the CIO post. Not only the CIO must understand the business; systems analysts, technology planners, systems architects, and others on the MIS staff must understand the context in which their work products or services will be used, or they cannot truly meet business needs. In fact, even computer operations personnel must be sufficiently aware of the business needs to establish service priorities or plan for disaster recovery.

One aspect that many CIOs have failed to recognize in the attempt to align IT strategy with corporate business strategy is that many companies are not in just one business. Many large corporations are composed of several divisions that are so big and so specifically focused that they may be viewed as different businesses. Each of these businesses contains different business processes and has different strategies to which information technology must respond. Knowing the customers' needs means knowing each of the businesses that MIS must serve.

Customer needs take several forms. They may be broadly classified as business and personal requirements. Business requirements for systems include functionality, timing, responsiveness, availability of information or information resources, and confidentiality. Personal requirements include ease of learning, ease of use, flexibility, polite service, and career ambitions. The last of these may be the actual driving force for many systems development projects, so it should not be ignored.

Know how the competition works. Not only is it wise to know about the information technology applications of competitors, but it is critical to understand how and how well these applications support competitors' business processes. Much of this information may be gleaned from trade publications and conferences, but companies are frequently turning to benchmarking exercises conducted by consultants to evaluate their use of information technology and the effectiveness of their business processes. Bare figures of performance, response times, availability, unit costs, and so forth tell a small part of the story. Anecdotal information and subjective evaluations may provide more useful ideas than do statistics or accounting. When line executives sponsor benchmarking studies, CIOs need to be involved and add their concerns for examination. More important, CIOs need to have benchmarking studies of their own that focus not only on cost and efficiency but on user satisfaction.

Identify satisfaction factors. The market study aspect of improving MIS services can never be ignored. Any business that becomes inward-looking and forgets its customer focus does so at its peril. So too with MIS.

The CIO has many tools to use in this task. Periodic (regular) customer surveys may be conducted by internal staff or supplemented with consulting assistance. Such surveys should make a point of asking users not only to rate their satisfaction but to assign weights indicating the relative importance of the factors. (Anonymity may help to get honest responses.) Feedback mechanisms that formalize complaints and follow-up responses may be logged, tracked, and analyzed. Feedback from user-support functions should be recorded. The equivalent of product comment cards may be used to gather information. Prototyping and the associated prototype testing by end users provides a feedback method at the time of system design.

Once satisfaction factors and their relative importance have been identified by these methods, supplemented by personal contacts of MIS staff with all levels of the customer community, they may be gathered and analyzed to establish a baseline of satisfaction for each major application domain. Although most application domains have much in common, such an approach is necessary because each application domain or business process potentially represents a different "market." Satisfaction factors (or criteria) for accounting systems may differ substantially from inventory management or computer-aided design (CAD) systems.

Create customer delight ideas. Most users are rarely able to identify new ideas that will add to their satisfaction, primarily because they do not know what is possible from the technology. It is therefore incumbent on the MIS staff to identify features and functions of their service that will create delight on the part of users, just as the automotive engineers did in the product development example.

The tools at hand for this task were established in the tasks described earlier: familiarity with users, understanding of business processes, understanding of customer motivations, knowledge of competitors' solutions, ranked satisfaction factors, and knowledge of what MIS and the technology can do. Using these tools, the MIS staff can hold "brainstorming" sessions to bring out ideas. Such sessions should be approached in the following manner:

- Select the brainstorming teams for each application domain; include representatives from each of the MIS areas that provide services to the concerned users.
- Appoint a session chairperson who is familiar with brainstorming or focus group techniques and who has no direct interest in the session outcomes. (An external consultant may be of great value in this role.)
- Provide copies of all the information gathered from all domains to all team members. Information gathered from one domain may provide ideas for others.
- Conduct the brainstorming session according to specific rules:
  - The agenda should take on one aspect of the domain at a time. A good approach is to follow the system life cycle from initial request through ongoing delivery.
  - Do not allow any idea proposed to be rejected or disputed. The value of ideas will be discussed later.
  - Record all ideas so that they are visible to all members of the team during the meeting. Many use flip-chart paper for this and tape filled pages to the walls of the meeting room.
  - Following the session, document all ideas and distribute them to team members.
- Ask team members to rank the ideas and submit them to the chairperson. The chairperson collates the rankings and prepares a handout and slides for the next session.
- Conduct a second session to discuss the results of ranking the ideas and to discuss the technical and cost feasibility of the ideas. The result of this session should be a list of feasible user delight ideas that are within the capability of the company to support. (Note that ideas should not be rejected on a cost basis, since users may be willing to pay for extra benefits.)

Validate customer delight ideas. The ideas created above provide material for the next step, which is to validate the ideas with users.

First, MIS should ask the users in an application domain to join a focus group on user satisfaction. Participants should be selected from each functional unit in the organization that has an interest in the domain. They should be provided with a copy of the ranked satisfaction factors originally gathered and analyzed as a basis for discussion (not the user delight ideas resulting from the MIS brainstorming). With this as an introduction, the focus group session should be conducted in the same manner as the brainstorming sessions within MIS. If participants have difficulty initiating new ideas, some of the ideas on the MIS user delight list may be introduced.

The session should continue until all the ideas on the MIS list have been proposed and users have no further ideas. In the same session, the participants should be asked to rank the resulting list of ideas by voting on their relative importance or value.

Second, the outputs of the user focus group should be evaluated by MIS in terms of feasibility, cost, and anticipated benefit, then presented to a meeting of supervisors and middle managers. The purpose of this meeting is to examine the ideas and rank their value and importance from the perspective of this group. The intent of this ranking is to provide "buy-in" to the ideas and the cooperation of these management levels. The ranking will also reflect the group's perspective on user delight and the value of the ideas to the company.

Implement customer delight ideas. The lists of user delight factors created through the validation process provide input for a meeting at the executive level to obtain concurrence and approval for implementation.

Typically, many of the ideas may be implemented by MIS without the need for executive concurrence. Ideas such as training MIS staff to handle user requests in a polite, businesslike manner are completely under MIS control. However, other ideas may involve changes to applications or equipment that require substantial investment. Presenting such ideas to senior executives requires preparation so that all aspects of the change are understood. MIS groups should be familiar with the methods used for preparing justifications for system changes.

When the proposed changes are recommended to management, the process through which they were obtained should be provided as background, and the results of the validation sessions should be presented prior to the specific proposals. A CIO familiar with the business and with the characteristics of the executive customers to whom the proposals are being presented should have little trouble orienting the presentation to sell the ideas.

ACHIEVING USER DELIGHT

Delight is in the eye of the beholder. This is another way of pointing out that user delight is a function of the current situation. An attribute that represents satisfaction in one situation may represent delight in another, and we quickly come to take for granted those features that are initially novelties. As a result, striving for user delight is a never-ending effort.

The Steps in Achieving User Delight

It would be impossible to identify all the factors that represent delight to users. The following are some proven suggestions.

Processing user requests. In many companies, users are discouraged from making requests for application changes or new services by the extensive procedures and approvals required. If MIS is truly to serve the business interests of the company and enhance business processes, the company as a whole must empower users by removing roadblocks to obtaining service. Reevaluate your current user request processes with this objective in mind. Devise methods by which MIS can assist users to formulate and process requests.

Defining user requirements. Evidence continues to mount that simply automating existing business processes does not achieve the gains intended. On the other hand, dramatic breakthroughs continue to be reported when business process redesign (BPR) techniques are used. BPR methods result in redesigned business processes that are often enabled by information technology. New applications or changes to existing applications have a much better chance of achieving business goals if the requirements are based on BPR project results.

BPR projects make use of techniques akin to joint application development (JAD) approaches to requirements definition. That is, they incorporate end user teams in the process. However, where JAD starts with requirements definition, BPR starts with improving the business process and considers information technology as an enabler for the new processes. Don't confuse BPR with new systems development.

The delight factors resulting from a BPR approach are not only those that come to users from a feeling of involvement but also those that extend to management from projects that reach business objectives.

System design. Many users have become accustomed to the ease-of-use characteristics of PC and expect the same characteristics in mainframe or minicomputer applications. This elevation of user expectations is one cause for dissatisfaction with legacy systems that may otherwise perform the necessary functions.

New applications, designed to permit PC interfaces, should be designed to use the features (such as pull-down menus, and point-and-click icons) that are used by the resident PC applications. This will remove context-switching as a barrier to ease of learning and ease of use.

Where legacy systems still perform the appropriate functions, converting the old terminal interface to a PC interface will often extend the life of the application and lead to user delight (and probably improved productivity).

A substantial part of the emphasis in system design should be on the ergonomic aspects of the system. Since many analysts and programmers know little of ergonomics, it pays to employ an ergonomics consultant to work with the team on design of the human interface. Users will be delighted with the results.

System development. Two elements of dissatisfaction that may be addressed in system development are the unanticipated cost of development and deployment and the length of time required before results are available for use.

Aside from MIS project overruns, unanticipated costs arise from a failure on the part of users to understand that deploying most new applications requires at least as much effort by the user organization as the effort spent by MIS in development. The solution to this is straightforward: When a project is proposed, inform users of the level of commitment required on their part and the specific tasks for which they will be responsible. Such tasks include creation of test beds (databases, transaction data, test scenarios, etc.) prototype testing, acceptance testing, end user training, design reviews, system roll out, and so forth.

To address the time issue will require that MIS borrow techniques from companies that face competitive time-to-market constraints for releasing new products and services. Many such techniques can be adopted. One steals some lessons from rapid prototyping. Rapid prototyping techniques break down a large effort into more doable chunks and then, with customer participation, assign priorities to the chunks. With this approach, large systems development efforts frequently can be turned into incremental efforts delivering interim products that demonstrate benefits. Delivery of useable components every six months will delight a customer far more than waiting three years for a major development project to be completed. Furthermore, MIS risk is reduced and the opportunity to make interim design adjustments to keep up with changing business needs is improved.

System acceptance testing. When a project manager must be responsible for debugging a system during acceptance test, fine-tuning performance characteristics, managing the development staff, collecting user observations and complaints, and managing the acceptance test procedure, none of these tasks are done well. Either MIS or the user organization must assign a full-time manager for acceptance testing and create a formal procedure for feedback of test results and follow-up on corrections. (Incidentally, this also applies to system roll out.) Imagine the delight of the users when they know who to call, find that person available, and obtain prompt and intelligent responses.

Computer and telecommunications operations. As online applications increasingly dominate the use of mainframes and minicomputers, it has become apparent that user delight means the total transparency of operations. It is only when operations fails in their assigned tasks that their existence becomes apparent.

It does absolutely no good for MIS to publish statistics that prove that the mainframe is available 99.97 percent of the time when users are concerned about the availability of their applications. (This is just as true of the customer who is confronted by a bank teller offering the excuse that "the computer is down.")

Failing 100 percent transparency (which most of us find virtually impossible), the next best things are preparedness and honest communication. Well-prepared contingency plans and recovery plans should be in place and be understood by both operations staff and users. Recovery drills should be run with user cooperation and an understanding of the reasons. When failures do occur, *all* concerned parties should receive frequent candid bulletins on system and application status until recovery is completed. If network failure is involved and e-mail bulletins are impossible, it is not going too far to use the telephone to keep users informed.

In addition to these measures, each user should have a point of contact to report problems and obtain status reports. That point of contact should be staffed continually during business hours. Furthermore, the contact point should be informed enough to respond appropriately, and not merely refer the caller to another staff member. If another specialist is required to respond to the user, that specialist should call the user.

End user support. End user support personnel are the frontline troops of MIS. Supporting end users, especially in systems composed of personal computers, workstations, or client-server systems, takes application knowledge, technical knowledge, diagnostic skills, on-the-spot repair skills, an understanding of business priorities, patience, politeness, and communication skills. If your current support staff lack any of these qualities, they will fall short in providing user delight—in fact, they will fail at user satisfaction. The keys to success lie in rigorous attention to staff selection, continuous training to keep staff up to date, and "immediate" availability of support.

Since immediate availability is generally not cost-effective or feasible, the alternative selected by many companies is some level of user self-support. Two methods may help in this approach. First, users should be well-trained in the use of equipment and systems. We would not expect an employee to operate machine tools without adequate training; neither should we expect employees to operate computers and applications without training. Second, in each department or region of an office or plant, there is usually one employee whose fascination with the technology has led him or her to become more expert than others. A growing number of companies have deliberately identified such employees and appointed them as "gurus" to create a first line of diagnosis and defense before calling the MIS support person. Far from conflicting with job duties, such appointments have generally brought higher productivity to the workgroup.

End user support provides one of the greatest opportunities for promoting user delight. A few months ago I had a hard disk drive failure on my PC just as I was nearing the end of a report on which I had worked all week. The last time I had backed up the drive was the previous week, so I faced the prospect not only of repeating a week's work but of missing a deadline. I called our company's end user support group for help and explained the situation to the technician. He came to my office an hour later to pick up my computer, promising to do his best to salvage the data on the drive and replace the drive.

When I arrived at my office the next morning, I found a computer installed and a note from the technician explaining that the new disk drive would have to be ordered and so it would take a few days to have my machine repaired. For the interim, he had provided an equivalent machine from the central pool. In addition, he had loaded the operating system and the word processing software I was using and had loaded all the files that he could salvage from the old drive. He also left directions for me to examine the salvaged files and find the ones on which I had been working. Fortunately, the critical files were undamaged. I called him immediately to thank him for his help in the emergency.

I found out later that the technician, realizing my predicament, had worked four hours after his shift ended to provide me with the ability to complete my report on time. After I completed my report, I wrote a letter to his manager expressing my appreciation for the extra effort the technician had provided. I was delighted.

My company has a "spot award" system that allows each manager a budget to make small on-the-spot monetary awards for efforts above the usual. I recommended in my letter to the manager that such an award was appropriate. The award was presented to the technician within the next week at a meeting of the end user support department, which I attended.

Other ideas. Among other ideas that have been observed in business, some that may be adopted by MIS follow:

- Anticipate users' needs by tracking their complaints and help requests on a weekly basis. When the frequency of complaints or help requests from one application or one organization rises, contact the unit managers and investigate immediately. See what can be done to alleviate the problem before it becomes noticeable.
- Initiate a quarterly outstanding user award. Establish and publicize the award criteria and make a small ceremony of the award presentation.
- Encourage feedback from users; do not penalize it. Edward Koch, mayor of New York in the 1980s, used to walk the streets and question citizens about his performance, asking, "How'm I doing?" When a user offers suggestions or makes a complaint, try to have an MIS staff member visit the user and record the user's comments for your tracking system. If a visit is not practical in a short time, make a phone call and take notes for action. Follow up user interactions with a brief note on results or recognition of the user's contribution (with a copy to his or her manager). Make friends of users.
- Measure the quality of MIS service by how it affects users and their customers. Such statistics are more meaningful than technical performance measures.
- Establish online bulletin boards to permit users and MIS staff to share problems, experiences, and solutions relating to specific applications or systems (e.g., a new accounting application, a personal computer operating environment, spreadsheet software).
- Keep promises to users. Project delays and computer outages will happen, whatever precautions are taken, but the prompt return of promised phone calls will go far to minimize users' irritation.
- Manage by walking around. A CIO encased in a remote office will only receive second- or thirdhand interpretations of reality. Walking around provides a firsthand view of how the business of MIS is conducted and offers opportunities to reinforce the messages about quality, service, and user delight.
- Empower MIS staff members to solve user problems without the approval of several layers of management. Let them start on solving the problem while concurrently informing supervisors. Don't penalize mistakes made in the attempt to provide better service—use them as a teaching opportunity.
- Take advantage of technology to provide user support. Use remote diagnostic tools and screen-sharing tools so that technicians can see what users are doing while they discuss their problem.
- Large "help desk" operations should install automatic call management systems so that the first available operator answers the call.

(AMP, Inc., of Harrisburg, Pennsylvania, has a goal of answering customer calls on the first ring.)

- If your customer support group maintains company PCs, printers,
  and other devices, make sure you have a good spares inventory management system so that repairs or replacements do not have to wait for
  parts. (If you outsource such maintenance, require your vendors to
  maintain adequate inventories and track their performance.)
- As increasing numbers of company personnel use mobile computers
  and communications devices, anticipate their needs and establish service units to support them.
- Ford, Xerox, Dow Chemical, and many other companies have found
  that the factors that differentiate them from competitors are coming
  less from their products and more from their service. Call in your
  company's sales and marketing or customer service managers to advise you on how to delight MIS users.

CHANGING THE MIS CULTURE

MIS personnel are usually selected for their technical qualifications, and
such qualifications are clearly important. On the other hand, superb technical capability is no guarantee of the ability to achieve user delight. For
example, 3M measures the performance of its customer representatives in
terms of core competencies that include problem solving, communications, and interpersonal skills. Such skills may not be inherent in the members of the MIS staff.

Several major MIS organizations have adopted mission statements
that set forth the goal of becoming a "customer-oriented" service organization, but such statements in themselves rarely change the attitudes or the
skills of employees. As S. I. Hayakawa, the famous semanticist said, "The
map is not the territory." That is, saying it does not make it so. However, it
is within the power of the MIS organization to make it so. It can be done
through several measures.

- Identify staff members who will directly interface with users.
- Conduct (or hire a consultant to conduct) training sessions for all staff
  members on customer service attitudes and on their responsibilities to
  achieve customer delight. Pay special attention to staff currently in
  user interface positions. Do not assume that MIS managers already
  know about customer service—make sure they take the training, too.
- Adopt a total quality management program for MIS and add TQM
  training for all staff members.
- Identify employees who will probably never be suitable for close rela-

tionships with users and find other, equivalent positions for them in the organization. Some otherwise productive employees may need to make careers in positions that do not expose MIS to adverse user reactions.

- Make user satisfaction and user delight pay off for employees through award systems for special performance and by measuring the performance of those in user interface positions according to user satisfaction.
- Encourage and reward ideas that will contribute to user delight.
- Reward exemplary performance promptly and publicly. Doing so is a CIO's investment in his or her future.

Finally, never stop seeking new ideas for customer delight. Changing technologies, applications, and business needs will always create new opportunities. Most of the employees of a company want to do a good job. Their advancement in careers, and sometimes even their job retention, motivates them to be as productive as they can be. Satisfaction, and delight beyond satisfaction, is achieved by providing tools and support that help users do their jobs well and that do not get in the way.

CONCLUSION

Achieving user delight is a significant factor in the success of an MIS organization and in maintaining the job tenure of the CIO. This chapter has described the steps to identify factors that will lead to user delight, has provided some initial ideas to delight users, and has recommended the steps to take to create a culture oriented to user delight in your MIS group. Implementing these ideas, and the others that you will discover by following the above steps, will not only ease the friction between MIS and users, but will lubricate the wheels of that relationship.

DISCUSSION TOPICS

- Is this chapter the most important in the book? Why or why not?
- What other means can be used to change the culture of an organization to a service culture?
- What other techniques can be used or adapted from other functions in the company to achieve customer delight?

REFERENCES

1. King, J. "Hold onto your Head," *Computerworld* (August 9, 1993): 85–90.
2. Peters, T. *Liberation Management: Necessary Disorganization in the Nanosecond Nineties*, Knopf: New York, 1992.

A Final Word (or "What does all this mean?")

Economic forces in the early 1990s drove companies to massive "downsizing" of their workforces, to reorientation of the business through acquisition and diversification, and to globalization to secure markets. The demographics of advanced countries are changing as populations age and as the need for workers shrinks. The "information age" is rapidly becoming a reality. The acceleration of technological breakthroughs and innovation continues to bring new tools to the market, and those tools change the competitive environment of the firm. Times are turbulent as this book is written, and they will probably continue to be turbulent for some time to come. After all, the turbulence created by the industrial revolution spanned over two hundred years.

This book set out to be a means of exploring how information systems and technology must be managed in the years beginning in the mid-1990s, and a means of sharing my experience and that of the many CIOs I have observed during a 35-year career in information systems management and consulting. This sharing of experience has taken the form of explaining "best practices" observed at a level that provides practical advice and methods.

As stated in the beginning, this book was not intended to explore every aspect of information systems and technology management nor treat every topic explored equally. Instead, it has reflected my experience with those issues that have proven to be most troublesome to CIOs and MIS managers.

The February 1, 1994, issue of CIO[1] showed the results of the Index Group's 1994 survey of 556 CIOs in companies with more than $250 million in sales (the majority had over $1 billion in sales). Shown below are the top management concerns of the CIOs surveyed, ranked in order of importance.

	1994	1993	1992	1991	1990
Reengineering business processes	1	1	2	1	1
Aligning IS and corporate goals	2	2	1	2	4
Organizing/utilizing data	3	4	4	5	7
Instituting cross-functional systems	4	4	6	3	3
Creating an information architecture	4	7	3	8	9
Improving the system development process	6	3	9	4	6
Updating obsolete systems	7	8	18	NR	13
Improving the IS human resource	8	12	5	13	11
Integrating systems	8	11	13	9	16
Changing technology platforms	8	10	NR	NR	NR

NR = not rated that year.

This book has addressed eight of the top ten issues facing CIOs today. The reader might consider how the top issues have changed, or if they have changed.

Aside from providing practical methods to solve critical problems, this book has set forth a vision of the coming paradigm for success in information systems management. CIOs in the future will have to manage by influence rather than direct control, and they will have to be intensely involved in the business of the company.

One theme permeates this book—the need for information systems professionals to gain and maintain a knowledge of the business organization they serve and of the industry in which that business operates. It is not sufficient for CIOs and IS staff members who hope to advance their careers to be super-technicians. In truth, it never was enough.

Now, and as they will be in the future, information technology and the systems built from that technology are an integral part of business operations, relationships with suppliers and customers, and the formulation of the competitive strategy of the firm.

All this considered, the final chapter of this book may be the ultimate key to a successful career as a CIO. Satisfying the customer and moving beyond satisfaction to "customer delight" are the keystones of business success. All the methods and techniques described in this book are oriented to this end.

From reading this book, readers who are CIOs may pick up useful ideas practiced by others in their position; readers who aspire to be CIOs may be better prepared for the role; and readers who are managers in other functions may develop a better understanding of the problems faced by the CIO and some of the solutions to those problems.

REFERENCE

1. Champy, J.A. "An Ambitious Agenda." *CIO* (February 1, 1994): 24–26.

Transaction Analysis Methods

INTRODUCTION

Transaction analysis (TA) is a technique developed by SRI International for determining the satisfaction level of internal "customers" in an enterprise with the services they receive from other functional units or processes. The technique is also useful for prioritizing the needs for those services on the basis of perceived value (or importance) to customers. When supplemented by interviews, TA can lead to specific problem definition helpful to the BPR project.

In addition, TA can aid in identifying the types of information and support provided, the flow of information and support, the overlap and interdependence of organizational units, and any potential redundancy of activities.

There are six basic steps in TA studies:

1. Identification of functions and activities involved in a process
2. Identification of the providers and receivers of information or support
3. Survey of the providers and receivers
4. Validation of the survey responses through supplementary interviews
5. Analysis of the survey results
6. Reporting conclusions (as input to the BPR project)

In the following task descriptions "providers" is the term used for those functions or organizations that participate in a business process by providing outputs to internal customers. The internal customers who make use of the outputs are known as "receivers."

TA techniques may be used in two ways: in a broad survey approach or in a workshop approach. The broad survey approach is described first.

THE BROAD SURVEY APPROACH TO TA

The broad survey approach assumes that a significant population of the enterprise makes use of the outputs of the business process being studied. It further assumes that this population is scattered throughout the enterprise and uses the various process outputs for different purposes. The approach is described in the following series of tasks. The description assumes the use of an external consultant to conduct the study in order to maintain the confidentiality of the responders and the interviewees. Experience has shown that employees are usually more candid about the measures being taken if an external, objective party conducts the survey and they are assured anonymity.

Task 1: Identification of Functions and Activities

In the first task of the study, the consultant, working with a client-appointed project coordinator, identifies the various outputs of the business process. Initially, the team must identify the organizational units or functions that are output providers in the business process. Managers of these units are interviewed to determine what outputs they produce (or activities they perform) in support of the receivers. These outputs are described in high-level terms that identify the information or the support activities provided to receivers. For example, an activity may be "providing accounting information" but this does not indicate the title of each accounting report provided (unless the report is a critical output). Similarly, a support function should be described as "diagnosing-production line problems," not as "diagnosing roller-bearing failures" unless that level of detail is needed.

The art of identifying activities is in limiting the number of activities to those that can be reasonably comprehended by the receivers responding to a written survey, and in providing clear and unambiguous definitions of activities. The level of detail is held at the highest level consistent with the idea that if individual receivers indicate lack of satisfaction with or importance for the activity, they may be interviewed to obtain the necessary detail. A survey that contains more than 20 activities is probably too detailed or the process being investigated has been too broadly defined.

Once the activities have been defined, each activity is numbered and a list is prepared to accompany the survey form. This list will also be input to the TA analysis database for transaction verification and file structure purposes. (SRI International uses a database management system to sort and compare the responses of providers and receivers.)

Task 2: Identification of Providers and Receivers

Again, working with the managers of the provider groups, the organizational units to which these groups provide outputs are identified as well as the individuals who work with these outputs. Furthermore, the providers are asked to list the organizations that provide inputs to them and the individuals who provide these inputs. (Remember that most organizational units are both providers and receivers of services. The survey should be broad enough to contain the business process itself and to indicate the interfaces to other processes. The specific boundaries of the business process may change as a result of the survey.) The individuals listed normally should be at the first-line supervisory level; however, they may include technical specialists with unique capabilities.

Most enterprises have an organizational numbering structure and a naming structure (usually resulting in abbreviated titles or acronyms). Either or both of these may be used to identify the organizations participating. It is usually necessary to obtain the mailing addresses and/or internal mail stop numbers for the individuals to be surveyed and their phone number so that they can be contacted for follow-up. Detail at this level must be gathered to ensure that responses to the survey are complete. At the conclusion, a list should be prepared of all organizational units and key individuals known to be involved as providers or receivers in the business process. This list has three purposes:

- To accompany the survey as a key for respondents to identify their providers or receivers
- As a mailing list for providers and receivers
- As input to the TA analysis database for transaction verification and file structure purposes

Task 3: Survey of Providers and Receivers

The first part of this task is setting up the survey forms for data collection. The data collected through these forms will be input to a database application. The application consists of an input module that validates data against the organization and activity lists and builds the database and modules that permit the printing of reports from the database. These reports allow review of the information and compare the results of receiver and provider inputs against each other by organization and activity. (See task 5.)

Each person surveyed receives two sets of forms plus the lists prepared in previous tasks. One set of forms is for the person to respond as a provider; the other set, for the person to respond as a receiver. The survey forms should have a heading that indicates the person's name, organization affiliation, address, and phone number. In addition, it should clearly indicate whether the person should respond as a receiver or as a provider of the activities he or she lists. Finally, the heading should leave space for the survey team to enter a transaction number so that records may be uniquely identified in the database.

The basic form consist of ruled spaces into which data may be entered. The vertical axis of the form is not labeled since all entries are directed by the horizontal column headings and the spaces should not confine response length or the number of items. The headings across the top of the columns depend on the information to be collected for the survey. Usually these headings identify columns for

- *Transaction number.* Each entry should be separately numbered in sequence by the responder. Each activity/organization code combination listed is a separate transaction. The transaction number for data entry consists of both the form number assigned in the heading space plus the line number for the activity.
- *Providing organization or receiving organization.* This column should indicate the organization code of the provider or receiver (depending on which form is being filled out). The codes should be obtained from the list attached to the form. In some organizations, inputs are received from external sources. If these inputs are to be included in the analysis, codes should be provided in the list. Since a single receiver may receive a number of activities from one provider, the organization code need be entered only once to cover all activities in which that organization is involved; ditto marks can be used for subsequent lines.
- *Activity number.* From the list of activities created earlier, the responder should obtain the appropriate activity number. The space should be large enough to enter a brief description if no listed activity seems suitable. It is always possible that some activity has been missed in the listing. For any description entered, the consultant and client coordinator should determine the appropriate code or create and assign a new code before the transaction is entered into the database. A single provider may provide the same activity to a number of receivers. In such cases the activity number need be entered only once and ditto marks used in subsequent lines for each receiving organization. Each activity/organization code combination listed is a separate transaction and should have a corresponding line number.
- *Level of effort.* This column requires entry of the person-hours or person-weeks per year devoted to the activity. (Be clear as to which measure is being used so that responses are consistent. In some cases person-months or person-years may be the right measure.) For providers, the amounts shown on all entries made should total the number of person-equivalent hours/months or years available to the organization. A proof listing made after all entries are collected and recorded in the database permits verification of the total against the actual labor expenditures of the provider organization units. Receivers enter their estimates of the number of units of labor time they have

received for each activity from each provider. These figures will later be compared as a further indication of the perceived value of the service provided by the activity. The amounts entered by receivers are subjective and are not expected to equal actual expenditures.

- *Importance of the activity.* On a scale of 0 to 3, with 3 being "most important," both receivers and providers indicate their perception of the relative importance of this transaction to the *receiver*. Since BPR is designed to respond to customer needs and satisfaction, this measure is designed to identify significant differences in perceptions of the relative importance of activities to the *receiver*. These scores will be aggregated in the analysis and compared by receiver/provider pairing.

- *Satisfaction with the activity.* For each transaction the responder enters a 0–3 rating, with 3 being "completely satisfied." Again, as a measure of perception differences, receivers should indicate their satisfaction levels and providers should enter the satisfaction level they think the receiver has.

Before the survey is distributed, management should inform all those to be surveyed of the nature of the project and survey, and that responses to the survey and interviews will be held confidential by the consultant. The forms should be distributed with a deadline for responses. The consultant should anticipate the need to be available for questions by responders during the survey period.

After collection, the responses will need to be reviewed and the transaction codes entered in the survey form headings prior to entry into the database. Any obvious errors or problems in activity descriptions should be remedied before data entry. The data entry process provides editing for errors in activity codes or organization codes and proof lists for verification. The proof list takes totals on level of effort, which should be validated with providers' budgets before proceeding to ensure that they are reasonably close and that no major blocks of time have been over- or understated.

Task 4: Supplementary Interviews

When a preliminary validation of the survey data has been completed, an initial comparative analysis should be obtained from the database. This comparison should be made for both the importance levels of activities and the satisfaction levels. Severe discrepancies noted should be traced back to the responders for follow-up. (Note that in most companies, it is important for the consultant to assure responders that their responses will be held in confidence and that sources will not be revealed to client management without specific permission.)

Interviews should be scheduled with receivers whose responses indicate the greatest discrepancies from those of the providers of the activities in question. The purpose of these interviews is to obtain specific details on the reasons for the discrepancies (without disclosing that such discrepancies exist and thereby jeopardizing internal company relationships). These details will be used during the BPR project as a guide to improving performance. They will also be used to substantiate, by example, the findings of the TA study.

In addition to these interviews, some companies will expect senior managers to be interviewed and possibly some key employees or middle managers. It may be necessary to conduct these interviews to ensure overall "buy-in" to the results of the project. This should be determined in advance with the company management, since it can add substantially to the cost of this task.

Task 5: Analysis of the TA Survey Results

The comparison reports generated by the TA database application produce several analytical reports:

1. *Labor transaction ratio.* For each activity provided, the actual labor expended by the provider divided by the perceived amount of labor reported by receivers yields a ratio that can be used to bolster the results found in the two critical measures of importance and satisfaction.
2. *Ranking of importance.* For each activity provided, a comparison is made of the perceived importance of the activity from the provider and user perspectives. This information can serve as a BPR guide to determining whether activities are necessary at all or are required at the levels currently provided. It also serves as a measure of how well providers understand their receivers' needs.
3. *Satisfaction.* This analysis compares the perceptions of the providers as to how well they are satisfying receivers with the perceptions of the receivers. It serves as a BPR guide to business process areas that need improvement to meet receiver needs. It also serves as a measure of how well providers understand their performance in receiver terms.
4. *Satisfaction versus importance.* This analysis compares both satisfaction with and importance of activities to each other in receiver terms and in provider terms. It indicates, for example, places where satisfaction may be high but importance is low. Such a finding shows that perhaps too much effort is being expended on a relatively unimportant activity while other activities suffer from the opposite.
5. *Transaction/transaction value count.* Counting the number of transactions between pairs of providers and receivers and adding the total value of the transactions counted (in labor units of measure) can provide the first clues to the possible combination of organizations to improve processes. Where a large number of transactions with high labor

content are exchanged, there is a clear indication that the organizations involved are symbiotic and perhaps should be combined.

6. *Activities by provider*. Listing activities by provider indicates the extent to which different providers offer similar (or perhaps redundant) services to receivers. This may lead to a potential combination of providers or to the elimination of redundant services.

Task 6: Reporting Results

The results of the TA study are reported to management as a part of step 2 of the BPR project described in Chapter 15. This report is generally presented in a workshop setting in which management is able to comment on the results of the study and add its own perceptions and insights to the findings.

In addition to these findings, the results of the survey provide input to the next steps in the BPR project. As process flow diagrams are developed, the survey provides an immediate trail to the providers and receivers of each activity, thus speeding up the diagramming task. The database contents can also be used to determine which organizations appear to be providing similar services to receivers. Further interviews can determine if actual redundancies or overlaps in activities or functions exist. Finally, the survey results can provide information on the extent of interdependence of organizations, which may lead to opportunities to consolidate activities, organizations, or functions during the BPR project.

THE WORKSHOP APPROACH TO TA

The workshop approach is an alternative to the broad survey approach. Its intent is to obtain similar information to that obtained in the broad survey approach from a smaller group of first-line supervisors of providing and receiving organizational units.

This approach requires a series of workshops in which the participants are a workshop leader and assistant (the consultants) plus a group of first-line supervisors generally not exceeding six or seven. The size must be limited in order to obtain the level of interaction required from each participant. The assistant's task is to take notes during the workshop.

The first two tasks described in the broad survey approach and the first part of the third task leading to the construction of the survey form are the same for the workshop approach. However, the survey form is distributed only to those who will participate in the workshops. When these forms are completed, the workshops may be started. Each person completing a survey form submits the form to the consultant, but retains a copy of it for use in the workshop.

Task 4 of the broad survey approach is skipped.

The completed survey forms are input to the database application and analyzed, as in task 5 of the broad survey approach. The workshops are used to replace the interviewing process in the previous approach, thus completing the equivalent of the first five steps excluding the interviews.

The next three tasks are described below. Note that if the group surveyed is small enough and there is deemed to be little risk of confrontation among the participants, the workshop may include both providers and receivers.

Task 7: Receiver Workshop(s)

With the assistance of the participants, the workshop leader constructs a high-level process flow diagram on a white-board. (If an electronic white-board is available to make immediate copies, it is very helpful.)

When the process flow diagram is finished, the leader reviews the activities from the survey and describes the findings using overhead slides prepared in advance. The participants are asked to discuss the findings and provide specific examples of any negative results. A list of the comments is made by the workshop leader, with the assistant recording supplementary details. This list is used as additional input to the provider workshop.

Task 8: Provider Workshop(s)

The provider workshop is conducted in the same manner as the receiver workshop. The process flow diagramming exercise is used to identify any differences in perception between the two groups. After the survey findings are presented, comments are solicited, just as in the previous workshop, and a list is made. When the list is completed, it is compared to the list of comments made by receivers and additional comments are solicited.

The output of this workshop is a consolidated list of comments that supplements the findings of the survey forms and provides the specific perceptions of both providers and receivers for the final report and management workshop.

Task 9: Reporting Results

Task 8 is identical to task 6 of the broad survey approach. Note that although the workshop approach has more steps, it is used for a smaller group of participants and is therefore less time-consuming.

Index